Joe Orton was born in Leicester in 1933 and was battered to death in August 1967. He left school at sixteen and went to RADA two years later. He spent six months in prison for defacing library books. In 1964 his first play, *The Ruffian on the Stair*, was broadcast and his first full-length piece, *Entertaining Mr. Sloane*, was staged in the West End, as was *Loot* two years later. *The Erpingham Camp* was televised in 1966 and staged at the Royal Court in 1967 in double-bill with *The Ruffian on the Stair*. His television plays, *The Good and Faithful Servant* and *Funeral Games*, were shown posthumously in 1967 and 1968. His play, *What the Butler Saw*, was not staged until 1969, and his novel, *Head to Toe*, was not published until 1971. *Loot* and *Entertaining Mr. Sloane* were both filmed but *Up Against It*, a screenplay commissioned for the Beatles, never reached the screen; it was first published in 1978. His *Diaries* were first published in 1986.

Head to Toe

A Novel

&

Up Against It

A Screenplay for The Beatles

Introduction by John Lahr

by

JOE ORTON

DA CAPO PRESS • NEW YORK

Library of Congress Cataloging-in-Publication Data
Orton, Joe.
    Head to toe; & Up against it: a screenplay for the Beatles / Joe Orton.
        p.   cm.
    ISBN 0-306-80836-6 (alk. paper)
    I. Orton, Joe. Head to toe. II. Orton, Joe. Up against it. III. Title. IV.
Title: Up against it.
PR6065.R7H4   1998
823'.914—dc21   97-39767
                                                                   CIP

CAUTION: The screenplay *Up Against It* is fully protected, in whole, in
part, or in any form under the Copyright Laws of the United States of
America, the British Empire, including the Dominion of Canada, and all
other countries of the Copyright Union and is subject to royalty. All in-
quiries concerning any kind of performance of all or part of this screen-
play should be directed to the author's sole agent: Margaret Ramsay,
Ltd., 14a Goodwin's Court, St. Martin's Lane, London W.C. 2, England.

The publishers wish to emphasize that the material quoted in John
Lahr's introduction from Orton's private diaries is fully protected by
copyright and that no further use whatsoever may be made of this material without the express permission in writing of the Estate of Joe Orton, c/o Margaret Ramsay Ltd., 14a Goodwin's Court, St. Martin's Lane,
London W.C. 2, England.

First Da Capo Press edition 1998

This Da Capo Press paperback edition of *Head to Toe & Up Against It*
consists of an unabridged republication of the edition of *Head to Toe*
published in London in 1990, here reprinted by arrangement with St.
Martin's Press, and the edition of *Up Against It* published in New York
in 1979, here reprinted by arrangement with Grove/Atlantic Inc. (*Head
to Toe* was first published by Anthony Blond in 1971; *Up Against It* was
first published by Eyre Methuen Ltd. in 1979.)

Head to Toe copyright © 1971 by the Estate of Joe Orton, deceased
Up Against It copyright © 1979 by the Estate of Joe Orton, deceased
Introduction to *Up Against It* copyright © 1979 by John Lahr
Extracts from the private diaries of Joe Orton copyright © 1979 by the
Estate of Joe Orton, deceased

Published by Da Capo Press, Inc.
A Subsidiary of Plenum Publishing Corporation
233 Spring Street, New York, N.Y. 10013

All Rights Reserved

Manufactured in the United States of America

Head to Toe

One

The creature onto whose head Gombold had strayed was some hundreds of miles high; it was impossible not to think this unique. He stood for a moment lost in thought, contemplating a landscape of waving hair. And then he heard a voice. He waited. It was his own imaginings. Or (now he became touched by fear) was it one of the odd beasts, savage composite carnivores invented and forgotten? He stood without breathing. The sound came again. Was it the pig of Othrys? Once more the sound was repeated. Or was it the vulture which copulated with its victim before devouring it? The cry came a third time. He quickly realised why it came no nearer. It was trapped in a hole. His mind ran on to the toad which lured victims by simulating cries for help. He approached a large hole and called out. No answer came. Straight ahead was another hole. Advancing he looked over the edge.

The gap in the rock was about four feet wide at the top and narrowed as it went down. Undoubtedly the danger of attack could not be great: the beast was sufficiently far down to be invisible. Gombold felt his spirits rise. On the ground by the rim of the hole he noticed a pie-dish, a half-empty jar of pickles, a cheese, a fork and asparagus tongs, a samovar, a box of biscuits and a pot of Relish.

'Can I help you?' he called down in a loud voice.

'Have you a rope?' came the answer.

'I'm afraid not,' said Gombold, heartened to find the creature human and civil.

'It is easy to find a stray hair on one of the paths. They are strong and excellent for the purpose.'

Gombold moved away, his eyes glancing at the ground. Under a particularly tall tree (for they seemed to him to be trees) he found a hair about fifteen feet long, its surface grey in streaks. He hauled it to the edge of the hole. Lying on the ground he leaned over the rim and lowered it as far as it would go. The end disappeared.

'Can you reach?'

'I can't see it.'

Standing up Gombold laid the hair by the side of the hole and went to search for another. After a few minutes he found one, red in colour. He knotted the two and lowered them.

'Can you reach now?'

'Yes,' the voice said.

Gombold braced himself. The pull came. He dug in his toes to prevent himself sliding. He could hear a scraping below and knew the man was clawing his boots against the wall trying to lever himself up. The pain of the hair cutting into his flesh was unbearable. He felt it bite into his palms, saw the blood beginning to spout. He could hold on no longer. And then it was over. The man's hand appeared; he pulled himself out of the hole.

He was perhaps forty and extremely fat. He could be called gross. His cheeks were quivering moons, his head a great globe, his body a swollen pear. Gombold wondered which minion of his invention this could be. They came crowding into his mind: Ballpander, Grendoll, Catsbody and Frag; Olimpicol, Devilday, Wormforce and the Lord of Difference. He remembered

6

Blazon and the incumbent of the Strangler; the man who rode upon a fly and the philosopher Sheenshite. It was impossible to recognise the man before him.

After dropping the makeshift rope down the hole, the man's first action was to seize Gombold by the throat with one hand, pummelling him with the other. At the same instant there came a crashing in the undergrowth. Gombold, feeling sure this was a savage beast, could not in his present condition give way either to fear or curiosity. Death seemed certain and imminent. The bushes parted and another man came into view. Seeing the struggle taking place on the edge of the hole he ran forward and separated the combatants. As Gombold drew away his rescuer began to beat the fat man about the head and finally bundled him back into the hole. Seeing how people appeared to treat one another and making sure of his own fate, Gombold piddled in his clothes and prayed for some heavenly power to guide him out of this fearful country.

Ignoring the cries of distress coming from the hole the man collected the food lying beside it. Then he turned and asked what Gombold was doing in the wood. Gombold attempted to explain the state in which he found himself, but the man waved his hand impatiently and walked away. When he was almost out of sight he turned and called, 'You can come with me if you wish.'

Gombold followed at a distance, reasoning that it was better to endure the man's company, however boorish, than to remain alone in such new and terrifying surroundings. The man stopped in a clearing to point out a hole the twin of the one from which the fat man had been rescued.

'Does each hole contain a prisoner?' Gombold asked.

The man made no reply. He sat under a tree and motioned for Gombold to do the same. They talked as though they were spending an afternoon on a pleasant excursion. The man was powerfully built and had a ginger moustache (which Gombold did not care for), and his teeth were bad.

'My name is Vulp,' he said. 'I am very rich.'

It did not occur to Gombold to doubt this, though it crossed his mind to wonder why he could not afford a shilling for a toothbrush. Actually Vulp had bad teeth because if you are rich it does not particularly matter whether you disgust people or not.

'Are you rich?' Vulp said, relaxing his mood. 'I'm sure you are.'

'No,' Gombold said, rising and walking down one of the paths.

Vulp gave him a minute's start and followed. Gombold was beginning to feel tired; he stopped and allowed Vulp to catch up. He wondered if there were any wild beasts in the forest. It might be safer to continue their talk elsewhere.

'Oh,' said Vulp, 'it doesn't matter. The animals never harm anyone. They sniff around and go away.'

'I'm sorry to offend you,' said Gombold, 'but I think we ought to try and find a way out of the forest.'

Vulp put an arm around his shoulder and promised to guide him through the wood by a secret path. He received Gombold's thanks with a charming smile. The two set off and to Gombold's surprise were soon in the middle of the forest once more. Not wishing to appear impatient he said nothing, trusting that his guide knew better than he the way to safety. After wandering for some considerable time they approached a dark clearing and as they did so Vulp excused himself saying he wished to be assured of a detour. He promised to rejoin Gombold within a minute. No sooner had his guide gone than Gombold began to be alarmed by the silence and gloom of his surroundings; no bird or insect disturbed the stillness, no wind blew among the boughs. The cloud had thickened overhead and the gloom deepened until he fancied he saw shapes, faces, creatures all claw and teeth intent on destroying him. He called. No one answered. Again he shouted for help. Not even an echo. He waited until he could be certain that Vulp had cruelly deserted him and then struck out into the wood once more.

He had not been walking for more than hour when he heard the sound of voices. The prospect of receiving help from the people who inhabited the country seemed remote and in order not to reveal himself too soon he pushed his way through the undergrowth with great care. Upon his approach the noises he had taken for voices changed into snarls, shrieks and grunts. Staring from behind a bush he saw an eagle, bald, mad, a single eye, claw, wing and a few tailfeathers – half a bird. Beside it was a cock and an aged lion, a dead mare and a she-wolf wearing a mitre. The scene filled him with terror. He hardly dared to breathe in case they should hear him, for if he had received such rough treatment from human beings what could he expect from beasts who by nature are enemies to man?

'You're not fit to take decisions,' the cock said, ruffling its feathers. 'You're a baby that can do nothing but play with itself.'

The lion rose to its feet. The cock moved too. In one leap it was off the ground into a tree. The lion bared its gums.

'I won't stand that kind of talk from a capon.'

'A capon!'

'I refuse to be associated with your dubious schemes.'

'Mon Dieu!'

The eagle intervened trying to patch up the quarrel. The lion and the cock laughed at its accent, at its blindness. Then another eagle, identical in every respect to the first, though younger, bolder, came up saying with a shifty gleam in his eye:

'Gentlemen, gentlemen. We are friends. Allies. Remember our association.'

The quarrel was resolved. A few minutes later, however, they had another. And then another. Each time the second eagle called upon them to remember their alliance. The animals snapped and roared at the bird until it went off in a huff. The cock and the lion shouted insults as it flapped into the forest.

'Parvenue!'

'Idiot!'

The bald, mad eagle talked to itself, and during the uproar the wolf remained silent except for an occasional howl of 'Pax vobiscum – ' or, less frequently, 'Gloria in excelsis Deo ... '

Deciding that the creatures were the contents of a private zoo, Gombold turned down one of the many paths and almost ran into a bear which was staring into the dark. From the gloom came the sound of hissing and the shimmer of scales. Gombold ran on avoiding all clearings until he was too tired to do anything but lie under a tree and sleep.

After a night of extreme discomfort he gathered what strength remained to him and stumbled on in search of some kind of dwelling inhabited by human beings. It was only when he had given up hope of finding help that he saw a disreputable young man sitting on a rubber mattress with a rucksack and a stick within reach. As Gombold approached the man scratched his head and whistled tunelessly between his teeth. Gombold hesitated; he had reason to regret his affability in the past. At this point the man called and introduced himself by the name of O'Scullion.

'Is there a way out of this wood?' Gombold asked.

'It isn't a wood,' O'Scullion said.

'Is there no way out?' repeated Gombold, already regretting that he had spoken.

O'Scullion tapped the enormous trunk beside him.

'I expect you think this is a tree.'

'As a matter of fact I don't. It's a hair.'

'Whoever heard of a hair seventy feet long. You must be simple.'

This remark was made in such an unpleasant tone that Gombold turned and walked away.

'That path leads nowhere,' O'Scullion called as he plunged into the undergrowth.

Gombold came back.

'You may as well sit down.'

'Which direction is best?'

O'Scullion pushed the mattress into a hollow between the roots of the tree and lay down.

'It depends upon where you want to get to,' he said closing his eyes.

'I don't care.'

'Then it doesn't matter which path you take.'

'But I want to get somewhere. I don't want to be lost in a wilderness for ever.'

O'Scullion raised himself on one elbow.

'Why are you asking me? Do you imagine for one moment that I would be here if I knew the way out?'

'If we pool our resources we could help each other.'

'What a ridiculous suggestion. I have no resources. Have you?'

Gombold hesitated.

'No,' he said at last.

'Then kindly don't waste my time,' said O'Scullion lying down and closing his eyes once more.

In a minute he was asleep. Gombold stood watching him for a while and then decided that there was no point in remaining in his company. Before he left he searched in the rucksack but found nothing. With a heavy heart he stared at the paths stretching into the forest. Identical in every respect and all, he was convinced now, leading further and further into the labyrinth. He closed his eyes and stumbled forward.

After a short time the trees thinned and he arrived at a hollow whose sides were covered in reddish clumps of reeds. Hanging in the branches of a distant tree he saw clusters of fruit. He made his way towards it hoping to find the fruit edible. He stretched out his fingers and touched the semi-transparent globules. Immediately he did so the thin skin broke; he was drenched in a liquid resembling blood. He tried again. Each time the ruptured membrane poured a bloody liquid across his hand. He put his fingers to his lips and allowed it to drip into his mouth. At once he was conscious of his heart beating slow and even. From between the roots of the tree an incongruous monster slithered. He marvelled at the ingeniousness of its construction evading the obvious. As the reptile vanished into the reeds he heard a number of voices. He was no longer alone; the whole landscape was alive. The reeds flapped like the tongues of dogs, the holes in the rock were mouths which called to him. Crouching down, his ear all but brushing the earth, he overheard the conversation of a melon and a daisy.

'How small you are. You are neither civilised nor a highly coloured barbarian. Why, not even a potato could call you exotic.'

The daisy shrugged its petals.

'And you are nothing but a vegetable. I would rather be a jacaranda than a pumpkin.'

The melon's round bulk shuddered; its skin heaved in agitation.

'You are confusing my species. I am a fruit.'

12

'There are hundreds of your kind thrown upon garbage heaps every day. Tasteless, insipid, possessing nothing but a glamorous skin.'

The melon did not speak and the daisy's laughter rose. Gombold walked on. The flowers and fruit called to him, but he did not answer. Beyond the hollow was an orchard, and this he entered, climbing the fence. He heard the sound of laughter. It was not the laughter of the daisies, it had a malicious ring and came from a patch of loganberries. They showered into the orchard over a broken wall. Gombold admired the bulbous bodies among the thorns.

'Oh, I prayed a bit, I admit. You couldn't stop me. But it wasn't prayers that saved me.'

'What then?'

'It was my thorns.' The loganberry who spoke paused for a moment. 'I've never seen such a scratch. She won't try to pick me again, I can tell you.'

'Well, Claude,' said a leaf, 'we're glad to have you still with us.'

'But you should have seen her fingers. Five hideous things plunging down. It's enough to turn a raspberry pale!'

Gombold sat on the edge of the wall, crossed his legs and listened. A buzz of voices rose from the ground. A wind blew and from wall to wall the orchard was full of sound.

'It must be fifty years since *Simple Vegetable Arrangement* was published. Now the same author has written *Vegetables for Decoration*.'

'I'm glad I'm a weed.'

'I couldn't bear to be arranged. They strip you before they do it. Imagine Primrose here without her leaves.'

'Don't!'

'It is a beautiful book. She suggests Carottes Nantaises – we don't have any present, do we? No? Then

13

I can speak freely – are excellent varieties for display. "Why not," she says, "arrange them with mint for a cocktail party? Or bowered in roses for a sophisticated supper?" '

'Bowered in roses? Such cheek! I wouldn't be closeted with a carrot for all the tea in China.'

'I hardly imagine she meant a *dog* rose, dear.'

Leaves and grasses moved in a great wave of light across Gombold's field of vision. A voice throbbing with the suppressed energy of an organ in a church came to his ears. He was compelled to listen to the patriarchal bass.

'My forefathers came from Africa,' said the sycamore, leaning over the wall, 'the essence of beauty is there. You can't imagine the tawny lion. You can't begin to visualise the gazelle . . . '

'May I ask what the climate is like, sidi?' said a starling.

'Indescribable.'

Gombold looked up: sharp eyes glittered among the twigs: his gaze met the starling's.

'Do you know any songs?' the bird said.

'I have been taught a few, but I am shy and afraid.'

'Of course you are. Such a strange new world.'

Flapping down the bird alighted on Gombold's shoulder.

'I hope you are happy here. We shall do all we can to help you.' As Gombold remained silent it was the starling that spoke again. 'There is a dove who lives in a church nearby and who knows the ways of your world. I shall ask him to come here. I think it may be good for you.'

'That would be kind,' said Gombold, 'but I shall not be staying long.'

The bird nodded. Again it looked about, then flew back to the branch. By now Gombold could distinguish the dry tones of the grasses and the accents of the annuals from the coarser, native wit of weed or lichen.

'*Plants of the Bible* – a really lovely book. Have you read it?'

'I had the opportunity of glancing at a few pages when one of the family was out here the other day,' said a tall-stemmed iris.

A thistle tried to edge into the conversation by calling shrilly, 'What is it? A text book?'

The irises and the grass stiffened and pretended not to have heard.

'A really lovely book,' repeated the grass, lowering its voice to a hiss. 'Five hundred colour plates illustrating everything from Eve's apple to the truffles served at the Last Supper.'

'Truffles? Now that is interesting.'

'He had a taste for them, did He?'

'Well, I don't say the Lord Himself did, but one or two of the disciples had a savoury tooth.'

'Isn't it wonderful the appeal of the Bible,' said a beetle, 'contemporary but timeless. I prefer the New Testament to the Old myself, though I suppose there is less to interest a plant.'

'What a wonderful person He must have been.'

'Even the humblest flower in the garden knows that He feels for her. Is there a root that at some time has not felt the benefit of religion?'

'Much of the success of the New Testament is due to Jesus' personality, but some is undoubtedly the result of careful teamwork.'

The thistles began to jeer. The flowers trembled and the air was full of seed as the grass shook with rage.

'I wonder,' said Gombold, striving to make himself heard above the bray, 'if any of you could direct me?'

'You'd better decide where you're going,' said a thistle.

15

Determined not to be browbeaten Gombold kept his temper. He bent his head until it was on a level with the iris.

'Is there a house nearby?'

'I'm not tall enough to see,' the iris said.

'I can see a house,' said the sycamore. 'Just beyond the fence.'

Gombold thanked it for the information and went on his way. Around a corner of the orchard he came upon a large and stately house. It had a crest of chimneys, a green-tiled roof and a verandah running the length of one wall. The door was open. He searched for a bell but found none. He called. No one answered. He went inside.

Scarcely had he taken six steps than he felt himself sinking into the floor: his feet had vanished into the luxurious pile of the carpet. He stood looking about him, little inclined to extricate his feet only for the sake of plunging them in again; the house was silent. Was it possible to create oneself a kind of phantom Gombold from the void of onanistic satisfaction? This creature was nothing but a spurt of mental fluid. Nothing else could account for the situation.

Just then a door on the landing above his head was opened and Gombold recognised Vulp, dressed only in his underclothes and clearly in search of someone. Gombold realised that an explanation was called for.

'Can I have a word with you, sir?' he said.

Vulp's reaction was to disappear suddenly from view. When he came back he was pulling on a dressing-gown. He hurried down the stairs.

'Who are you?' were his first words, surprising Gombold to such an extent that he could not reply. 'Did you imagine the house was empty?'

'No,' said Gombold, convinced that Vulp was playing a heartless trick.

'Are you alone?'

'Yes.'

Vulp fiddled with the end of a stick which he had brought down the stairs and narrowed his eyes.

'What right have you to be here?'

'You promised to guide me through the wood. Don't you remember?'

This put Vulp into a rage.

'Don't tell me lies,' he cried. 'I promised no such thing.'

His moustache twitched. Gombold was aware that a woman had entered the hall; she stood watching them.

'Not even capable of dealing with a burglar, I see,' she said, casting a withering glance at Vulp. She opened the door an inch or two and called, 'Con. Give us a hand.'

The doorway was suddenly blocked by an enormous policewoman. Gombold noted that physically she was the biggest woman he had ever seen in his life: her arms alone were thicker than most men's thighs: she was a real giant. She stood with her legs apart sensing the situation.

'What's the game?' she said at last, her cheeks wobbling. Before Gombold could reply she addressed him again. 'Where's your I.D. chit?'

'I didn't realise I had to have one.'

'Must have a chit,' she said, and there was an ironical contempt for Gombold in the way she cast a sidelong glance towards Vulp and his wife and smiled.

'I shall have to get one,' said Gombold.

'Where from?'

'From whoever issues them.'

'I issue them,' she said with a certain finality.

She looked at him out of pale eyes, a wart under her left eye was almost invisible being covered by a film of face powder. She hooked a finger round Gombold's tie and led him into the room.

'Sit down.' The tone was one of unmistakable authority. 'Where do you live?'

'Nowhere.'

She screwed up her eyes; the wart slipped into a trough of flesh.

'Who told you to come here?'

'Nobody.'

'Are you a tourist?'

'I suppose I am.'

'Ought to have a chit then. Come a long way?'

'Yes.'

'Takes a long time to travel down the whole body. Expect you want to see the lot?'

'Yes.'

'Some things are more interesting than others.'

'Naturally.'

'I've been around a bit myself. Are there parts which attract you more than others?' Her voice had taken on a deeper shade of meaning; Gombold fidgeted in his chair. 'Sometimes, and for people living in certain regions, the life of a parasite requires a strong nerve.' She pursed her lips. 'I'll make you out a chit,' she said at last. 'If you're in no hurry Con could show you round, eh?'

These words were spoken in such compelling tones that Gombold could do nothing but nod his head. With a lurch the policewoman propelled herself towards the door. As though she had been listening outside Mrs Vulp appeared.

'Give him a room,' Connie said.

'A room?'

'As a favour for Con.'

Mrs Vulp glanced at Gombold.

'But he may be dangerous. He looks as though he is.'

'Nonsense! Give him a room. Make sure it's a good one.'

She strode down the hall. Mrs Vulp beckoned Gombold to follow her.

Two

He was in bed. He lay motionless through the night. He knew voices and darkness. His aloneness was vast about him. Then, through it, very soft, there came a sound. He knew someone was moving at the foot of his bed. He pretended to be asleep as Connie moved backwards and forwards. She was searching his clothes. She went away. The noise faded. He slept and dreamed. He dreamed of his tongue, long, red and loose; he dipped it into a crack in the floor; the end began to swell, a great bulge appeared. The swelling increased until it formed a face; red eyes stared at him, the tight mouth opened and spoke. As it did so he experienced a feeling of pain. He tried to answer but could not.

Connie came to his room early. She sat beside him while he drank a cup of tea. He told her of his dream; her reaction was not encouraging.

'You want someone to look after you,' she said. 'I think I can squeeze you into my place.' The prospect of living in close proximity to her terrified Gombold. He turned pale. 'A little sweetie, aren't you?'

For a moment he thought she was going to assault him, and to escape he slid beneath the blankets. She leaned back in her chair and half-closed her eyes.

'Too much on my own,' she said, taking the tray from the bed and placing it upon a table. 'Smoke like a chimney; fag ends all over the shop. You can do a bit of tidying up.'

21

Gombold stiffened. Did she expect him to clean the place? A feeling of indignation which he did nothing to control swept over him. His skin prickled. He felt the bed shaking as though in an earthquake; she was sitting beside him. The bedclothes were on him at one moment, the next he was exposed; she mauled him in a most unexpected manner. His teeth shook. He lay on his back and stretched out his arms. A faint moan escaped his lips as she enveloped him; he completely disappeared under her; he was suffocating; he gave himself up for dead. She was killing him. In a state of near unconsciousness hours seemed to pass in which he was haunted by the fear of being crushed to death. When, after an unknown period of time, a knock was heard on the door he heaved a sigh of relief; she must go away now.

'It's the phone, Con.'

'Who is it?'

'I don't know.'

Gombold watched as she heaved herself from the bed, but could not bring himself to speak. Without saying a word she turned on her heel and left the room. In a panic, hardly knowing what he did, Gombold flung himself against the door and forced the lock into place. He began to dress. It crossed his mind to run away. To escape from her. And then he heard her footsteps returning. The door rattled. He stood petrified. Would she break it down?

'What are you doing?'

'I'm dressing.' His voice sounded feeble and appeared to come from a great distance. 'I won't be long.'

She grunted and went away.

A road wound down between the lines of red hairs. Gombold sat next to Connie hardly daring to speak.

The urge to escape was still strong, but something held him back. She did not speak a word during the journey: her eyes were fixed upon the road. He was a prisoner. He watched her hands upon the steering wheel. She had only to command for him to obey. His spirits sank as he realised the truth.

They stopped before an impressive building, the police headquarters. She strode through the doors and came back carrying a sheaf of papers and a brief-case. She opened the car door and helped Gombold out; he found himself leaning on her arm, half enjoying the feeling of dependence. In the lift he snuggled closer to her. She smiled and put an arm around his waist. Her flat was at the top of the building. At the far end of the living-room was a cupboard and against it rested a bag of golf clubs and a sort of ornamental battleaxe.

'No great shakes,' she said. 'We'll be moving out in a bit.'

Gombold sat down on one of the chairs. Connie went in search of a corkscrew. There was a pile of what looked like newspaper clippings on the table, mostly concerned with political demonstrations, a camera, and some odds and ends of foolscap covered with illegible writing. A studio portrait stood on the sideboard. After studying it for some time he came to the conclusion that it represented a handsome young woman in her middle twenties, possibly Connie's younger sister. Connie came back into the room. She saw him looking at the photograph.

'A little pet I knew,' she said. 'What do you think of him?'

Gombold was too taken aback to reply. He watched as she took off her uniform jacket and sank into a chair. She pushed her legs forward and afterwards he could not remember what had impelled him to kneel and unlace her boots.

'Over there,' she said, pointing to a cupboard. 'I want to be able to see my face in them.'

In the cupboard were forty or fifty pairs. He ran back and took her tie which she held out to him. She loosened her collar, put on a pair of glasses and poured herself a drink.

'Busy tonight,' she said. 'I'll be wanting a light meal about seven. Nothing fancy.'

Gombold followed her into the bedroom where she opened the drawer in a dressing table.

'Let's see about a proper rig-out for you.'

The clothes she produced for him to wear had a curiously unfamiliar feel. A lightness in the heels made him want to skip. Connie made him walk up and down as though in movement she had more power of judgement. When he was dressed she watched as he minced before his image in the mirror.

'Promise one thing,' she said, standing above him, 'never wear Daddy's clothes.' Gombold was too busy tying on a frilly apron to listen; she shook him. 'Understand?'

'Yes.'

'If you wear so much as a sock belonging to me I shall be ever so angry.'

Gombold smiled and ran off to prepare a meal. Connie poured herself another drink.

The words Connie had used had the opposite effect to her intention: they stimulated his curiosity. Why must he never wear clothes belonging to his husband (for he increasingly, and without the slightest trace of alarm, thought of her as his husband). The urge to disobey the order was strong, but he attempted at first to resist the temptation. The consequences of such an act were unknown and the mere thought of Connie's anger was enough to instil in him a regard for her wishes. Yet there were times as he knelt in the kitchen cleaning the soft leather boots that an all-consuming desire to wear them took hold of him. The urge became stronger when he brushed the tweed of her coats, or ironed the linen of her shirts. Power resided in her clothes: if he wore her clothes he would become powerful like her. Almost without realising it he took down a coat from the peg and tried the effect. Perhaps he had the power, but it would avail him nothing, to challenge her authority. He leaned against the wall, his hands pressed together, oblivious of everything but his own thoughts. Then suddenly his attention was distracted: he stared, listening intently, into vacancy. He turned round, he could hear nothing; but he ran on tiptoe and locked the door. Then back to the mirror with flushed cheeks and on to the wardrobe where he rummaged through the clothes.

A new-found confidence caused him to wave caution to one side; he was soon in the street, walking among a crowd who did not notice his elation. His first discovery was that men no longer showed him those little politenesses which he had come to expect. He boarded a bus. No one glanced his way. No one attempted to rise when he could not find a seat. He was near the city centre. He stepped down from the bus as a column of marching men approached. At their head, waving a banner, stood O'Scullion. Gombold drew back and the column passed on. And then, thinking better of it, he hurried to catch the men up. Not until he was level with the head of the column did O'Scullion turn his head.

'Are you joining us then?' he called, turning into a large square where the marchers halted.

'I have no idea what you stand for.'

O'Scullion gave him a contemptuous glance and mounted a platform.

'Now then,' he said, 'listen to me.'

The crowd cheered. Gombold cheered with them,

25

though he did not understand the reason for the cheering. Pressing his way forward, he was soon directly under the platform on which O'Scullion stood, with the crowd around him: drinking up words, drinking up closeness, touching, feeling with a great surge of emotion that he had found something new. The mystical quality of crowds, thronging together. Tumult and shouting; jostling one with another.

'Come with me,' O'Scullion said, at the end of a series of speeches.

Gombold followed him down a side street. He was surprised to see that darkness was falling. It had been early afternoon when he left the flat. Only a short time ago it was daylight, and now night was upon them. Connie would soon be returning. Almost as soon as the thought crossed his mind he dismissed it. He felt fully confident, dressed as he was, to deal with her. Tantrums and threats did not trouble him. O'Scullion turned a key in a door and motioned him forward.

At the top of a flight of stairs stood a man holding a birdcage in his hand. Not until they were close did he put the cage upon a hook and greet them.

'I've brought a new recruit,' said O'Scullion, hanging up his coat.

'You're late,' said the man after a short pause.

'It was a long way.'

'But the meeting was just round the corner.'

O'Scullion nudged Gombold into a lighted room without further explanation. The owner of the house followed. A table and a few chairs were all the contents of the room. Sitting on the chairs were a dozen people, mostly men but a few women included. O'Scullion and Gombold sat at a table, saying nothing. As the evening wore on Gombold tried to find out a little more of the activities of the organisation.

'How am I to know what you stand for?' he said.

O'Scullion smiled.

'People generally ask that.'

'What are your aims?'

O'Scullion considered the scratches upon the surface of the table and said, 'You are very keen, aren't you?'

'What qualities do you require?'

'You have them.'

'I should know.'

'I quite agree with you.'

A man had been wandering around the table for some time; now he spoke to O'Scullion in a low voice.

'Just a minute,' said O'Scullion, rising, 'this is a new recruit and I am discussing private business.'

The man went away.

'My most important charge to you,' said O'Scullion, sitting down again, 'is never to reveal to anyone private conversations I may have with you.'

Some time after this Gombold realised that the life of the Prime Minister was in danger. There had been previous attempts on the lives of various members of the Government. A bomb had been thrown at the opening of Parliament; no one had been hurt, though. Something had gone wrong and the bomb had lodged in one of the chandeliers. Even this might have had some effect but the timing mechanism was so faulty that the police were easily able to evacuate the building before the bomb exploded.

'Surely the damage was considerable?' said Gombold.

'Actually no,' O'Scullion confessed. 'I don't know much about bombs. It didn't go off.'

Gombold sympathised. And repeated his expressions of sympathy when told of the attempt to shoot the Foreign Secretary (Fay something or other) when she returned from a disastrous goodwill tour. Gombold could not make out what had happened on that occasion. Nor could he fathom the reason for the failure

27

to assassinate the Home Secretary, or why, after a comparatively successful demonstration outside the War Office, eighty per cent of the organisation resigned.

'They were disheartened, I suppose,' said O'Scullion.

The room had cleared of all but three people; a bald-headed man with a magnificent beard, a youth and a woman. O'Scullion called them over. They sat down, saying nothing, facing Gombold across the table.

'Can you shoot straight?' O'Scullion asked abruptly.

No one answered and Gombold realised that the question had been addressed to him.

'Yes.'

'Good.'

'Very good indeed,' said the woman.

'These are your accomplices,' O'Scullion said, pointing to the three.

'But I don't require any.'

'Can you do the job on your own?'

'He must be a genius,' the youth said.

'Is he familiar with telescopic sights?' asked the woman after a short pause.

'Yes,' said O'Scullion, after another pause.

'He has had experience then?'

'Undoubtedly.'

'Does he know what we require of him?'

'I believe so.'

'We are proud to help him.'

An abrupt silence fell. Gombold felt that they expected him to address them, but could find nothing to say. His tongue seemed to stick to the roof of his mouth when he tried to speak. The woman smiled across the table in a kindly way.

'You are in a difficult position,' she said. 'You cannot tell us apart. Is that it?' She stopped and went on involuntarily, 'Many people have remarked upon our similarity.'

The man smiled too.

'Is that what is bothering you?'

'I have no difficulty in distinguishing a man and a youth from a woman,' said Gombold in a sharp tone.

'How sure he is of himself.'

'People usually tie themselves into knots attempting to tell us apart,' the woman said in self-justification.

'I can hardly believe it,' said Gombold.

'Believe it or not as you wish.'

'I hope he isn't going to disbelieve everything.'

'Treat us as though we were one.'

The woman seemed to be doing her best to help; Gombold sensed disappointment in his reply:

'I couldn't possibly do that. Think of the complications. Suppose I had three jobs. It would waste time sending you all on the same job consecutively. Whereas if I divided the work we should get it done in no time.'

'That is only a theory,' said the woman, breaking the silence which followed Gombold's words.

There seemed no other way to solve the problem than by agreeing to treat them as one, at which they expressed themselves ready to serve him faithfully in all he did. The time was close on eleven o'clock and the meeting began to break up.

'Will you require us to prepare an itinerary for tomorrow?' said the woman.

'No.'

'At what time are we to call on you?'

'At 10 a.m.'

'We shall follow your instructions.'

The man, who had listened with close attention, asked to be allowed to make a note of the time Gombold had mentioned. Gombold assented. The man took out a pocket book and made two or three quick jottings.

Gombold rose to leave. He had been studying the three for some time, and now he gave them a final glance; it was impossible to mistake them for each other. To pretend they were one and the same was absurd. Since they forced him to acknowledge that they were of one substance he must publicly call them one; in private he knew they were three and looked and sounded different. He shook hands and said good night.

When he arrived back at Connie's flat he saw at once that the blinds were drawn; she was waiting up for him. It did not cause him alarm. Though he had disobeyed her orders and was dressed in forbidden clothes he felt no twinge of fear. He swelled his chest and mounted the stairs. Then he descended to the hall and took the lift; the liftman gave him a quick glance and said nothing. Gombold rehearsed in his mind the things to say.

She was standing by the fireplace with her back to him as he entered. The door banged shut and she turned. She yelled at the sight of him with the full force of her lungs. The sound thundered through the room. She stood above him.

'Take off those clothes,' she said, and could not keep her voice from trembling. 'I have something to say to you.'

'I like them.'

'Take them off!'

'They give me confidence.'

'I told you never to wear Daddy's clothes.'

'You aren't a Daddy. You're a woman.'

The blow fell on the side of his cheek; she had struck with the fingers balled into a great fist. As in a dream (of course he struggled a little but she was too strong for him) he felt her tearing at him, removing the forbidden garments, he felt as though he were being dismembered. As each one fell from him a lassitude crept over him until, naked at last, he trembled before her. The realisation of what he had done appalled him.

'What did you do it for?'

'I don't know,' he said, the tears streaming down his face.

She helped him into a housecoat.

'Who put you up to it?'

'Nobody.'

'You'd never do it on your own.'

'I did.'

'Then you're a wicked little bitch!'

She hit him again, and this time the blow knocked him to the floor. He seemed to have lost the strength he had had during the afternoon and evening. She took him by the arm and led him into another room. It was quite dark, Gombold could not see her face, her figure was only vaguely discernible. He stumbled into a chair. Immediately she dragged him out of it. For an hour or so, her arm hooked through his, she walked him round and round until Gombold was ready to drop from exhaustion.

'I'm tired,' he said.

She stopped.

'You've been a bad girl. A regular little tarty. What did you want to go dressing up in Daddy's clothes for? People will think you are a man.'

'But I am a man.'

'Don't be silly, dear.'

'I am. I am.'

'Are you out of your mind? This is your bedroom. Is it a man's room?' She switched on the light; Gombold blinked. It was a pretty, frilly, pinky room. 'No man would have a room like this. You are a woman.'

The remark was made with much assurance and in an accent of derision, Gombold felt a little afraid. She took hold of his arm.

'You are a woman,' he blurted out.

'I am your lover.'

'You are a strong woman.'

'I am your husband.'

She was practising some kind of torture upon him. The light hurt his eyes. They set off once more round and round the room. By now he was a little unsure of his facts. The effort it cost him merely to keep going made him lose control of his thoughts. She was almost dragging him along, he felt sick. She was killing him. His head swam. She switched the light off. And on again. What was the matter? Why was she behaving in such a strange manner? He fell forward. He dipped, without knowing the moment, into oblivion. When he came round he clutched at the hand that was held out to him so firmly that he heard a grunt of pain.

'Daddy's here.'

'What happened?'

'You fainted.'

He was near to tears. 'I'm such a bad wife.'

'You're the best in the world. You mustn't be such a naughty little tart, though. Going out and disobeying your Dad.'

'I won't do it again.'

Strong arms enfolded him. He was safe. However difficult it might be he would never disobey her again.

The next day three people called upon Gombold who were so alike that he could not tell one from another. They insisted that he knew them. They said that he had employed them for some purpose. Gombold shook his head.

'Who are you?'

'Your accomplices.'

'Are you?'

'What has happened? Have you lost your memory?'

They sat down and stared. He had a feeling of panic. He wanted them to go away.

'Why are you wearing those clothes?'

'I always wear them.'

'But they are women's clothes.'

They were mad. He knew it. He was shut up in a room with three lunatics. He put out his hand and touched the handle of a paper knife: should they turn violent he had some means of protection.

'Why have you changed your clothes?'

'These are my normal clothes.'

'But they are women's clothes.'

'I am a woman,' said Gombold, feeling sure of his ground.

'Who has given you this idea?'

He studied them for a minute or so; each sitting together, smiling. Whether their smiles heralded the onset of a murderous frenzy he could not say. If they had not escaped from a mental home he would be very much surprised.

'Is there any reason why you should imagine yourself to be a woman?'

He was determined to stop their nonsense.

'I am the mistress of Connie Hogg, the Chief of Police,' he said.

'The Chief of Police is a woman.'

'What utter nonsense. Do you think I am incapable of telling the sex of my lover?'

And here he involuntarily lifted his chin a little, and gave them a triumphant glance.

'You will, no doubt,' they said, smiling to prevent the atmosphere becoming too charged, 'be ready to furnish us with proof of your sex?'

It was rape they were contemplating then? He would resist. A complaint should be made to the authorities.

'You ought to weigh your words,' he said, amiably but without returning their smile. He had a weapon for dissuading them from the step they intended to take. 'I have influential friends.'

'We merely wish to be assured whether your claims are justified.'

Their effrontery was boundless. He experienced a sudden spasm of disgust. Three great men, who must surely be brothers they were so alike, forcing their way into a flat and molesting a woman who had done them no harm.

'Should we withdraw?' two of them asked.

'Why?'

'We are men. Should you prove to be a woman we would not wish to embarrass you.'

'One of you is a woman?' Gombold asked with some surprise.

'Certainly.'

He stared: was there nothing with which he could identify the woman?

'I am the woman,' said one.

Gombold looked at the creature enquiringly. She smiled and said nothing. The others retired. The woman took his hand.

'You are the victim of a delusion,' she said. 'Remove your clothes and I will tell you to which sex you belong.'

'I have no doubt.'

This remark proved to be ill chosen, for it seemed to arouse the woman; she gripped his arm and said with no attempt to conceal the change in her attitude:

'I have a very real doubt!' And then added: 'Are you going to be reasonable?' As Gombold did not reply she continued in a low voice with a menacing note: 'I insist that you face the truth. Off with those clothes.'

She seized him round the waist and fell with him to the floor where the nightmare of the previous evening was repeated. Gombold let out a continuous squeal of fright and rage. The creature straddled across him ripping at his clothes like a fury. He was being outraged, he was sure of it; he closed his eyes and screamed as loud as he could. He implored his assailant for mercy. With utter disregard for his feelings he was stripped as naked as the day on which he was born. With some idea of protecting his modesty he crawled away behind a settee, which afforded the only possible cover in the room.

'You are a man. I knew it all the time.'

'And so are you,' said Gombold, as with a gasp of surprise he allowed his assailant to help him to his feet.

The woman who had attacked him was no woman: she had a bald head and a beard. She came towards him carrying a suit of clothes. The door opened and a youth and a woman entered. There was silence for a little as Gombold dressed, then he said:

'Your behaviour was generous, but rash.'

'You admit that you were deceived as to your sex?'

'Reluctantly I do.'

'And the sex of your husband?'

'I cannot understand how the confusion came about.'

'Do you still have difficulty distinguishing us from each other?' asked the woman abruptly.

'Certainly not.'

'What is wrong with him?' said the youth.

'When I thought I was a woman I imagined you were indistinguishable; now that I am a man I see you are quite recognisable apart.'

'Perhaps with suitable study you could learn to face the truth. We are indistinguishable.'

'You are not!' said Gombold in an angry voice. 'You are not!'

'We are.'

'You are three people: a man, a woman and a youth. How can you be indistinguishable?'

'Are you sure of your facts?'

'Quite sure.'

'You were sure that you were a woman.'

This was undeniable. He said nothing. They were trying to make him believe something that was not true. They were as bad as Connie. He gave them another glance: three separate and easily identifiable entities. Not indistinguishable. They smiled and dropped the matter for the moment.

'We have other business on hand,' said the woman. 'When we are the Government you will, I think, have no difficulty in agreeing with us.'

Three

After weeks of planning the day arrived upon which the Prime Minister was to be assassinated. The morning had been cool, but the early afternoon was close and sultry; there seemed a brooding atmosphere in the streets. Followed by his three accomplices Gombold left for the hall where the Prime Minister was to hold a news conference. Tall and slim, with heavily made-up eyes and a wide-brimmed hat, he resembled perfectly a woman of authority and fashion. The furred and feathered accomplices kept close to him, talking of the woman to be killed. They entered the forecourt of the Conference Hall. A brief inspection and the giving of the password 'Irresistible', and the control post let them through. Sentries with tommyguns were on duty. The building was surrounded by a high wall. A second check took place; Gombold tilted the hat further over, throwing his face into shadow. In the distance he saw a column crowned by a lioness holding a cock between its paws. He shuddered at the symbol.

In the ante-room they presented their forged credentials to the Duty Officer. In the faint light of the room, where the windows were obscured by half-drawn blinds, a secretary pushed four chairs towards them.

'Take the weight off your legs,' the Officer said, rummaging in her enormous desk.

Gombold wasted no time. His manner was correct

and official.

'Here are my passes. You will see they are in order. I wish to go up immediately.'

'That is impossible.'

'Why?'

'Regulations.'

'What regulations?'

'I have my orders.'

'I wish to know who gave you those orders?'

For a second there was dead silence in the room; no sound but the rustle of leaves in the garden. Gombold swallowed hard and audibly. The situation was tense. The Duty Officer's face had not changed nor did it change now, but Gombold, who had never taken his eyes off her, felt that her manner had grown colder.

'It throws our calculations out.'

'I don't see why?'

'Who are you representing?'

'The South-west division.'

'Really?' Her eyebrows rose. 'I had no idea that a new candidate had been elected. Dodi–' she said, interrupting her speech to address the secretary who was flitting about the office in incomprehensible activity. 'Have a look in the file, perhaps you can find the South-west division?'

'I don't think there is any need for this.'

'Neither do I, but we cannot be too careful.'

Gombold watched the secretary approach an enormous filing cabinet: it dominated the room: light gleamed on its surface. The secretary stood on a stepladder and opened the top drawer. A dozen or so papers escaped and were blown by the draught from the electric fan into every corner of the room. The secretary wobbled on her ladder; more papers fell. The Duty Officer swung round in her chair and attempted, without rising, to pick up the papers nearest to the desk.

'Shall I try another drawer?' the secretary asked in a faint voice.

The Officer did not reply, she was reading the papers she had picked up. The secretary, taking her silence for assent, stepped down from the ladder and struggled with the bottom drawer which, opening unexpectedly and with a rush, deluged the room in more papers.

'We get through an enormous amount of work here,' said the Officer nodding her head, 'and what you see is only a fraction of it. What happened to the notes I made last week?'

The secretary, who was staring at the floor with a distracted air, suddenly came to life. Ignoring the Officer she began picking papers up, crouching low near the desk, scuffling them together and breathing heavily. The Officer shouted and she stopped.

'What happened to my notes?'

'I filed them.'

'Where?'

'Under "N".'

Nothing was said for a minute or two, and then, without a word of warning, the secretary pushed the drawers of the cabinets shut and planted the papers she had collected in front of the Officer.

'I'll fetch someone,' she said, stamping through the scattered documents to the door.

'Find my notes,' said the Officer turning in her chair. 'Ask about the South-west division.'

The door slammed. The Officer cleared her throat.

'She's a great help to me as a rule,' she said. 'I have to scold her now and then, but I couldn't wish for a better secretary. These official records are a *pest.*' She spat out the word with venom. 'I've another girl for the typing. That's who she's gone to get now. A different person entirely. A bit common, you know.'

'Do you keep all the records here?' Gombold asked.

'I don't think so.'

'Don't you know?'

The woman flushed an angry pink.

'No, I don't,' she said.

'Who is in charge here?'

'I am.'

She sat up in her chair. Her manner had become aggressive. She gave Gombold and his accomplices a stony stare.

'It is impossible to get things straight in this place,' she said. 'I have too much to do; things get left lying around. You would be surprised by the amount of work I get through.' She leaned back in her chair. 'I know you think we sit on our bottoms. Well, I can assure you we don't. Work, work, work from morning till night. You have all the fun. I'm sure I don't.'

'I'm sorry,' said Gombold, who thought the time had come to make amends. His words had already made the Officer hostile if not suspicious. 'I'm so on edge.'

'Is it your first conference?'

'Yes.'

'You needn't be worried. You'll love everybody.'

'I was so terrified that my clothes were dowdy.'

'I think you look very smart.'

'And my hair – where do you get yours done? It's so lovely.'

The Officer smiled.

'I'm so glad you like it. Most people think because a girl's in uniform she doesn't have to worry about her appearance. They couldn't be further from the truth.'

She had relaxed her manner; she took out a hand mirror and studied her face.

The secretary had returned with three other women. They were all kneeling before the cabinet attempting to prise open the bottom drawer which had become wedged.

'Couldn't I give you a hand?' said Gombold.

'Leave them to it,' the Officer said. 'I don't think there is any real need to check up. I'm not the suspicious type. It's just that we cannot be too careful.'

A stillness fell upon the room, only the rustling of the papers was to be heard; it looked indeed, for a few minutes, as if the Officer were dozing. A faint moan came from the first secretary. The contents of the entire cabinet were sifted; it took an hour and a half. At the end of that time no document relating to the South-west had been found, neither had the Officer's notes. A loud rapping on the door made Gombold turn round. A big, heavy woman with flaxen hair barged into the room.

'Ready?' she asked.

'I can't come yet,' said the Officer.

'Why not?'

'Busy.'

'Can't it wait?'

'No.'

'Nonsense.' The flaxen-haired woman scanned the room with a pained air. 'You're off duty!'

This seemed to have a profound effect upon the Officer. She stood up and stared at her companion in a dazed fashion. The secretaries hastily shuffled the papers into one drawer of the cabinet and slammed it shut with a crash. The Officer reached for her hat and coat and, while struggling into them, said:

'Contact Christine, will you?'

The first secretary got the connection. She passed the receiver over. A voice came over the wire quite audibly.

'Is that you, Chrissy?' the Officer said. 'I'm sending you a new girl. I want her to be shown the hall. I know she's early. As a favour, dear.'

At the other end of the line Christine did not seem to understand for she began to ask questions. The Officer paused for a moment; then she said she was going off duty and would send Gombold along. Gombold rose to his feet. The first part of his task was over and done with; other, and in their way, as pressing duties awaited him. He said goodbye to the Officer who shook hands, and said she hoped for a wonderful conference. In the handshake there appeared an unexpected comprehension and agreement.

Acknowledging the salute of the guard, Gombold and his accomplices took the lift to the second floor. They walked slowly down the carpeted corridor to the hall. The shots were to be fired from a balcony at the further end. This would not be in use during the conference. The rifle to be used had been dismantled and each assassin had a part in her large and ultrafashionable handbag. It was not long before the conference was scheduled to begin, but Gombold found he had plenty of time to mount his rifle and to take sight tests. As the minutes ticked by a feeling of numbness crept over him. His heart pounded. The clock struck three.

Down below him a few women had arrived. They settled themselves into the big, comfortable chairs.

'Now, my dear, what are you going to wear for the disarmament conference?'

'I did think my –'

'Too perfect. Too perfect.'

'I'm against any relieving of international tension, and I know Lillian thinks –'

'Lillian thinks we should wear –'

'I think it would be wonderful if our delegates wore matching costumes.'

'Fay! What a perfectly wonderful idea.'

'We must tell Lillian.'

'Yes, Lillian must know about Fay's idea.'

A number of women rose and crowded round the Prime Minister as she entered wearing a wool two-piece, simplicity itself, yet with a sort of dash and elegance. The Normandy blouse was longer than average. Her shoes were brown with bronze calf as contrast. Gombold found himself straining to catch her words which were spoken to the Chancellor of the Exchequer:

'You can tell Mrs Vulp that if she wants a Life Peerage, she'll have to put her bloody hand in her pocket.'

A tall, not unimpressive figure, she was something of an expert in her own line, though many said this specialisation had been won at the cost of character and humanity. She settled herself at the head of the table; she lit a cigarette.

'Now, dears,' she said, blowing a stream of smoke into the air, 'we have had the most heavenly cabinet meeting –'

A pretty woman in a grey dress struggled to her feet.

'Oh, Lillian! And I wasn't there. I wasn't there. How could you!'

'But darling –'

'You promised.' She burst into tears. 'It was promised.'

'The very next time.'

'No. You've betrayed my trust. I wouldn't come now if you begged me.'

She sat down and then thought better of it. Dabbing her eyes she ran from the room. The Prime Minister sighed.

'She gets so excited by the smallest things. Where was I?'

'– the cabinet meeting.'

'– the cabinet meeting.'

'We held it at Molly's house. And we have decided at last.'

A flutter of voices rose:

'Yes?'

' ... yes ...

'She's going to have it re-decorated in Chinese white lacquer and natural oak woodwork.'

'How marvellous.'

'Did you have the final say?'

'Of course.'

'I knew you would. You were all for natural oak, weren't you? She wanted some dreadful dark-looking muck she'd picked up cheap somewhere.'

'Fay!'

'Well, it's true.'

'It is *not*.' The woman called Molly stood up, her eyes blazing. 'How dare you say such things. And to my face as well.'

The Prime Minister smiled. 'All right, dears, calm down.'

Gombold, waiting for a favourable opportunity to do his work, stood rolling an unlit cigarette between his lips.

' ... the International field ... I've made a big decision. I'm going to the disarmament conference in a great flowing dress in white broderie anglaise with heavenly flounces. The price was simply outrageous.'

'Will there be an official statement?'

'Yes.'

'Is that final?'

'Yes. The doors are closed to further negotiations. I decided quite definitely this afternoon.'

'Good.'

'Lillian, if you are asked to take part in a four-girl meeting in the autumn will you go?'

'Well, dear, it depends on the aims and terms of such a meeting.'

'Diplomatic rumours say you are against any change in the hemline.'

'I think it would be a grave psychological risk to

shorten the hemline now. It might have far-reaching repercussions.'

'Are you in favour of direct contact with our rivals?'

'In certain circumstances I am. Though after the disgraceful things they said about my drawing-room curtains last time, I don't think I can make too great an effort to be polite.'

'But Lillian, that would be fatal.'

'They were the latest screen-printed furnishing fabrics: matt-black with an azalea motif. And – well I just don't want to dwell on the things that woman said.'

'Poor Lillian.'

'But what about the Conference?'

'Yes, what about the Conference?'

'It's arranged to coincide with the autumn showings. So we can have a look round the Houses as well as attend the Conference.'

'Lillian you – are – a – genius.'

'Lillian you're so wonderful.'

'I admire you so much Lillian.'

'And the election? Is it true?'

'Perfectly true.'

'There's going to be one before the Conference?'

'Yes.'

'You are sure of being returned with an increased majority?'

'Perfectly sure. It is clearly right that the ladies of this country should have an opportunity of deciding as soon as possible who is to represent them. Topline discussions lie ahead. I say to all women, "Put your strength into winning this election. Victory, I know, will crown our efforts. It is vital in the interests of the free world to stabilise the hemline."' She paused and looked around the table with a worried expression. 'Now, dears, bad news, I'm afraid. Are we having scalloped bedspreads over separate floor-tipping frills, or plain eiderdowns which keep their beauty like an heirloom? *That* is the crux of the matter. The efforts to reach agreement came to an abrupt end last night. Naturally there is dismay in official circles. Failure came after several hours of extra talks, optimism, and the postponement of "Pixie" Heath's trip abroad.'

'Poor dear.'

'I know she was so looking forward to –'

'Yes, yes, she was.'

'Girls! please! There's been a tremendous effort on all sides to try and ram through a last-minute compromise solution. For nine hours "Pixie" postponed her holiday, acting at the request of Dr Maud and the Rev. Daisy Greene. "Pixie" hoped to have good news for us. But she left with the problem still unsolved.'

A rustling of feathers, silks and linens floated towards Gombold; the exquisite scents tickled his nostrils. He began to sweat as the moment approached. The three accomplices sat in the shadows watching him. He listened to the Prime Minister, rolling the cigarette between his lips, feeling it ... crumble ... as the afternoon wore on. They were sipping drinks in cool, long-stemmed glasses; ice tinkled. A young girl stood up.

'Lillian,' she said, 'about the strike.'

The Prime Minister patted a seat beside her. The girl sat down.

'Darling, darling! What a good little puss you are for reminding me. I nearly forgot.'

'Well?'

'Yes?'

' ... I'm so on edge ... '

'It's not really my problem. Edith here (come along we're all friends), Edith is in charge of that particular thorn in my flesh. It's not my pigeon.'

Edith rose and cleared her throat. She was about forty with beautiful hair; her hands too were a joy to behold.

It was an open secret that she was the brains behind a chain of beauty salons.

'This is my first report as a member of the Government,' she said, 'and I would like to commence by paying to the ladies of the cabinet an immediate tribute. What a wonderful set of women they are. And how they manage to run the country and remain so attractive I do not know. If I may be forgiven for bringing personalities into it, I think it is due to their all being young at heart. We are fortunate in having as our "P.M." a woman of energy, imagination and infectious good humour (and may I say, Lilly, I think you're looking simply splendid after your new facial). Our "P.M." is backed by a body of able and skilled enthusiasts without whom we would all be in a sorry state.'

She cleared her throat and consulted her notes.

'The strike – I told Lilly earlier in the day that the situation is very difficult. Yet the fact is that hope has been kept flickering by something Madame Jeanne said yesterday morning at the start of our marathon talks. "I believe," she said, "that something could be done without compromising the findings of the Streeter report." This appears to be the clue to a settlement. Madame Jeanne, as some of us know, is notoriously difficult to deal with.'

Several of the women laughed; a few applauded.

'Anyway,' Edith said, 'there's no need for us to feel gloomy. There will be no proclamation of an emergency until the last possible moment when hope has been abandoned.'

She sat down to a round of applause. She could be heard saying to her neighbour, 'I think we'll be able to get the wheels rolling before long.'

'Well, that seems to be everything,' said the Prime Minister, rising to bring the conference to a close.

Gombold, high in the darkness, brought her into focus; he could now see only a small region of flesh, a few strands of hair, a section of her hat. She turned and smiled at someone, a young voice was saying:

'Isn't this room exquisite? You know, I've been admiring it so much I've hardly heard a word anyone said.'

The Prime Minister moved; Gombold swung his sights to the left and right searching for her.

'Polly! you minx ... '

'And can't we see Gertrude's long friendship with "Spooky" Sutherland reflected in the entrance hall with its unique collection of ... '

' ... and she has a deep interest in the work of ... '

' ... who designed the ... '

'You've got to hand it to her, the whole place *is* Gertrude.'

Gombold stood above them like a scientist in a laboratory. He did not have much longer. The Prime Minister held up her hand for silence. The whispering ceased, noses were powdered, lipstick re-touched, hair straightened. Gombold saw nothing but the pale skin of the woman below. He felt his finger on the trigger. He squeezed, was conscious of the rifle kick, saw consternation beneath. The bullet hit the Prime Minister above the frontal sinus at seven minutes nine seconds past four, rupturing the dura mater, which lines the cranial cavity, and entering the brain. At seven minutes ten seconds past four the Prime Minister was as dead as fifty dodos.

Gombold laid the rifle down. There was no risk of finger prints; he had worn a pair of white gloves throughout the operation. He walked as quickly as the unfamiliar skirt and shoes would allow away from the scene of the crime. Before the gallery could be screened off he was down in the garden mingling with the astonished crowd.

Rumour of the outrage soon spread through the city. Within ten minutes Police Chief Hogg was thrusting her way through the crowd. She forced her way inside the Conference building. Then she tried to clear the sightseers who found nothing to look at except the public rooms. Soon nobody could remember exactly where the shot had come from, what part of the building had housed the assassin. So they stood outside in dull amazement.

Police Chief Hogg took a lift to the scene of the crime and continued to walk in a baffled manner until a deputy came to report that a set of women's clothes had been discovered in a men's lavatory two streets away. Immediately Duty Officer Maisie remembered that she had talked to a new delegate who, she said, 'walked funny', and, it appeared from the few words spoken, 'talked funny' too. So the secret of how the murderer had gained entrance to the building was revealed.

'Get me a man,' said Hogg abruptly.

An officer and two or three women searched and found her a man.

'Do you know anything of this?' Hogg asked.

'I don't know, miss,' the man said. 'I came to deliver a parcel. What's happened?'

'Bring him upstairs,' Hogg said.

They took him upstairs. In an office at the top of the building Hogg perched on the edge of one of the couches. She sighed.

'I want to know what you were doing here,' she said.

'I came to deliver a parcel,' the man said. His voice was sullen, attentive to the danger he was in, but covertly attentive. The other women were behind him, where he could not see them. He wanted to turn and look, to see what they were doing, but he did not dare, the hair on the back of his neck rose. He stared at Hogg's lips with an intense concentration. But it was not in her lips. The signal came from her eyes. The man felt the steel bite into his neck; he winced, jerking forward, away from the nail-file, baring his teeth.

'Is that the truth?' Hogg said. 'Be sure you're telling the truth.'

'He's lying,' one of the women said. She was the deputy who held the nail-file, pointed end inwards. She pressed it gently against the man's neck. She was watching her chief. It needed only the smallest flicker of an eyebrow, a nod.

Hogg sat erect, scarcely sagging the springs of the couch. 'I think he hardly realises the serious position in which he finds himself. I'm not making threats but – if he should be lying – then I cannot answer for those women out there. They might decide to take the law into their own hands. I couldn't stop them.'

Perhaps there was another signal, it did not appear this time even in her eyes. The man expected pain. The file sank into. the flesh above the collar, the point twisting a little in the wound.

'Well?' Hogg said.

'I came to deliver a parcel,' the man said.

His voice was flat, not angry, quite expressionless. 'I don't know what happened here. I've nothing to do with it. It isn't my business.'

'Let him go,' Hogg said.

They watched him walk through the doorway.

In the forecourt of the building and in the nearby streets there were many who believed that it was an anonymous male crime, committed not by a man but by Man. And presently some of the women with revenge in their hearts began to canvass about for a male to crucify. But there wasn't one. Every man in sight had disappeared. Except the man who had come to deliver a parcel. He pushed his way through the crowd. They were baying now, with intolerant assurance and perhaps pleasure. The sounds they made were notes of wailing, while others shouted words of incitement. The noise seemed to come from a single throat, as though an animal were loose.

They closed in; he heard their voices now only as myriad and interminable insects. Falling into the gutter, breathing the sickening smell of blood, thinking how when he was younger, a boy, a youth, he had loved the sight of female flesh and the sound of women's voices, of walking or sitting alone with them under trees. He never knew the danger. Then the pavement, the stones, became actual, savage, filled with, evocative of, the claws of birds, maddening, terrifying sounds. He was afraid.

And then he died.

Four

It was dark when the rebel forces went into action. Decisive steps were taken while the Government still argued. The East garden police headquarters were raided – a magnificent coup. Eighty women were killed and several hundred taken prisoner. News came quickly upon this that the Government were preparing to flee the capital. The rumour was unfounded. No one quite believed it. It was officially denied, and proof of the authenticity of the denial was soon forthcoming. Rumours such as this were rife in the city. A person who was never discovered announced that at an appointed time women workers, won over, would open the gates of a small-arms factory. But it was when the body of the Prime Minister was taken from the Conference hall to the chapel of the Strangler that the revolution can really be said to have begun.

With official pomp, increased by security arrangements, the makeshift coffin was transferred. Two battalions with covered drums, ten thousand of the National Guard, and policewomen drawn from the important city districts followed the hearse. Three top-ranking officials carried laurel wreaths, and after them came a countless multitude of women from all branches of society: on the pavements, in the trees, in the streets, on balconies, at the windows and on the roofs, there was an even denser throng of men. An armed crowd passed, and a startled crowd watched; the Government had its finger on the trigger.

The procession proceeded from the Conference hall to the holy monument. It rained at intervals, but the rain produced no effect on the crowd. Several notable 'incidents' occurred, such as the coffin being carried twice (by mistake it appeared) around the Haymarket; stones thrown at Sir Shelumiel Cush, who was noticed on a balcony with his hat on; the emblem of masculinity torn from a popular flag; a policewoman wounded; and an officer of the Townswomen's Rifles causing havoc among her companions by crying aloud, 'I'm a man!'

The hearse passed the park, followed the river across the North bridge, and reached the esplanade of the Amazon, where it halted. At this moment a bird's-eye view of the crowd would have offered the appearance of a comet, whose head was on the esplanade, and whose tail was prolonged as far as the Conference hall. A circle was formed round the hearse, and the crowd was hushed. All at once O'Scullion appeared on the outer edges of the crowd with a flag, though others say with a stick surmounted by a cap.

When he spoke he did so with the fire of conviction. He said why a revolt had been necessary. His speech was so convincing and so detailed that his audience were spellbound. The assembly listened till the end; they did not interrupt. They gave no sign of either agreement or dissent. But their silence weighed heavily on those present. O'Scullion's voice rose, he came to the end of his speech.

Other leaders of the rebellion made in no way inferior calls. Gombold was pressed to denounce the private life of Police Chief Hogg but refused. He said it would be extremely embarrassing for him to do such a thing. The crowd showed great emotion when the speeches were over. The day had been carried. Only then did disaster strike. The rumour came that several young women on the edge of the crowd had been raped by the revolutionaries. As cries of 'shame' were heard the Government forces could be seen approaching. Women in armoured cars sped along the left bank to stop the passage of the North bridge, while on the right soldiers emerged from the Convents of the Strangler, the Enemies, and the Holy Thing. It was the counter attack.

At the moment when the Government forces and the rebels came into contact Gombold found himself lost in a sea of hands, arms, backs, breasts; the noise hid the sound of shots. Who gave the signal for the attack? No one could say. Some thought that a bugle-call sounded the charge, others that a woman was stabbed. The truth is that three shots were suddenly fired, one killing Emily, Countess Climax, the second an old deaf woman who was closing the window of her house, while the third grazed an officer's cheek. A man cried, 'They've begun too soon!' as the government forces swept down upon the crowd killing members of their own party and the rebels in an indiscriminate slaughter.

Gombold fled to the rebel H.Q. O'Scullion was not there, and as Gombold waited he heard what had happened in the provinces. Everyone knew something, no one knew the whole story, everyone wanted to know more, as was natural in this obscure situation. The curious, the anxious, even the indignant, came and went. To them Gombold said with a shrug of the shoulders what was true, that he knew nothing definite. He could do no more than now and again express his own indignation at the outrage committed, or agree with the indignation of others. It seemed to be the general opinion that the incident was a carefully calculated invention.

His own feeling he could show only to the comrades

who were conspirators or sympathisers and to whom he could speak in full confidence. Their first question was: 'Is all lost?' He could but shrug his shoulders for he did not know any more than they. Filled with deep apprehension he received news of a counter-offensive. Unexpected reinforcements were arriving. Preparations were immediately made to defend H.Q. to the last man.

As the night progressed the news became more and more depressing. Early victories dwindled as the Government showed its strength. Soon H.Q. was isolated. The Government waited until first light to move in. And yet the rebels were not disheartened. Although death was certain they kept up their spirits. The ideals were noble it was conceded; if they died they died in a good cause. And so they waited. The sky grew pale. The sun rose. Over the city there was silence. Everyone waited.

Suddenly bullets ricocheted from the corners of houses, broke windows, wounded men. The impression produced by the first round was chilling; it was of a nature to make the boldest think.

'Comrades,' O'Scullion cried, 'Let us not waste our ammunition, but wait till we see them before returning their fire.'

'And before all,' a youth called Offjenkin said, 'let us hoist the flag.'

He picked up the flag, which had fallen, not having been properly secured. Outside in the square the troops were clearly seen. He held the flag in his hands.

'I'll raise it myself,' he said.

This was such a grand gesture that the men around him cried, 'Don't do it.' But he was determined to hoist the flag. With each step he ascended, the scene became more terrible, his handsome face and the expression upon his lips were calculated to bring tears to the eyes of all beholders. When he stood on the roof of the building, in the presence of twelve hundred invisible gun-barrels, they knew they were watching a hero.

Brandishing the flag he cried, 'Long live the revolution!'

Shots rang out and Offjenkin tumbled from the roof, bleeding, heroic and dead.

'Comrades', O'Scullion said, 'Let us place his corpse under cover; let us each defend this dead man, and let his presence in our midst render us impregnable.'

A murmur of assent followed these words. O'Scullion bent down, raised the young man's head, and kissed him on the forehead; then, stretching out his arms as if afraid of hurting him, he took off the dead man's coat, pointed to the bloodstained holes, and said,

'Let this be our flag.'

An army greatcoat was thrown over Offjenkin; six men made a litter, the corpse was carried to a large table in one of the ground floor rooms.

It was while O'Scullion and his rebels were paying their homage to the courage of one of their number that the first assault of the Government forces was launched. Someone called, 'Watch out!' The men hurried from the side of Offjenkin's corpse, but it was too late; for they saw a flashing line of bayonets. One second more and the rough defences around the H.Q. had been captured. O'Scullion shot seven or eight women as they clambered over the barricade. The Government held the whole city except for the house itself.

For the next hour or so an uneasy calm was preserved. The whole attention of the women was directed to the front of the house, which was the easiest place to cover. From the back access was difficult. As Gombold, after making a routine inspection of the defences, was reporting to O'Scullion, he heard his name called from the rear of the house:

'You there, Gombold.'

He started, for he had seen no one during his rounds. He took a step to leave the yard.

'Gombold,' the voice repeated; this time he could not doubt, for he had heard distinctly; he looked around but saw nothing.

'Over here,' the voice said.

He was drawn to a garden shed. It was a young man he had never seen before. No one had suspected that he could have got into the H.Q. without being seen. He had a letter to deliver. It was from Gombold's mistress, Beatrice. Gombold read it. The young man said he could lead Gombold out of the danger area. Gombold was tempted but could not leave his comrades. The letter from Beatrice told him to meet her at the house. She had something of importance to say to him. Gombold saw that the handwriting was genuine; no one could fake the style. He hesitated and while he did so a loud explosion was heard. The Government had blown up the building. There was no hope now. So Gombold followed the young man with a clear conscience. His brave comrades were undoubtedly dead. He would not want to view their mangled corpses. He had in his pocket a photograph of O'Scullion. It was a memento of a great man and a noble cause.

He followed the young man. They climbed over broken walls, outhouses, and round the backs of office buildings. When they reached the North bridge they parted. Who the man was Gombold never knew; a brother or a cousin of Beatrice perhaps. Avoiding the main thoroughfares, which were thick with riot police, he made his way to the house. Beatrice was waiting for him in the garden.

She was like ice, cool, pure and white. Her face was as beautiful as ever and as he kissed her he saw, for the first time, the police closing in on him. She watched him led away. Her eyes blinked, but it was not tears. The moon shone down. The stars were hard. Gombold was taken to police headquarters, beaten up and thrown into a cell.

Afterwards he slept and when he woke it was evening again. The cell appeared more comfortable than he had been led to expect, and it did not, therefore, alarm him. In the darkness his sense of hearing became more acute: at the smallest sound he rose, convinced they were coming for him, but the noise died away, and he sank back onto his bunk. At last steps were heard, a key turned in the lock, the bolts creaked, the door opened, and a steam of light filled the cell.

He was taken into a yard where a lorry waited, the driver was in his cabin; Gombold climbed into the back of the vehicle with his guards. He felt himself urged forward, and having no intention to resist, he was in an instant seated at the front between two soldiers, the others took their places and the lorry moved off.

He glanced around. The faces were blank. Gombold had no idea of direction, no clue as to where they were taking him. After an hour or so the lorry came to a halt. The soldiers descended first, then Gombold was ordered to step down. They were on a wharf. He saw the reflection of rifles by the lights of the lamps on the quay. The men looked at Gombold with curiosity. A woman officer gave the order and they marched their prisoner towards a boat tied up at a landing-stage. Gombold got into the boat. Four oarsmen rowed him out to sea.

His first feeling was of joy at breathing fresh air again; but he soon sighed and wondered where they were taking him. The boat could not make a long voyage, there was no vessel at anchor outside the harbour. He was not bound, nor had they made any attempt to handcuff him; this was strange. He waited, trying to see through the darkness.

Half an hour later he saw rising from the blackness a building, with towers, columns, stairways and buttresses. And he knew where he was. Castle Sanguine had for a long time been a fortress for political prisoners.

Gombold said, 'What are we going there for?'

The soldiers smiled.

'I haven't had a trial.'

'If you're guilty a trial is a waste of public money.'

Gombold was silent. A shock made the boat tremble. One of the soldiers leaped ashore, a rope creaked as it ran through a pulley, and Gombold guessed they were at the end of the voyage.

The guards, taking hold of his arms, forced him to rise, and dragged him towards the steps that led to the gate of the castle. A corporal followed, armed with a rifle.

Gombold made no resistance, he was a man in a dream, he saw soldiers who stationed themselves on the stairs, he felt himself forced through a door, it closed behind him; all this he did mechanically, nothing fixed itself on his brain. They halted for a minute, during which he strove to recollect his thoughts. He looked around. He was in a courtyard surrounded by high walls, he heard the tread of sentries, and as they passed before the light he saw the barrels of rifles.

They had a ten-minute wait. Gombold could not escape, the soldiers released him, they were awaiting orders. The orders arrived.

'Where's the prisoner?' said a voice.

'Here,' said the corporal.

'Follow me.'

'Quick march!' said the corporal, pushing Gombold.

He followed the warder who presented him with three blankets, a pillow, a toothbrush and a chamberpot. They walked the length of a reeking corridor. The warder opened a door.

'Here's your cell for tonight,' he said. 'It's late, and the Governor is asleep. He might change you tomorrow.'

Before Gombold could open his mouth, before he had noticed where his bunk was, the man slammed the cell door and switched off the light. He was alone in darkness and silence. He drew a deep breath.

With the first light of day the warder returned to take Gombold to the Governor. He found the prisoner in the same position, as if fixed there.

'Had a good night?'

'I don't know.'

'Hungry?'

'I don't know.'

'Want anything?'

'I want to see the Governor.'

The warder shrugged and nodded his head in the direction of the corridor. Gombold followed.

He was led into a room. He felt a carpet under his feet. A bowl of roses gleamed upon the long oak table. Gombold gave his name and number. The Governor smiled, listened with a sympathetic ear, promised to do all in his power to help. The prison chaplain expressed his concern at the condition of Gombold's cell; at the idea of detaining a man without trial. The interview came to an end. Gombold left for his new quarters in a calmer state of mind.

The next morning the gaoler said, 'Well? How are you today?'

Gombold made no reply.

'Want anything?'

'I want to see the Governor. He promised to see my quarters were better – these are worse.'

'You can't see him today.'

'Why not?'

'It's against the rules.'

'Against the rules?'

'No more than one visit to the Governor a month. You've had your month's supply.'

'What is allowed, then?'

'Better food, books, and the occasional woman – if you care for that kind of thing.'

'I don't want books, I'm satisfied with my food, and I don't want a woman. I must see the Governor.'

'If I have any more lip I'll cut your bread ration.'

'Have you a pencil I could borrow?'

'Yes.'

Gombold took the stub and the warder left. At lunchtime he returned.

'Don't brood,' he said, 'or you'll go mad.'

'You think so?'

'The old boy before you went crackers.'

'How long ago was this?'

'A few years.'

'Was he freed?'

'No. He was a doctor.'

'Listen,' Gombold said. 'I'm not mad, perhaps I shall be, but at present I'm not. I'll make you an offer.'

'What is it?'

'I'll pay you well if you help me to escape.'

'I'd lose my job.'

Gombold brushed this aside. 'If you refuse to help me I'll hide behind the door one day, and when you come in, I'll brain you with this chair.'

'Threats!' said the warder, retreating and putting the door between them. 'You're certainly going off it. The doctor started like you. In three days they had to give him an injection.'

Gombold whirled the chair around his head.

'Oh,' said the warder, 'it's like that is it?'

'That's right,' said Gombold, dropping the chair and sitting on it.

The warder went away.

A month later Gombold saw the Governor again. He told him of the condition of his cell. The prison chaplain had gone into the case. The Governor sighed. 'I hope you aren't going to be a troublemaker,' he said. 'We do our best.'

'What exactly is your problem?' said the chaplain coldly.

'My cell is filthy,' said Gombold.

That something had to be done was agreed. The Governor and the Chaplain both shook hands with Gombold. They hoped that he had come to his senses. When his term of imprisonment was over he could go back to the outside world and become a useful citizen. Gombold noticed that there were chrysanthemums on the table. He left in a calmer state of mind.

The warder led him to his new cell. After numberless steps had been descended, Gombold saw a door. It was opened, the warder pushed him forward, and the door was shut with a loud bang. The air Gombold breathed was thick. He was in a privy.

Five

All his emotion burst forth; he cast himself on the seat, crying, and asked himself why they tormented him so. One thought in particular came to him – that during his journey he had sat still, whereas he might have plunged into the sea, and have reached the shore. Or have been shot. He would have been happy, but now he was confined in the castle ignorant of his future. The thought was maddening, and he could hardly bear it.

And then, he studied how he might liken this house of ordure to the world: first, the pissoirs they were the mob, gurgle, gurgle, gurgle into infinity. And the lavatory pans were the politicians – there were fewer of them and these came in the same shape and size but not colour. The chains were artists and thinkers – pull one and release a fresh shower of water, cleaning away the shit. Industrialists were toilet paper – some of the cubicles (which he took to be countries) had too much, some hadn't any, in one he had to push his way through festoons of the stuff. These ideas flowered in him; his head almost burst; he did not know where they came from, they were inexhaustible.

The warders locked him into a single cubicle. All he could see was the courtyard below his tiny window, and the rest of the room through a hole in his prison door. Soldiers came to use the urinal; he could hear the flushing of the water and smell the stale odour. He could not get out of this place. In his pocket he had the stub of pencil and there was enough toilet paper for every use. He wrote a specimen of his verse and poked it under the door.

'I am a young writer,' he added at the end, 'but I think this will show you I am a true writer. I beg you to release me –'

> I am a blue salmon,
>   I am a dog, I am a stag.
>   I am the speckled white cock's
> Desire for hens.
>   Primrose I am and hill bloom,
>   Tree and shadowy blossom.
> I am the ninth wave's stillborn foam.
>   I am berries at harvest-time,
>   Wheat on the stalk,
> The sun swift-rising in the long-maned sky,
>   The moon.
> I am the penance and the sin.
>   I love.
>   Karafy,
>   My arm shakes, my breast trembles,
>   My heart aches,
> I carry my head in my hand.
> I am autumn, frost, and winter.
>   I am the girl's delight,
> I am the stallion.
> (I am the girls I myself have enjoyed.)

At night he sat on the seat and stared into the darkness. He thought, planned, waited, and waiting plunged back into dreams. He was Danaë locked in her tower. O Zeus! He felt the hero in his belly. He was Ugolino; the key to his tower at the bottom of the Arno. He was Osiris in his coffin, St Barbara, Rapunzel.

66

The soldiers were outside – more than he had ever heard; artillery, infantry, guardsmen, squads and troops, whole regiments came here. Through the hole in the door he saw parts of uniforms; a tunic, a coat, a cap or a beret. Drums rolled, bugles blew, troops marched. They had regular bladders, Gombold saw the same ones several times. After many months he even knew their names. Boar, Honour, Speculate and Whitsalt, were the most noticeable. And Dogg the most assured. And Loosefish the most violent. And Crim the most handsome. And Cathole the most intelligent. And Snapturtle, Droop, Propagate, Lill and Rutt, the most quarrelsome.

One day Gombold made a paper dart of another poem: it was the kind of writing he had never done before, indeed he was convinced it was of a type no one had ever attempted in any language. After a second or two the dart was returned, unopened. His heart sank. There seemed no one here either to appreciate his writing or to engineer his escape.

Then he heard a voice say, 'You in there.'

Gombold looked up. An eye was pressed to the hole in the door.

'What?' Gombold asked.

'Stop writing poems.'

'I have to pass the time away.'

'There are other ways. I'm not picking up your muck every time I pass.'

'Who are you?'

'My name's Squall. I'm a corporal in charge of ablutions.'

'Don't go away,' Gombold said.

'I've got work to do,' Squall said.

Gombold heard the sound of his boots tramping on the stone. His voice echoed among the privies. Next day Gombold was dozing when Squall called to him again.

This time he stayed half an hour or so. Gombold found that he was keen on the army. He had worked in other jobs, but they had none of the advantages of the army . . .

'My first job was in an agency,' Squall said, wheezing through the hole. 'I was a young kid at the time. I worked for a dwarf. He wore special shoes, though. You'd never have guessed. His name was Jelf. Earnest Jelf.'

'He was a family man?'

'He had three daughters.'

Gombold roused himself from his lethargy, 'Were they dwarfs?'

Squall didn't answer. Gombold concluded he had gone away. After a silence Squall said, 'They were short-statured. Betty, Eileen and Susan. They were lucky girls. I'd dispute their being dwarfs. He trained them well, you know. He had the wherewithal to do it. His circumstances were vastly different from average. But he'd done it from small beginnings.'

Gombold saw Squall's eye disappear from the hole. He dozed. A few days later a visiting magistrate came to the prison.

At the sound of the key turning in the lock, and the creaking of the hinges, Gombold, who was sitting on the privy seat, raised his head. He guessed that the moment to address himself to a superior authority had come. He sprang forward.

The soldiers levelled their rifles and the magistrate stepped back. Gombold saw that he was represented as dangerous. In a voice full of humility he addressed the magistrate and sought to inspire her with pity.

'I don't know whether it is in your power to release me,' he said, 'but you can state my case to the correct authorities.'

'We shall see.'

68

Gombold fell on his knees. The door closed.

Days and weeks passed, then months; Gombold still waited; he at first expected to be freed within a fortnight. When this time expired, he reflected that the magistrate could do nothing until her return to the capital, and this might not be until her circuit was over; he, therefore, fixed three months. These too passed. Then six more.

Squall came and went. Sometimes he spent as much as an hour talking to Gombold, at others only a minute.

'That dwarf I was telling you about,' he said one day. 'Are you interested?'

'Yes,' Gombold said.

'I thought you might be.'

'What was his wife like?'

'She was a bit of a mystery. Her name was Emmy. She used to work for a firm of wholesale chemists before her marriage.'

'My mother's name was Emmy.'

'It's a name you feel confident with. My own Ma's maiden name was Annie. Annie Francine Bridie Trull. She died many years ago now. She passed away three weeks after my sister was married.'

Gombold said, 'Is she happily married?'

'She is getting a place of her own soon.'

'Has she any children?'

Squall drew in his breath. 'She's not likely to be breeding,' he said. 'She married Christ. She had a vocation.'

Gombold stood up. He felt he must keep his body in condition so he had evolved a system of exercises. He began to twist and bend.

'Don't do that,' Squall said. 'You'll strain yourself.' A pause, then: 'My Ma was embalmed.'

'Was she?'

'She expressed a wish to be scientifically preserved.'

He came back later on and watched Gombold writing. He said, 'Don't mind me asking but how come you were caught? We heard your mob was killed.'

Gombold told of his betrayal. When he spoke of Beatrice his voice grew low. He could hardly bear to accuse her.

'It's because she's rich,' he said.

Squall said, 'I was once kicked nearly senseless by some woman's husband. I'd wandered into her bedroom and she called him in and stood by while he nearly broke my back. And she was only an ordinary woman.'

Silence, the eye moved, and then: 'I'll be saying cheerio today.'

Gombold stopped. 'What?'

'I've been posted. It's been nice knowing you.'

The familiar eye was removed; the footsteps receded and Gombold was alone once more.

He passed through each degree of despair that prisoners suffer. He asked to be removed from his present cubicle, for a change, however disadvantageous, is still a change and might afford some relief from monotony. He begged to be allowed to walk, to have books and instruments. He spoke to himself for the sake of hearing a human voice; the sound, throbbing through the dark, set up echoes which seemed to be other voices talking. Odd fantasies took possession of him. In the solitude of his cell, and of his own thoughts, he was able to reconstruct ages past. His only communicants were men of his imagination;ʾ in the quiet hours they peopled the silence and told him of their lives. Gradually he turned from life and lowered himself, as in a diving bell, plumbing the ocean of mystic contemplation.

First the forests, worlds he knew so well. Landscapes gleaming in the light, and creatures part bird, part plant, flourished in his private dimension. A new twist had been given his brain, corridors of the unconscious stretched before him unexplored. Those benefits commonly provided by religious experience were his without fasts and castigations. Philosophical debate and meditation, intellectual discipline and the rigours of the desert procured for him. This was Eden, the earthly and heavenly; this the vision, the globe inhabited by devils and angels. This was death.

Tangible symbol of knowledge. Incantations, numbers, bewitching hocus-pocus, he could conjure from nowhere whatever he wished. And magic, apparently so incompatible with sense, was at his finger tips.

The three Graces, Voluptas, Castitas and Pulchritudo dancing: how marvellously round and incredibly fleshy. His brain spoke in riddles as he watched before him a catalogue of the richest kind. Hidden music played. Incongruous symbols mixed with holy things: a phallus, mitre, Hermes the mystagogue who guided souls, a woman lifting her forefinger to her lips; two men locked in a cupboard pointing rods at him. By use of images it might be possible to extract from fantasy a kind of reality.

Two halves of the cosmic egg split apart, curiously corrupt, perhaps a travesty. In the egg, intact but transparent, he saw the outline of a dormant Helen. Conceived by Chaos the egg destroyed a civilisation.

The Graces as three machines.

I.N.R.I. encircled by a crown of thorns, the letters standing for I Now Represent Idiots.

Enclosed in a privy he surveyed the world. Trooping by with a naked Venus came a wheel, its spokes like arms. Also casually juxtaposed in the scene was a wood and a revolving merry-go-round.

Mystical doctrines, rites, a whole lore of matters indistinct to the senses, legendary lists of Gods, his own name being included. Mother, cleanse my heart, give

71

me the ability to rage correctly. Let me learn why Prudence begins with a P.

Gombold, the prisoner, imprisoning reason, experienced an opening of windows, a smashing of barriers, and a cleansing. Saw again his wanderings. Saw the animals in the forest; wheels, springs and coils of sense and nonsense. He had succeeded in breaking down the walls so that his experience recorded clear and true, in its totality, was not a single unit, but many separate units, melting and fusing into a vision.

One day, early in the morning, a light sweat broke out and glazed Gombold's forehead. Around him the ruins of a church stretched upwards. He lived in the crypt, among bits of coffins and bones. He had succeeded to a reasoned derangement of the senses. He trod the rotting wood and dry bones under his feet. In his heightened perception, his expansion of consciousness, the world of men, their dreams, hopes, ideas, art, struggles and achievements were presented to him as a black bag. Musing on this symbol he found a coffin – a large one, and closed the lid. He looked through the sides. High-boned and skeletal faces stared at him. Lying in his coffin, he composed a poem which began 'Let us murder our mothers ... '

Forms blurred and faded. But there was a sound which did not fade. He listened. He raised his head: someone was knocking on the lid of his coffin. He shuddered. A continual scratching, as if made by a powerful toothed instrument.

The sound lasted nearly three hours; he heard a noise of something falling, and then silence. The warder brought supper. Gombold began to speak on many subjects, of the food, of the coldness of privy seats, grumbling and complaining, in order to have an excuse for speaking louder. The warder thought he was delirious and left him as soon as possible.

The sound became more and more distinct. An almost imperceptible movement among the stones at his feet. At last a voice calling to him.

'Who are you?'

'An unhappy prisoner.'

'Of what country?'

'I don't know.'

'Your name?'

'Gombold.'

The voice then asked a number of questions concerning the whereabouts of Gombold's cell. And upon being assured of certain facts cried aloud in disappointment.

'Oh, dear. The imperfection of my plans has ruined everything. An error of a line has been equivalent to fifty feet in reality.'

These words were uttered with an accent that left no doubt of the speaker's despair. The next instant a portion of the floor on which Gombold was standing gave way and he toppled into a deep hole which appeared at his feet. Finding no bones were broken he looked with keen interest at the man, who introduced himself as Doktor von Pregnant. He was tall, with bedraggled hair reaching to his shoulders, deep-set eyes, almost buried beneath thick eyebrows, and a long beard falling to his knees. Drops of sweat stood on his forehead, while his clothes hung about him in such rags as to make it impossible to guess their original state. He looked about 2,000 years old, but a briskness and an appearance of vigour in his movements made it probable that he had aged more from captivity than time.

'Let me see,' he said, 'whether I can remove traces of my work.'

He raised the paving stone as easily as though it weighed an ounce and fitted it back into place.

'I suppose you have no tools?'

'Do you have any?' Gombold asked.

'I made some. I have all that is necessary, with the exception of a file – a chisel, pincers, lever, brace-and-bit, two kinds of saw and a hammer.'

'I would like to see them.'

'Well, in the first place, here's my chisel.' So saying he displayed a blade, with a handle made of beechwood.

'How did you make it?'

'With the leg of my bed and a piece of iron.'

'I congratulate you,' said Gombold.

'Do not speak so loud. Guards are often stationed outside cells in order to overhear the conversations of prisoners.'

'But I am alone.'

'That makes no difference.'

'Is there any possibility of escape?'

'None whatever,' and as Doktor von Pregnant pronounced these words, an air of resignation spread itself across his face.

Gombold stared. 'Tell me why you are here,' he said.

The Doktor stared in a thoughtful way at Gombold wondering whether to trust so casual an acquaintance with his secrets. After a moment's reflection he started the story of his struggle. He too had been a rebel, but a successful one. For rebels are considered useful in the task of undermining. The rebels came to power. The Doktor did not. 'They hustled me into jail before you could say "knife".' He shook his head as he related his story.

Gombold remained motionless; at length he said, 'Then you have given up hope of escape?'

'Yes.'

'Why?'

'I was fourteen years making the tools I possess. I have been twelve years scraping and digging out the earth. And then I find myself under the cell of a fellow prisoner.'

Escape unaided had never occurred to Gombold. Some things appeared so impossible that the mind did not dwell upon them. At once he resolved to follow the Doktor's example, and to remember that what has once been done may be done again.

After continuing some time in thought, Gombold said, 'I have a plan.'

The Doktor jumped. 'Have you indeed?' he said.

'The corridor through which you have come is in line with the main sewer. If we dig further we can break into the sewer and so escape.'

'It may be possible.'

'We must begin at once.'

The Doktor shook his head. 'Listen to me,' he said, 'since my imprisonment I have studied the celebrated cases of escape. Among them are many failures. These I consider due to a haste wholly incompatible with such undertakings. To hurry is to lose. The successful escapes have been carefully arranged: Jeel Ciztaubort from C Block of Typoex, Greems from Inkle, the Signal of I from Hurlothrumbo. The ill-disposed chicken from Ido Towers. Husk, Cant, Carcelag, Cutboozy, the Fiddle, the owl, David's sow and the Wheelbarrow from Fort Marcoos. Neptune, Juno, Ceres, Vesta and Dis from the belly of their father. Truth from Dogmas, Jonah from the whale, every British Prime Minister since Pitt from Justice, my aunt from her wits, and many similar cases. I've come to the conclusion that chance frequently affords opportunities we should never ourselves have considered. Let us, therefore, wait for a favourable moment. You won't find me backward when the time comes.'

Gombold was still impatient to begin work. 'You could easily endure the delay,' he said, 'you were always occupied, and your philosophy encouraged you.'

'I didn't turn to that for support.'

'What did you do?'

'I wrote.'

'You were permitted to write?'

'Yes, except that I was not allowed a pen.'

'I see.'

'When you visit my cell I'll show you my life's work – A Concise History of the World and its Interests.'

'On what have you written this?'

'Upon several shirts. I invented a preparation for making cloth into paper.'

'Are you a chemist?'

'I have a little knowledge.'

'But you must have needed to consult other authorities – both for your invention and your history?'

'A slight effort of memory enabled me to recall the contents of many books. I could recite the whole of Shoxbear, Arrispittle, Grubben, Taciturn, Saint Trimmer-Ac-whinous, Saint Ginn of the Crutch, Goitre, Dinty, and Kneetchur. I committed to memory extensive commentaries on Mockbreath, King Lour, the choretricks and egglogres of Furgrill and the Purgreese List of Milltongue.'

'You are multi-lingual?'

'I speak five of the modern languages, that is to say, Finsh, Spoonish, Onlisch, Dallience and Greeman. By the aid of ancient Glook I learned modern Glook – I don't speak it well, but I am still improving.'

Stronger grew Gombold's amazement. He began to wonder if the Doktor were not one of his waking visions.

'Then if, as you say, you were not allowed pens, how did you manage to write the work of which you speak?'

'Oh, never mind. You ask too many questions.'

Gombold fell silent. A minute later he said, 'When will you show me your work?'

'Now.'

The Doktor turned, lifted the paving stone once more, led the way down the passage.

'But you yourself must be acquainted with languages?'

'No,' said Gombold, 'I have little Litthom and less Glook. I rely upon translations.'

'Well, well, better a translation than remain in ignorance.'

After having passed through the subterranean corridor, the two prisoners reached the further end. As he entered the Doktor's cell Gombold looked about him; but nothing unusual met his eye.

'Well,' he said, 'show me.'

'What do you wish to see first?'

'Your great history.'

Doktor von Pregnant drew from their hiding place three or four shirts, stacked one behind the other; they were numbered and covered with writing, so legible that Gombold could easily read.

'There!' said the Doktor, 'you'll find it quite simple – EGYPT (Old Kingdom) collar. EGYPT (Middle Kingdom) and EGYPT (to Persian Conquest) left sleeve. EGYPT (Psamathek III to Cleopatra VII, with notes on climate and religion) right sleeve. If ever I get out of prison and find a publisher courageous enough to give his imprint to what I have written my literary reputation is assured.'

'May I read?' said Gombold.

'Certainly. The Rise of Christianity (should you be interested) I have written upon a handtowel, added as an appendix to shirt one.'

Gombold examined the work with intense admiration; then he ran his eyes down a second shirt taking in any significant or interesting passage.

When he had finished reading as much as he could manage at one sitting, he laid the shirts aside and stood with his head drooping on to his chest, overwhelmed by the great work. While reading, his mind had been engaged by the idea of a man so intelligent, ingenious and clear-sighted as von Pregnant, parting with a little of the knowledge gained over a lifetime of study, to enrich a humbler mind.

'Of what are you thinking?' asked the Doktor.

'I was reflecting upon the enormous degree of intellect and ability you must have employed in reaching the perfection to which you have undoubtedly attained. If you do this whilst a prisoner, what would you not accomplish as a free man?'

'Nothing. From great pressures diamonds are formed. In freedom this energy of mind would be dissipated in useless endeavour.'

'It is an idea I can't believe.'

'Truth is not affected by your inability to believe.'

'Can truth be so depressing?'

'Truth is only depressing to the mind unused to thought. And now,' said the Doktor, putting the long-cherished shirts back into their original hiding-place, 'let me hear your story.'

Gombold obeyed, and began what he called his story, but which consisted merely of an account of his wanderings until he arrived at the Castle. From this period all was blank. He knew nothing, not even the length of time he had been in jail.

Doktor von Pregnant stared at him, shook his head and went on to speak of other matters. Although his conversation contained many useful hints and information he never mentioned escape. Gombold realised this was deliberate policy. He listened with attention to all the Doktor said; some of the remarks corresponded with what he already knew, but a part of the conversation was incomprehensible to him. However, it did open fresh views to an inquiring mind, and gave a glimpse of broader horizons.

'You must teach me a fraction of your wisdom,' Gombold said, 'if only to prevent your tiring of me.'

The Doktor said, 'When I've taught you a little, you'll know as much as I do myself.'

'I feel a great need of knowledge. When shall we begin?'

'At once.'

That very evening they sketched a plan of education to be entered upon the following day. Gombold had a good memory, combined with speed. He already knew Onlisch, and had picked up a little of the local language during his travels. By the aid of these he easily understood the construction of others. At the end of six months he spoke several foreign tongues and was making excellent progress in both ancient and modern Glook, Litthom and Hoobray, Trukkish and the many dialect forms of Greeman.

He never now mentioned escape; study took the place of liberty; absorbed in acquiring knowledge, days, months and years passed in one rapid and instructive course. Doktor von Pregnant educated Gombold by speaking sometimes in one language, sometimes in another; relating to him the stories of nations and great men. He never tired of adding to his history, and when a new passage was interpolated he discussed the item with Gombold . . . .

'Sir Thos. Browne didn't know everything, I can tell you. What song the sirens sang and the name Achilles assumed, he didn't know, he says; but I do. You can take it from me. Those girls used to sing a little cavatina (adagio) ad captandum vulgus, which I'd say, in my honest opinion, for what it's worth – I'd say it wasn't good enough.

'As for the name Achilles assumed – PHYLLIS. Little Phyllis they called him. And everyone knew he was a boy. Well, everyone except Odysseus. What a surprise for him when he discovered his mistake, eh? Only it wasn't quite the way he told it. No. That tale of Achilles seeing the armour and giving away his sex ... He never gave anything away in his life. Not that one ... The way Odysseus discovered was this ...

' ... put him off his stroke, I bet ... and Achilles said, "Don't let's argue about it, it doesn't matter two hoots." And Odysseus agreed – sort of. God alone knows who invented the other story ...

'Am I boring you? ... Then there was Laura ... "Isn't there anything you can do to help we girls break into print?" she says. "It's difficult enough to arrange for the publication of my own work," Petrarch says .... "I'm not a whore, dear, I'm a poetess," she says. "Well, I hope you perform the one function with a little more verve than you do the other," he says ....'

'Why did Hannibal turn back from the gates of Rome?' Gombold asked.

The Doktor closed an eye. 'You must read that for yourself,' he said. 'By the by, my boy, would you mind if I robbed you of your vest? I need an extra chapter on the development and influence of Smith with a Y.'

Gombold made no objection to the Doktor's request. He gladly gave his vest to the service of knowledge.

Six

One day a chance fall of rock inside the passage set Gombold thinking of escape once more. The Doktor agreed to his suggestion and they began to enlarge and extend the tunnel. That night in his cell, thought of toil forgotten, Gombold saw a scallop-shell, symbolising sexual love, venerated rushes and wild asparagus in a sunless, flowerless underground cavern – magnified hallucinations. And in the morning, scraping and digging, in little spurts and fits and starts, they clawed towards freedom. Mining their way through the walls, under privies, they searched for the main sewer. Scrabbling in the filth, nails cut, hands bruised, bleeding fingers and eyes tired of the impossible task before them.

The cycle revolved. Gombold slept and dreamed. He rose and worked and dreamed again – and went on dreaming. The Doktor talked constantly, continuing Gombold's education.

'What is the abiding value?' he said one evening.

'Truth,' Gombold replied.

'I have taught you nothing then,' the Doktor said. 'The rulers of whatever country you choose will designate as "true" that which is useful to them. Truth is relative, and always behind it stands some interest, furthering its own ends.'

Gombold could not bear this. He said good night and

returned to his own cell. It was only when he had composed himself that he realised he had forgotten to ask the Doktor what he took to be the abiding value.That night, whether as a result of the Doktor's premise or not, his dreams were more disturbing than usual. He saw a goat, father of Fornicationists, preaching chastity, a big-bellied virgin, a pair of pink combinations, the flayed skin of an ass, heard music from a cave. He saw twelve figures armed with sickles hacking away his testicles. The froth from which energy rose was produced by the castration of Gombold. The seed of the God gave form to the formless. The testicles of Gombold fell into the sewage beneath his cell and he woke crying. He continued to moan to himself until the warder entered with breakfast.

The passage which he dug with the Doktor's help grew larger and larger; from a narrow passage it became a wide corridor stretching for several yards under the castle. And still the work progressed, still they had not reached their goal. There were, of course, problems involved, for without scientific instruments the Doktor's calculations were not entirely trustworthy. But his ingenuity was up to the challenge. Recalling his efforts as a chemist and historian, at writing without pens or ink or paper, at painting when no paint could be obtained, he culled from his brain an instrument which served to guide them in their labours. And once he had perfected his technique it was a great success.

Several years after Gombold's imprisonment the task was completed. The corridor connecting the privies with the main sewer was finished, and the two men slithered into what they hoped was freedom.

Gombold's first sensation was blindness, for he could see nothing. In the darkness he heard noises. The sound of waves dashing against the cliffs reached his ears. Edging along their tunnel they reached the sewer.

Gombold stretched out one arm, then the other; he touched the wall on both sides; his foot slipped, and he understood that the pavement was damp. He advanced cautiously, fearing a hole, a cesspool, or some gulf, and satisfied himself that the pavement went ahead. He turned and beckoned to the Doktor. The old man shuffled forward holding his history beneath one arm. He had invented a crude torch which gave enough light for the first few minutes of their journey, then guttered and went out. A fetid gust warned them of the spot where they were.

They progressed northwards to a bend where the waters carried garbage from the kitchens. The swerve of the walls suggested the curve of a womb, hinting at rebirth. Again, the sea pounding the walls represented, on an elemental level, perennial invaders pummelling for his release.

After half an hour they were forced to stop, for a question occurred to Gombold; the sewer ran into another, which it intersected, and two roads offered themselves. Which should they take? They turned left. In a short while they were lost. In this unknown region each step they ventured might be their last. Alone, in the darkness of a cloaca, they had need of a guide. Suddenly Gombold noticed that the sewer was ascending. They heard the sound of voices, distinct and ominous, and saw shadows before them. Their own. Gombold turned, and saw behind them the light of a torch. Behind this several men.

It was an unhappy moment for Gombold and the Doktor. Discovery seemed certain. They had not been seen yet. It was difficult to tell whether the guards had reached the intersection. There was a chance that they might take the opposite road. The Doktor put out his hand and touched Gombold's arm. They stopped, hardly breathing, waiting. The guards came nearer and nearer. Then stopped. Gombold saw them make a circle, and then heads came together and whispered. The result of the council held by the guards was that the prisoners had gone right. The sergeant gave orders to right-wheel. Had they thought of dividing into two squads and going in both directions, Gombold and the Doktor would have been caught. The squad set out again, leaving the prisoners behind; and at this moment, the sergeant, to satisfy his conscience, fired several shots into the left tunnel. One of the bullets hit the Doktor who collapsed at Gombold's feet.

Kneeling down Gombold assured himself that his companion was alive and then, lifting him with difficulty, he dragged him along the passage. He hoped that soon they would reach the entrance. With dismay Gombold saw the Professor's history floating along the filth. It would be impossible to decipher the manuscript. The fruit of years of labour was lost.

At about six in the morning Gombold could distinguish the sides of the tunnel. As the light increased he saw that the Doktor's condition was serious. His hair was covered in blood, and blood was clotted at the corner of his lips. Noticing these things Gombold came to the entrance of the sewer. The tide was out. The waves roared on the rocks. He sat down, and remained for a time as if stunned. Then he raised the Doktor, carefully laid his head on his shoulder, and half dragged him to the shelter of a nearby cave.

Fetching water from the sea, he bathed the Doktor's face. He searched in his pockets for a rag to use as a bandage. There was nothing. Not even a handkerchief. Soon the Doktor regained consciousness. Gombold saw the situation was desperate.

The Doktor moistened his lips, 'Leave me,' he said. 'Make good your escape.'

'No,' said Gombold. 'I will stay here with – you.

84

Perhaps tomorrow you'll be better.'

'Tomorrow,' said the Doktor, 'I shall no longer be here.'

'What do you mean?' Gombold asked. 'We shall never part; you shall not leave me.'

The Doktor licked his lips; he had heard the sound of Gombold's voice rather than the meaning of the words. He murmured:

'It is true it would be charming to be free. Charming, but –'

He broke off, and said, 'It is a pity.'

Gombold took the man's hands in his. He said, 'Your hands are like ice. Are you suffering?'

'I – no,' the Doktor replied, 'I am quite well. It is only –' he stopped.

'Only what?'

'I am going to die.'

Gombold shook his head. 'No,' he said.

'Oh, you forbid me to die? Who knows? Perhaps I shall obey. I was on the road to death when you arrived, but that stopped me.'

'You are full of strength and life,' Gombold said. 'I shall take you with me.'

'No, no, no.'

All at once the Doktor rose. Gombold supported him, and tried to speak, but was unable to do so. After rallying a little, he sank back again. He caught hold of Gombold's sleeve.

'You are recovering,' Gombold said.

'I wish to die. I wish to die.'

Gombold fell to his knees and choked with sobs kissed the Doktor's hands. The hands did not move – for he was dead.

Gombold buried him on the seashore. Soon after this he realised he had to trust his body to the mercy of the waves. He took off his boots and plunged fully clothed into the sea. He had broken free from his chrysalis and emerged whole; now, he was part and parcel of the world, of the ocean, of the universe. So his thoughts would have run, if he could have collected them together under such circumstances. In fact all he was conscious of was – water. Great waves determined to dash him to pieces on the rocks, to smash his freedom before he had tasted it.

He paused for breath, and dived in order to avoid being seen. When he surfaced he was thirty feet from the shore. Before him, flying spray and foam roared. An hour passed, during which he continued to swim. And then, exhausted, he tried to tread water in order to rest but the sea was too choppy. The sky darkened. He felt a violent pain in his groin. He put his hand down and encountered resistance; he extended his legs and felt scales, and in an instant guessed the nature of the object he had taken for a submerged rock. It was a fish. Settling his haunches into the back of the creature, he pressed his knees against his sides, behind the fins. He saw the head in the water below him, thrusting through the emptiness.

They sped on. The waves slid past, white and green, ridge upon ridge, disappearing into drifts where the horizon erased the ridges. He shuffled his feet against the scales, which were firm and cold. The flesh sank beneath his touch. In the wilderness there was no movement except the waves. At the end of another hour he experienced a sensation of giddiness. He recollected that he had not eaten or drunk for a long time. And then he saw, a mile or so distant, driven on by the force of the wind, a huge bird. Its screech carried to his ears.

The fish moved on. Through the seas. Up and over the white froth. He looked back and the eagle was still behind them. He pressed his legs against the cold flank, as though to hurry it. Beyond the waves, under the racing clouds, sped the eagle. His eyes moved backwards and forwards. The waves rose, twisting spines around him, clefts and ledges, white streaks on the walls. From the clouds, the eagle, yellow in the sky, swooped. He saw its talons extended. Its shadows hovered above him. The feathers, hard, gold, tipped with a greenishness as of bronze, brushed his neck. He stared up, his heart pounding. A wave of emotion filled him; it brought a desire to exult, to shout in triumph. Soaring up to the clouds. Out of the waves.

The bird's breast was smooth. He was gripped by the talons, held firmly against the feathers, the beak curved across his shoulder. Space wheeled below. The remote waves gleamed. Waves against rocks, rocks, flatlands, hills. New snow firm upon peaks. Ridges and bulges of rock, streaming with ice. Wall and crag, rimmed against the air. Along the crest of the ridges and through the precipices, higher and higher, until they swooped over a mountain and saw another further off.

The lesser summits of the range were below. Rills, burnished knobs, smooth and holdless, crags, jutting and immense. The bird was not visible but the feathers pricked with light winked behind his shoulder.

White bannered, armoured like insects, the towers of a city lay among the boulders. Over bulges, over buttresses. The snow caulked with gold. Sweat beaded his forehead; his face caught the sun. The city was no more than a foot in diameter. Long minutes passed. His muscles ached. During a lull in the wind he heard sounds from below. The bird sank, the noise of bugles struggled upwards. In wheeling rebus, dim prospects rumbled under him, disappeared into foggy horizons, and were replaced by other images, vague but half-familiar. The flat plains of the belly, the navel, the red forest, the thighs and adjacent demesnes vast in scope and structure. Immeasurable gulfs of flesh rolling away for miles from head to toe.

The enormous anatomy began to disintegrate as the eagle floated down. The mountains were gone; they were falling towards the city situated between the navel and the groin.

Seven

When he arrived at the main shopping centre Gombold
was arrested for vagrancy. He spent three nights in jail
and was released with orders to move on. Paying no
heed to the advice he was arrested a second time. So they
got him a job rolling stones up a hill. He left after a
week. His next job was trying to catch water in a sieve.
This was better paid but the monotony made him long
for prison. A third job entailed keeping women
supplied with wool. He carted the wool to each
machine. Saw the basket of the operative was kept full.
The women were making winding sheets. Gombold
wondered that so many should be required. When he
asked if the undertakers were short of shrouds the
forewoman reported him for being cheeky.

The manager said, 'You can have your cards.' A
secretary said he ought to know the shrouds were never
sold. They were taken to another department and
unpicked. Gombold was not qualified to work burning
wheels, predicting clouds, painting feathers, or spin-
ning straw, so he ended up out of work.

One evening he was looking into a shop which sold
bridal gowns; but in reality wondering whether he
could pinch anything anybody would buy. While he
was examining his own reflection a man turned the
corner and entered the shop. After a second or two he
came out carrying a bridal wreath.

'Come with me,' the man said. Gombold was so surprised that he could not answer.

It was no use arguing with the people who live hereabouts, thought Gombold. So he followed the man.

'I'm called Pill,' said the man. 'I was once in service. But I was turned out because I had a mind of my own.'

'What are you doing with that wreath?' Gombold asked.

'I stole it.'

'What use is it?'

'I might get a few bob for it,' said Pill, 'Wait here.'

They had stopped beside a well-to-do house. Pill put his sack down and rang the bell. After a moment a woman appeared. She was thick-set and carried a pair of garden shears in her hand.

'Are you interested in leaves?' the man said.

The woman stiffened. 'Leaves?'

'For the garden. I noticed you had a good garden.'

'I'm not interested. I'm sorry,' said the woman, attempting to close the door.

Pill put his foot in the door. The woman pretended not to have noticed this. 'I saw the garden was well kept. I had an idea you were a plant lover. Am I right?'

'I have nothing to do with it.'

They confronted one another. Pill fastened his eyes upon the brooch pinned to the woman's dress. The woman glanced at Gombold.

'My sister's the gardener,' she said. Her voice came out a tone higher than she had expected. Her next words were so low that Gombold had difficulty in hearing. 'It's no good trying to interest her. She has the fertiliser delivered. They deliver it twice a year.'

'I'll chance it,' Pill said.

'We're not interested.'

Pill fetched a handful of leaves from his sack. 'These

90

are top quality. From the heart of the country. Judge for yourself.'

'I've told you – '

'What's the objection?'

The woman stepped back into the hall. 'Go away,' she said coldly.

Gombold, while listening, had mechanically pulled at the upper part of the cane Pill had given him, and a dagger blade became visible.

'Oh,' he said, as he thrust it back.

Pill winked. The woman standing in the doorway in her overalls said, 'I shall tell the police you're pestering me.'

'How am I doing that?'

'I don't have to answer your questions. Here,' she said, opening her purse. 'Now go away.'

She pressed a pound note into Pill's hand. Pill removed his foot from the door which was immediately slammed. 'It never fails,' Pill said. 'I terrify them. They think I'm some kind of a sexual lunatic.' Gombold followed him down the path and into the street. They walked through the residential area until they approached a stretch of wasteland by the river. Standing in the middle of a pile of rubble was a horse, forty feet high, constructed of wood and stone, once painted black, and now dirty and delapidated by time and weather. It was the horse used by the Greeks to sack Troy. In this deserted corner of the city the forehead of the colossus, its mane, its upreared head, and its feet like columns, produced a surprising outline at night. No one cared for it now. It was gloomy and immense; few people visited the waste ground on which it stood. It was falling in ruins, and each year, a little less was left of it.

Gombold followed Pill without a word. A ladder was lying alongside; Pill raised it, and placed it against one of the horse's forelegs. A trapdoor could be seen in the belly.

'Go on up, said Pill.

Gombold mounted the ladder and stepped inside the animal. Pill switched on an electric torch. The sudden light made Gombold blink. An entire skeleton was visible. Above his head a beam, from which sprang at intervals cross bars, represented the spine and the ribs. Printed on the walls were the words, 'This is one of the most exciting periods in history. I'm glad to be taking part in such a unique event ... ' The rest was erased by time and damp. Beckoning him to follow Pill wandered a little further and Gombold saw the words 'Brutus, great grandson of Aeneas, wrote this before embarking for a new life. It is our hope to found a kingdom in the west.' So, Gombold thought, Nennius knew what he was talking about after all. Pill thrust him forward to where his bed was. There was a mattress, a coverlet, and an alcove with curtains. The mattress was a roll of carpet, and the coverlet was a blanket of some hairy material left by the Achaean soldiery. The alcove was three long props driven into the horse's belly, two in front and one behind, and fastened by a cord at the top. These props supported a roll of wire netting so that it entirely surrounded the three poles. The bed was under a cage. Gombold followed Pill inside. Sitting on the mattress Gombold borrowed the torch and shone it on to the walls. He spotted a crude drawing of Helen. He had to admit that there was truth in the legend; she had a round face, a button nose, and straight hair, cropped like a boy's. He stared at the face for a long time.

'I'm switching out the light,' said Pill.

Gombold felt a sandwich pressed into his hand as the light was switched off. The light was hardly out before a trembling shook the wire netting under which they lay.

'What's that?' Gombold said.

'It's the rats, ' Pill said.

Gombold lay down again. The rats which lived

inside the horse had been held in check by the light, but as soon as it was put out they swarmed over the meshes in hundreds. Gombold fell asleep.

The night passed. A wind, which mingled with rain, blew in gusts. The police patrolling the streets around the wasteland took no notice of the horses. The monster, erect and motionless, stared with blank eyes into the dark. Towards dawn, a man came running across the rubble, and slipped under the horse's belly. He was soaking wet. On getting under the horse he called aloud, 'Hey, you!'

Immediately the trapdoor was opened and Pill put his head out.

'What?'

'We want you, come and give us a hand.'

Pill went back into the horse and roused Gombold. He was very tired and annoyed to be woken up.

'What's the matter?' he said.

'I've got a job on,' said Pill.

So Gombold followed him across the rubble into the city. While they were walking Pill asked Gombold for the story of his life. Gombold was able to oblige because he had grown used to people wanting his history. At the end of his recital Pill told him that Vulp was a big man around those parts. He owned a lot of land. 'How did you come to meet him?' Pill asked.

So Gombold told him of the incident in the wood. 'He told me he was stinking rich,' he said, 'and he told me how his mother had been the talk of the world in her youth. Throwing it about and all that.'

'His money isn't worth much,' Pill said. 'It can't bring happiness.'

'But he is happy,' Gombold said.

'And what about health?'

'He was healthy.'

Gombold added that the most disgusting thing about

Major Vulp was his teeth.

Pill said, 'I once new a man called Pearce whose teeth would turn your stomach. And he hadn't two hapennies to rub together. It goes to show.'

The pair walked toward Ninety-nine Days street, which led to the Market. Nobody took any notice of them. Soon they arrived at a building which had iron doors. It was the prison. Gombold shuddered. It was still hardly light and it was raining. The scene before them was depressing enough even in the sunlight. In weather like this it was calculated to make even a cheerful person feel gloomy. Three storeys up was a narrow ledge. A man, dressed in prison uniform, lay shivering in the rain. An old drainpipe ran along the wall to the spot where the man was lying. This pipe, which was full of cracks and holes, was very precariously fastened to the wall.

'We ought to climb up there,' said Pill.

They stood looking up at the man on the ledge. The rain was dripping from their hair.

'We want you to climb up there with this rope,' said the man who had fetched Pill. 'You're lighter than any of us.'

Pill examined the rope and the drainpipe, and pursed his lips. 'Why?' he said.

'There's a man up there who can't get down unless he has a rope.'

Gombold made a back and Pill tested the security of the drainpipe. He had the rope round his waist. At the moment when he was going to ascend, the man on the ledge, who saw safety approaching, leant over; the first gleam of day lightened his face, and in spite of a beard, Gombold recognised O'Scullion.

Pill reached the top of the wall, straddled across it, and fastened the rope. A moment after, O'Scullion was in the street. As soon as he saw Gombold he uttered a squeak of surprise. They waited for Pill to join them and then they went back to the wooden horse.

Gombold was very pleased to see O'Scullion again. He had escaped the holocaust only to be imprisoned in the same manner as Gombold. The man who had woken Pill up was a fellow prisoner. Gombold never saw him again after that night. O'Scullion wanted to hear Gombold's adventures. This took several hours to tell. Then O'Scullion told Gombold that Vulp now owned 17 banks, 38 companies and 4,693,000 acres of land on desirable sites in the main cities. With Beatrice marrying Lord Beersheba the extent of the Vulp fortune was colossal. The Major (who was now a Field Marshal) had been making statements which seemed to indicate he was going to build many more buildings on desirable sites. Sir Shelumiel Cush was the top hotel king. He had recently built and opened the Sweet Times hotel, All eyes, Wild Manners, the Sentinel, and was thinking of extending the Predator (which had 73 exits and 500 lifts). Gombold asked how his old love, Beatrice, was looking.

'She's more beautiful than ever.'

'I had hoped,' Gombold said, 'that she might have developed into a harridan.'

'The papers rave every time she appears in public,' O'Scullion said.

Gombold, who had comforted himself by thinking that Beatrice might be physically or mentally ill, or might have lost her looks, burst into tears and refused to be comforted.

He lived with Pill and O'Scullion for the next few weeks. O'Scullion was very good at the leaf game. Gombold could never intimidate householders enough. So while O'Scullion set up on his own account Gombold followed Pill and showed the dagger at the right moment. Soon they had enough money to do

95

nothing for a few weeks.

Every day they left the horse and searched through the streets until they met someone who could be persuaded to tell or retell an old story. They heard a mother of six give her version of the fall of Icarus; a judge, on his way to preside at a trial, was kind enough to comment on the temptation of Zoroaster; two old dogmeat sellers gave a variation on Solomon's Judgement which presented the king in an equivocal light; an elderly man, who had private means, lent a new and wholly unexpected twist to the buggery of Ganymede; a party of schoolchildren. unprompted, re-enacted the massacre of the Innocents, and a female tramp re-told, with vivid phrasing and appropriate gestures, the death of Procne. So the time passed pleasantly enough. It was seven weeks later that they resumed the leaf game.

Walking up to the door of a well-to-do house they heard voices coming from the open window of the drawing room.

'In the old days – ' said a voice.

She was interrupted. 'Don't talk to me about the old days. If only we had them back again. Do you remember . . . '

'*Can* I ever forget.'

Gombold and Pill sat on a green-painted tub and listened.

'Do you remember the picnic?'

'What an idyll!'

'If only we had the old days back again. When mother was alive.'

'Before the war.'

'Before our way of life altered.'

'Before father died.'

'Now what I always wanted to know was: what did Bertie tell you that day on the picnic by the river?'

Silence, then in softer tones: 'Ah, that picnic by the

river. And poor, poor Bertie.'

'Now what I always wanted to know *was* what did poor father have to say to you when you ... by the river, in the sun. We were so happy in the old days ... before the war ... '

' ... before father died ... '

' ... and mother ... died – '

' – and we lost our money and the climate changed unaccountably for the worst. Those were the days ... '

'Do you remember the swans by the river? Do you remember how Bertie fed them with a piece of cake from the hamper? Do you remember how ... '

A pause and then, 'What I always wanted to know was what did you say to make poor Daisy cry so – that day, by the river, in the sun, so long ago ... .'

Here there was an even longer silence and two sighs could be quite distinctly heard. Gombold and Pill stood up. Gombold tried to lift a lead gnome but it was fixed to the concrete in such a way that it was impossible to steal it. So with regret they left it. Pill rang the doorbell. A dog began to bark somewhere in the depths of the house. It sounded rather a large dog and Gombold suggested they should go away. Pill refused to do this and they waited until an old man came to the door.

'What do you want?' he said.

When Pill told him he laughed aloud and banged the door so hard that a pane of glass cracked right across. Gombold and Pill walked away down the path.

'It was the dog,' Gombold said.

'I was bitten in the leg last month,' Pill said.

'Were you?'

'I was walking along minding my own business when this animal comes sniffing round my trousers. I just stopped to ponder whether to give it a kick when it took a piece out of my leg the size of a half-dollar.'

They walked around for a bit. Gombold said it was

97

nice weather. Then it began to rain. So they sheltered under a shop awning for a few minutes and then they had to move on because the shopkeeper came out and rolled up the awning. They tried another house and got a pound. Another place had a moveable lead statue of a dancing elf. After they had sold it at a place where Pill knew they tried a house where an old lady of seventy lived. She gave them ten shillings but insisted on keeping the leaves. This had never happened before. Pill was taken aback.

As they were walking back to the horse, he said, 'She must be a mean old bleeder that woman.'

Gombold agreed and the matter was never referred to again.

Pill said, 'Did you see the paintings in the hall?'

'No,' Gombold said.

'I wondered if they were valuable. I seem to remember paintings of Jesus fetching a lot.'

This reminded him of an aunt who bought a picture to hang in her bedroom. She took the back off and found an envelope wedged there. And out of interest for something to do (she was an idle sort of woman) she wrote to the address.

'What happened? Gombold said.

'Nothing,' Pill said. 'I don't suppose her letter was worth replying to.'

They sat down under the horse's legs because it was a fine evening.

'The most likely explanation is that she couldn't express herself in a way any civilised person would understand.'

O'Scullion came back with a gash over one eye. He wouldn't tell them how he had come by it, but he thought as it was summer and growing warmer, they ought to leave town.

The next day they wandered along the shore. In the

98

afternoon they went for a swim in the sea. Lying in the sun, on the water, Gombold's thoughts turned to the strange, the improbable and the wild. The tide had carried them some way from the shore. They swam; through the breakers, over the white froth, between the walls of water. They swam for forty minutes and gained the shore. Their clothes had vanished.

Before the full realisation of this had touched them they saw three neat piles of clothes behind a rock. The owners were nowhere in sight. Gombold hoped the travellers were not in the vicinity. As they walked up the beach, over the sandhills and on to the road, O'Scullion found a purse in the pocket of his trousers and decided they must have a meal. They came to the Predator hotel. They went in and the tall, figure behind the desk said, 'The party are expecting you gentlemen; go straight in.'

'Thank you,' Gombold said.

Inside the main dining-room an enormous meal was in progress. A woman said, 'Tickets. Where's your tickets?'

Gombold felt in his pocket and produced a ticket. 'Is this it?' he said.

The woman snatched it from him, tore it in half, put one piece into a basket and gave the other half back.

'To be retained for supper,' she said.

O'Scullion and Pill were also able to find tickets tucked into their clothes. The woman pointed the way to a table.

'You'll find your places reserved,' she said. 'Hurry up. We're off again soon.'

Eight

After an excellent tea they were bundled into a coach which had 'Under 80 Travel Club' painted on the side. For the next two hours they were jolted along the roads at seventy miles an hour. O'Scullion was sick. They had to stop while he went behind a hedge to recover. He came back and sat down between Pill and Gombold in silence. The coach resumed.

'I suppose we must be approaching it now,' a fellow traveller said. 'It's a great favourite with tourists – one of the wonders of the world.'

'Is it?' said Gombold.

'Yes,' the man looked to see if his wife was listening, 'I didn't want to come at this time of year. But she insisted. It's the season, you know.'

'Oh?'

'Guides, hotels, picture-postcards. Little models. Crowds in the streets. I was all for coming out of season. She wouldn't hear of it.'

'No?'

'She's determined. It's more convenient, she says, in the season.'

This man, called Apewit, was small and wore glasses; he sat next to his wife in front of Gombold, but apart from talk of food and accommodation, that was the sum total of their conversation.

They stayed at the Conceit, a hotel converted at great

expense from a hunting lodge by Sir Shelumiel Cush. Over supper Apewit's wife said, 'I've seen you before.'

'I joined the party yesterday.'

She shrugged. 'I thought I knew everybody. Are you enjoying yourself?'

'Oh yes.'

'You get fabulous treatment on these tours. We did the island of butterflies last year. And the year before that we had a sixteen-day tour of historic places.' She edged another piece of pork pie into her mouth. 'Have you been before?'

'No,' Gombold said.

She looked over to her husband. 'He wanted to take advantage of the special 10 per cent Thrift Season round trip reduction. But I said, "No. In season or not at all." I want everything I've dreamed about. Unique experiences. Fantastic scenery. And meeting people with charming outlooks.'

Gombold agreed. After this he went to bed.

The next day the coach took them along the banks of a river and O'Scullion was sick again. It wasn't too bad this time, though. The whole company had got out to admire an old broken pillar which was historic. So O'Scullion was saved the embarrassment of stopping the coach. At midday they arrived within sight of their destination. The land had been flat, but now the whole area rose to a towering peak on the horizon. The sky sank ... the land soared. Gombold stared out of the window. Slowly his eyes slid across the scrub. Everything gathered itself together; the whole plateau leapt.

The party stepped out of the coach, staring until their necks ached and their eyes swam. It stood up from the ground, bulging and bristling, its walls veined by blue streaks. So vast, so steep, so mighty that it seemed a new world rising out of the old; a world of its own; beautiful and menacing. A vast erection of the earth. Gombold

102

caught his breath as he muttered, 'Suspirum et decus puellarum et puerorum.'

'Do you like it?' asked Pill, with an inflection that denoted contempt.

'Yes,' Gombold said. 'Don't you?'

Pill seemed taken aback and Gombold repeated his question in a modified form. 'What don't you like?'

'I thought it'd be bigger. It's not what I expected.'

'It's much finer than I anticipated. We have nothing like it where I come from.' To avoid saying anything wrong Gombold changed the subject and asked, 'How high is it?'

'About a hundred feet. You're not thinking of climbing it?'

'Can one?'

'I believe so.'

'Well then,' said Gombold, 'I might.'

Pill looked dumbfounded and went in search of O'Scullion.

That night they stayed at the Tetanus, a hotel built out of glass blocks. It catered for tourists with special interests and foibles.

Apewit's wife said to Gombold, 'Are you sure you were with us when we started?'

'Who?' Gombold said.

'You and your friends.'

Gombold pretended to be angry. Actually he was frightened. But he thought if he gave Apewit's wife a bigger fright than she had given him she might shut up. She went away after Gombold had insulted her.

Apewit came across and said, 'Have you insulted my wife?'

'Yes,' Gombold said.

He told Apewit what had happened. Apewit saw Gombold's point of view, but would he mind not speaking to his wife because then he could tell her that

Gombold had apologised. Later on Gombold said to Pill, 'I think we ought to get away from here.'

'Wait till tomorrow,' Pill said. 'They're going to see the sights. We can steal a few valuables.'

O'Scullion said, 'I thought you wanted to climb?'

Gombold said, 'I've decided not to go.'

It was late when they came down in the morning, and the dining-room was empty. As they finished breakfast Pill suggested they have a quick look round and get away before the party returned. Gombold remained downstairs while Pill and O'Scullion robbed as many tourists of their valuables as was possible in such a short time. While he was on his own Gombold questioned the desk clerk to find out whether a journey south would be possible, or if possible of any use. The most densely inhabited portions were in the east and south-east from the femur to the tibia. The idea of seeing the feet intrigued him. And what if he should perhaps step off the feet? Where would he be then? He did not have to wonder for long; he discovered where his first world was in finding out what lay under the feet. On the giant's shoulders was a globe; beneath his feet stood a rock placed on the back of a bull, Kujata, resting on an enormous fish, Bahamut, the Behemoth of the scriptures. Thus Gombold arrived at the reason for his presence in the forest: he had dropped like a louse from his own world.

O'Scullion and Pill reappeared carrying a suitcase stuffed full. Pill had three wallets, a handbag and seventy-eight pounds in cash which he found stuffed under a carpet. With this money they left the hotel and took the southbound express.

The train was uncomfortable. All the seats were made of wood except the corner ones which had cushions. When they entered the train it was full. They stood for the first hour in the corridor and then four old

104

men pushed their way onto the platform. Gombold, O'Scullion and Pill sat down in the seats which had been left vacant. Immediately Gombold noticed a man sitting on a corner seat. He was immensely fat. He recognised the man he had rescued from the hole in the wood. A sort of palsy overcame him at the thought. He was about to introduce himself when he remembered how uncivil his treatment had been on the previous occasion. However the man, turning to open a hamper of food, noticed Gombold and screwed his face up in an effort of memory.

'I've seen you somewhere before,' he said in a loud voice.

The other travellers pretended not to have heard. They kept their eyes fixed upon the magazines and newspapers they were reading, but their ears were cocked to catch the slightest whisper.

'Where have I seen you?' the man said.

Gombold told him. The man roared with laughter and began to eat a sandwich. Pill, who was very hungry, wondered if Gombold's friend could spare a bite to eat. Gombold decided the time had come to clear up one or two mysteries connected with his adventures.

He said, 'What were you doing down that hole?'

The man sighed. He looked out of the window and did not answer. In fact Gombold never received a satisfactory explanation.

After a silence Gombold said, 'Where is this train going?'

The man said, 'It depends on where you want to go.'

It was Gombold's turn to fall silent. Pill said, 'How come you're so fat? You must be the fattest man I've ever seen.'

Gombold thought this the rudest remark to date. He was about to apologise when O'Scullion said he felt ill and must leave the carriage. When the commotion had died down, the man said, 'I am the fattest man you are ever likely to meet.'

Pill's mouth dropped open; the man patted his monstrous belly and said, 'I am the fattest man in the world.'

This closed the conversation. A whispered argument could be heard between a woman and her daughter. The woman wanted to know whether the fat man had paid for two seats or only one? The daughter told her mother to be quiet and not to show them up.

'Yes,' said the man, 'I was fat from the time I was born. And whereas most children lose their fat I retained mine and added to it.'

There was no pretence now of not listening. The whole carriage sat rapt while the fattest man in the world spoke.

'I am proud of my size,' he said, addressing the carriage in a loud voice, 'proud of it. I seek out and select those foods which are said to increase girth. I have eaten wild ram, fresh-water snails, crayfish, seaslugs, lapwings, faggots and bread sauce. In the Humerus peninsular I've consumed the durian, which smells like an open sewer. In Gloose I've tasted octopus legs stewed with leeks, in Toeland seaweed under the name of Glory-be-to-God. I've devoured green mealies, Wien-erschnitzel, Prophetenkuchen, gli, gor, and atta. I've sated myself on the caterpillars that the natives south of the kneecap draw from holes with thorns. I've gorged the tails of Astrakan sheep, and by the marshes and mudflats of the navel eaten potted crocodile.'

He did not open his mouth again until he had succeeded in spearing an olive.

'These delicacies,' he said at last, 'and many more, expanded my size, spread my growth: pollulation embarrassed my friends but not me. This dilation, tumefaction and pandiculation infuriates my wife. O!

106

the superiority of my size. And still I eat. I sample pickled bear's paws, elk's nose and camel's hump, passover cake, kisher kid and hotcross buns. I've eaten yak's tripe and lamb's eyes. Of birds alone my palate has tasted ten kind of duck, including the shoveller, four kinds of plover, three of lark, stork, bittern, heron, flamingo, ortolan – a bird tasting of ripe figs and having an egg whose flavour is reminiscent of whisky - thrushes, quails, nightingales, wrens (it was a recipe for baked wren's dung which almost undid me) the eagle, the ossifrage and the ostrich. Whilst others seek rare birds in danger of extinction to photograph or catalogue, I do the same but at the end of my quest I eat the precious specimen. So I have become exaggerated, bloated; and swagbellied never to be congruous or harmonious again.'

'Would you be slim if you could?' said Gombold.

'No,' said the man.

'Are you a member of the Humpty-Dumpty club?' said O'Scullion who had just returned.

'I am founder member and President.'

'Is it true that seven members were carried from the eating room senseless after last year's eat?'

'Certainly not,' said the fat man.

'How about passing round the remains of your hamper,' said Pill.

The man offered a sandwich rather grudgingly. He got out at the next station and Pill said the sandwich was the most tasteless thing he had ever eaten.

The train stopped after half an hour. A lot of men boarded the train near the engine and began working their way along. When they were three carriages away O'Scullion said, 'Passports! It's the frontier.'

They searched their clothes to see if the tourists had had passports. As none of them intended travelling to the frontier no passports were found. So they jumped from the train and ran down a steep incline into the bushes at the side of the track. The train moved off. They skirted the frontier post and found themselves in wild countryside.

Nine

An ugly old hag passed them. She said that if they continued walking they would come to a city. They did as directed for about three hours, and when they were nearly exhausted reached a pleasant place where they saw a town of some size. The people inhabiting it exhibited rhythmical consecutive sexuality. In all cases the initial sex was male, followed by a series of alternating female and male phases throughout life. As a rule the adult completed one male and one female phase every five years, but in some cases individuals had as many as three changes of sex, with a period of hermaphroditism, during that time. In addition the population contained a number of true males who retained the male phase indefinitely.

They were a happy people. Gombold and his companions stayed the night. The next day they attended a lecture which discussed the beneficial effects of living under the threat of extinction. After this they were shown an art gallery, a book-shop, a concert hall and a new theatre. They were extremely cultured, they said.

At the next town they ran into a number of men with dog's heads. Gombold was frightened at first, because they surrounded him and his comrades and asked what business they had in the area. Gombold replied that they were on a sight-seeing tour.

'The only sights to be seen are yourselves,' said the leader of the dog-men.

Everyone laughed, and the encounter passed off peacefully. The inhabitants of this town were part dog-headed and part horse-bodied. At first Gombold supposed that these people were the centaurs of antiquity. But closer examination proved this erroneous. They were rather more than half a horse. Many were equine to the breast. They were ruled over by a queen who was horse to the neck. The dog people were dogs down to the navel; some even further.

While the three comrades were looking round the main square a sound of hooves was heard, and cries of 'Here she comes,' 'Make way,' heralded the approach of a white filly attended by geldings.

'Isn't she wonderful?' said a woman bystander whose face was so poodled that Gombold had difficulty in thinking of her as a human being. 'What a perfect mare she is.'

'Did you notice her bridle?' said another.

'She dresses wonderfully.'

'She's a credit to the country,' said the first woman, moving away.

Later on Gombold met a man who said he'd been put in prison.

'Yes,' he said, 'For political offences. It was one bank holiday and I was looking for a place to sleep. I had a terrible head on me. And my guts was playing up. I dropped into a place I know for a tonic water. And I got into an argument with a man who maintained the queen helped the export drive. "These people abroad," he says, "give a look at what saddles and bridles she wears and they want one like." In the end I lost my temper and said, "Sod the queen. And you as well." Then the police rush in and the next thing I'm up for lèse majesté.'

This was a shocking thing to hear. But when the man had left Gombold was told not to believe a word of what had been said. The man had been put into jail for thieving. Gombold didn't know what to think. O'Scullion said he thought the people who lived in these parts were hellish.

Later, a smart cob approached and asked if they would like to see the queen. This was a strange thing to ask. But the man seemed so keen to show Gombold and his friends the only attraction the town possessed that Gombold said yes.

They were led into the queen's hall, and there they saw how she and an old pony ('that's her husband', their guide said) passed the time. They talked of Nobility, rank, condition, distinction, gentility and order. Then they spoke of Commonalty, democracy, the principles of Government and self-respect. Everybody in the room cheered. After this display the guide drew Gombold and his friends to one side and told them of the wonderful things the Queen did, and the way she conducted herself. She washed three or four times a day; she was never rude to the servants; she was a good mother; she led an exemplary life; she slept at night; she used her vocal cords when she spoke; she walked on her legs; she had hair on her head; when it was hot she sweated; when it was cold she shivered; she had been conceived and born in the normal way of mammals; one day she would die and the worms would eat her. Gombold and his comrades expressed astonishment at the number and variety of the Queen's talents.

While they were listening to the music playing in an adjoining room, the Queen appeared, attended by court, and the three young men were dazzled. One of the geldings standing by handed her a sheet of paper. She approached and said:

'It must not be thought that I am responsible for

111

anything that happens, or might happen, or be caused to happen. Advisers advise and I accept. Though in theory I need not accept yet in practice I do. If in practice I did not accept, the theory would not be workable. But it is also erroneous to suppose my position is merely nominal; it has the appearance of being nominal but in reality it is not. I am accepted as theoretical, or quasi-head of a number of people, widely differing in character and interests, who accept me as their quasi-head, as I accept them as my quasi-theoretical subjects.'

Having made this speech, she retired for a while with part of her court. Gombold questioned his guide as to the nature of the advice given to the Queen and was told she always sought it on every subject. For this reason, Gombold was told, she never spoke except after sifting the advice given by her ministers.

'Does she never speak impromptu?' asked Gombold.

'Never,' said the guide.

He doubted whether anybody had ever heard her say anything of which her advisers were not informed in advance.

'But you could try.' he said.

They waited until the Queen returned. She was certainly beautiful. Gombold approached her and clearing his throat asked if she would speak to him. She smiled and held out her hand. Gombold asked once more. She glanced to one side, and her chief adviser stepped forward with a sheet of paper. Gombold, seeing that she was about to read another speech, turned away. There was a flutter behind him and the Queen, realising what it was he wanted, said in a charming voice, with a suggestion of a neigh, 'So kind of you to call,' which the guide declared to be the most gracious and intelligible thing he had ever heard from her.

After the pleasure of listening to the Queen speak

unaided, Gombold went back to the lodgings. The next day they stole a car and drove towards the kneecap. The roads were dusty, on either side was desert and scrub, it was an unpleasant part of the afreet's anatomy. They ran into a belt of dwarf pine and across a zone of moss and scraggly shrubs. The air grew colder. At the next town they opened the suitcase and sold the most valuable pieces. O'Scullion bought a book called 'Onanie in der Pubertät,' and Gombold bought one called 'Les derniers jours de Pompei'. Pill drove very fast. Then he had an accident and the car was no use for driving anymore. They thumbed a lift.

The man driving said, 'Where are you three laddies going?'

'We're touring,' said Pill.

'Where are you making for?' said the man.

'Nowhere,' Pill said.

The man looked surprised and said that he was on his way to view a house and would they like to accompany him? Gombold thought the man looked extremely sinister. He was about to refuse the offer when Pill accepted. The man said his name was Beersheba.

Pill said, 'Are you the Lord?'

Lord Beersheba smiled. Gombold thought it was the most horrible smile he had ever seen. Even more horrible than Major-General Vulp's. When Lord Beersheba got out of the car to buy something or other (O'Scullion said he was probably going to dope the three of them), Gombold said they ought to make a getaway. Pill asked why.

O'Scullion said, 'I think he's peculiar.'

Pill wanted to know what he meant. O'Scullion said he knew perfectly well. Pill said why was he being coy? O'Scullion said he had to be because Lord Beersheba might overhear. Pill said that he was in the shop.

After a pause Pill said, 'I met a geezer like him once before.'

O'Scullion asked what happened, but Pill wouldn't say. Instead he launched into a tale of a friend of his who met a man who wanted him to pose for nude photos.

'He was flashing his money about,' Pill said, 'and Mickey was hard up. With the employment situation being difficult. He did take a few photos. And the beauty of it was that Mickey was picked up by the police on a charge of attempting to break into a shop that sold artificial flowers. It was a complete fabrication. Mickey said, and I believe him, that the breaking was done by the police. They had it in for him. And when they were searching him they found these photos. He says they're of himself. But the bleeders didn't understand. They showed them to the judge and it went against him. He got a stretch for carrying obscene photos. He spoke up in court. He said they were of himself. But the law didn't recognise any difference, so he told me.'

While they were thinking of this, Lord Beersheba came back. Pill went on with his story and he said in a loud voice, in case Lord B. had designs on them,

'I'm modest by nature. I had an upbringing a monk would envy.'

Lord Beersheba ignored Pill. He said, 'One of you laddies come and sit by me.'

O'Scullion nudged Gombold who climbed into the seat beside the driver. Lord Beersheba put his hand into a carrier bag.

'Open these,' he said. 'You'll find a gadget next to you.'

Gombold opened the bottles of beer. O'Scullion made a face: 'I suppose we'll wake up in some house having been outraged,' he said. Pill drank three or four bottles and Lord Beersheba had to stop and buy more.

114

'I once knew his wife,' Gombold said. 'Shall I ask him about her?'

O'Scullion said he hoped it would be a conversation which wouldn't lead anywhere odd. Pill had gone to sleep. When Lord Beersheba came back Gombold asked him how his wife was keeping these days. Lord Beersheba slammed the door of the car.

'She's very well.'

'I knew her once.'

'Did you?'

When they had travelled another six miles Lord Beersheba said they ought to call him Bernard. They came to the house which Bernard was to view and the agent showed them over the place. Pill didn't come because he was asleep.

O'Scullion said: 'What are these under the dust-sheets?'

'I'm glad you asked, sir,' the agent said. 'These are the family, Lady Jill, Lady Anne, the Hon. Nancy, Charles and – er – ' He stopped and scratched his head. ' – Uncle Willy.'

Lord Beersheba stared out of the window. He was only interested in the house which he wished to turn into a hotel.

The agent said, 'One condition of the sale is a written guarantee to protect and cherish the inhabitants of this lovely stately home.'

'Poor things,' said O'Scullion. 'They don't look as if they get enough to eat.'

'Please don't remove the dust-sheets, sir,' the agent said, as Gombold lifted a cover to find a Brigadier staring at him, 'They're a means of protection. We have here a remarkable collection. The set is almost complete. In fact I don't mind telling you, this is one of the finest collections in existence. If only we hadn't lost Lord John ... we need him to complete the set.'

'We must be going.' said Lord Beersheba. 'I don't think the house interests me.'

Gombold was surprised he showed so little concern for the family. O'Scullion said they looked a nice bunch. They didn't have awful expressions on their faces like Bernard. But Gombold remembered that Bernard had only been Lorded for owning desirable sites. So it didn't count.

'Those pictures were worth something,' Pill said when they got back. 'I had a look round.'

'Were they interesting?' Gombold said.

'Every one was of Jesus. Did I tell you about my auntie?'

'Yes,' said Gombold.

'The artists of the past were obsessed by holiness,' Pill said. 'You can tell. They led a totally different life from today. They studied more. They believed in something. It made them work faster. I have no use for the unholy turn the century's taking.'

Lord Beersheba agreed with Pill. He became excited when he talked of work. When they reached the outskirts of the next town he said he must drop them off.

'Did you say you knew my wife?' he asked Gombold.

'She won't remember me,' Gombold said.

'I'll give her your regards. What's your name?'

Gombold decided not to give his real name because he was still on the run. He said his name was Pill, which rather surprised Pill.

Pill said, 'Can you lend us a few quid?'

Lord Beersheba gave them a pound each and drove away.

Ten

For the next few days they wandered in a southward direction. At one time there was a general panic because it was thought the afreet was dying. In actual fact the danger was past when the panic began. The Government had no intention of spreading alarm until the crisis was over. They found a wallet on the third day containing: an aerial photograph of a woman's head, the Maundy money ceremony; view from the ground. A fibula, a small bottle-holder, a candelabra, a rectangular clasp for a pocket bestiary and a nanny-goat's postiche. None of these were of any use so they threw the wallet onto a rubbish dump. When they arrived at the next town on the fourth day they saw an advertisement offering a reward to the finder of the wallet. They went back to the rubbish dump and searched for it. When they found it the bottle-holder had disappeared but the rest of the contents were intact.

On the sixth day they reached a house where seventy-seven women and two men were absorbed in reading one book.

'Is it a personification of a mass for the dead?' said the first woman.

A second woman who kept her hat on even in the house said, 'Ah, is it?'

The seventy-seventh woman said, 'Kemmerling has interpreted the work in a platonic sense. Henpate thinks it is a symbol of the unconscious.'

One of the men who presented a disgusting sight with tobacco ash spilled down his waistcoat said, 'A political interpretation is given by Eustis.'

Everybody shrieked with laughter. The man seemed upset. Gombold felt sorry for him in spite of the waistcoat.

'It's sold a million copies,' the first woman said.

The second man, smooth, plump rather than fat, with pudgy hands, said: 'Various attempts have been made to interpret the allegorical meaning of the work. Turnipot sees in it allusions to Dante; Pockwelter, Noddypeke and Fewmet to a carnival song; Henpate is alone in seeing it as reproducing the rhythms of an Ambrosian hymn. I have my own theory, which is *quite* original. It will occupy me for the rest of my life.'

A girl in a pretty dress called to the first woman, 'Can't we get him to lunch?'

Here there was such a deafening noise of shrieks, squeals of delight, whistles and groans that Gombold had difficulty in hearing what was said. As the din died away a babble of voices rose:

'Yes, yes, get him to lunch.'

'He can be here in time if he takes the 11.15. Oh, will someone ring him?'

'Or send a telegram.'

'Yes, a TELEGRAM.'

'It's too late to ask him now,' said the first woman, who was the owner of the house.

'Yes, it is a bit late,' O'Scullion murmured, close to Gombold's ear.

The girl in the pretty dress said, 'I can't wait to meet him. He's a genius. He's my favourite writer.'

'What do you think, Stanley?'

The man in the dirty waistcoat said nothing.

'He's in one of his tiresome huffs again,' said the seventy-seventh woman.

'I think we ought to have him to lunch,' said Stanley.

'I do really feel – yes, I expect in spite of his bitterness, he would like ME.' This from the seventy-sixth woman who wore thick glasses. 'Would he like me, do you think?' she said.

'Certainly.'

'Arthur knows him a little,'

Arthur said, 'Only a little.'

'Ring him then. Dare you?'

' ... he evokes a scene beautifully, such a stringent eye for character.'

Arthur went away to telephone the author and Gombold heard one of the women say, 'He doesn't know him, he's never met him.'

Gombold went behind the house and stayed there for an hour and then rang the front door and told the maid he was the author they were expecting. The maid announced him.

As he entered the room the woman who owned the house was saying to Arthur, 'I think one may observe in the best of his work a close relationship between the state of contemplative awareness and the intellectual attraction for pure dialectic.'

She beamed with delight when Gombold was ushered in. O'Scullion tittered; Pill looked unhappy, standing by the girl in the pretty dress.

'You must meet everyone,' said the hostess, who was called Jenny.

After Gombold had drunk two sherries ('ever so dry' he said) and had talked a lot of nonsense to the seventy-sixth woman. Stanley asked if he would write something.

Gombold had given up feeling sorry for him even when he was snubbed by the seventy-sixth woman. Borrowing Stanley's pen and a piece of notepaper from Jenny he wrote:

119

In the ruins of the British Museum old aunt Bear went about her work. She had long finished up the honey that her husband had left behind the statue of Ramses. Uncle Bear owned a hock-shop (or rather he lived part of the time in the basement of a ruined mont-de-piete, which is the same thing), but he would wander off and leave her with nothing in the house to eat.

Gretchen, the rat woman, moved back and forth. 'He's good-for-nothing,' she said. 'Running off and leaving you to starve.'

'He didn't run off,' said aunt Bear. 'I've already told you: his mother, Frau Bear, is ill and needs him. And besides there are enough beechnuts to last.'

Gretchen scurried back to her nest on the Fates and aunt Bear lay down. Old aunt Bear they called her; she was not old; not more than five. But her fur was patchy, her eyes watery behind thin eyebrows. She was a good Bear, but not a happy one. There were footsteps along the main aisle. But it wasn't Uncle. It was Frances O'Malley Whipsnade Polar.

She was a big creature – not tall, but broad and stoutly built – and her shoulders filled the view.

'My dear,' she said, 'what you need is a good blow. To take you out of yourself.'

'I couldn't,' aunt Bear said, 'not till H.G. gets back.'

'Where is he?' Frances O'Malley Whipsnade Polar asked in her gruff commanding tones . . . .

'What's this nonsense?' said Jenny. She stood behind Gombold with a tall man in a grey suit. 'How dare you behave in this outrageous way.'

She was furious; her eyes blazed.

120

'Who are you?'

Gombold realised there was nothing to be done. He held out the wallet.

'Is this yours?'

Jenny brushed it aside, 'How dare you,' she said again. 'How dare you.' She looked as though she wanted to hit him.

'We understand you were offering a reward,' Pill said.

Jenny swung round. The whole room had gone quiet.

'A reward?'

'We saw the notice.'

'If you don't go, I shall call the police.'

In the garden O'Scullion said, 'What a pity she found out before lunch.'

Pill said, 'That young bird was eating out of my hand.'

'We never got our reward,' Gombold said and tossed the wallet and its contents into a bush.

They walked down the road. O'Scullion said they ought to have something to eat. While they were wondering where to go, a car drew up and the girl in the pretty dress opened the door.

'Hi,' she said.

None of the three moved.

'Want a lift?'

Pill said yes. They got into the car and Gombold began to drive. The girl, who was called Stella (what a rotten name), sat in the back seat with Pill. After a few minutes there was a scuffle and she called, 'Please, help me, you two.'

O'Scullion glanced over his shoulder and went back to reading his book. Gombold stared at the road ahead and wondered whether Stella knew Beatrice. A squeal of fright came from the back.

O'Scullion said, 'What are you going to do when we reach the toes?'

'I hadn't thought,' Gombold said. 'Go up the other side, I suppose.'

After a silence, O'Scullion said, 'Are we on the left leg or the right?'

'I believe, the right,' Gombold said.

Stella was crying.

'What's the matter with you?' Pill said.

'We shall have to cross to the left?' said O'Scullion.

'Yes.'

After a long time Stella said, 'I want to get out! Let me get out!' She tried to open the door.

Gombold drew up beside the kerb. Stella looked dishevelled. She stepped down and came round to the front.

'Well?' she said.

'What do you want?' Gombold said.

'It's my car. Have you forgotten? It's my car.' She was hysterical.

'I thought you was going to take us to one of your parties?' Pill said.

'Don't be ridiculous.'

Pill made a rude noise. When she asked for the car he made a louder noise.

Gombold said, 'We can't pinch it.'

'Why not?'

Gombold could give no reason. An argument ensued as to whether or not they should steal the car. Finally O'Scullion said they ought to take a train. It was quicker. They got out of the car and Stella leaped in front of the steering wheel and drove off at a furious rate. Pill said it was a pity to let her go; he had hoped they might rape her.

About half-way between the knee and the ankle (on the right leg) the motor road runs parallel with the

122

railway. As the train reached this spot they saw a police car speeding along the road. In order to take no chances they jumped out of the train and found themselves in a desolate area of scrub. Above them an aeroplane wheeled. They crossed a river and walked for seven days. On the morning of the first day they saw a dying aster attacked by rats. In the afternoon they met a woman teacher who was conducting a Nature class. She was a nice woman. Sincere, O'Scullion said. They came across her in the middle of a patch of woodland.

'But then,' O'Scullion said after she had gone, 'human beings behave like rodents, so it's not surprising.'

On the second day they saw an elderly man dressed in a well-cut suit being kicked and beaten by a tramp. If this had taken place in a lonely spot Gombold would have gone to the man's aid. But the incident was enacted in a public square. The more the tramp kicked him, the more he smiled. A crowd gathered. As the man was kicked and beaten, the audience applauded. Finally, when he lay exhausted and covered in blood, the tramp pissed over him. The audience went wild. The tramp bowed and the elderly man, still smiling, was helped into an ambulance.

On the third day they met a woman who said the ruling spirit of the Universe was Love.

'I wish we could see the glory of the Infinite Morning, when love and unbiased friendship is for everyone,' she said.

Pill borrowed three pound ten on the strength of it.

'Until men can love men and women do not fear to trust their own kind we shall see no peace,' she said.

She took them around the town with her and bought one or two things. She also gave them the address of a friend of hers who might put them up for the night. Her last words as she waved them goodbye were, 'Many cannot tolerate the idea of an Infinite Intelligence directing our little parish of the Universe. To them I say – look around you.'

On the fourth day they slept.

On the fifth day they met an old woman who suffered from deafness and couldn't afford a hearing-aid. Actually it wasn't necessary for no one wished to speak to her.

On the sixth day a man took them back to his house on a suburban estate. Et in Suburbia ego, O'Scullion said. Pill thought the place was quite nice. Gombold said it was good for the kiddies. When they arrived at the man's house they found his wife had hanged herself.

On the seventh day they came to the ankle. It had the appearance of a cape jutting away from the main peninsula. Occupying approximately one sixteenth of the land area of the foot it held four-fifths of the civilised population.

On the eighth day it rained and Gombold had the toothache.

On the ninth day they had pains in their bellies because of something they'd eaten and Pill threw a stone which broke the window of the Registry office.

On the tenth day they reached the big toe and took a room for the night in a tramps' hostel.

The next day they went to the edge of the toenail and paid half-a-crown each for a view of the afreet in a diminishing glass. He was gross and ugly in appearance, pot bellied and coarse; naked except for rawhide sandals. He carried a club so large that it would have needed a hundred men to lift it, and it was, therefore, mounted on wheels. It was extremely nasty weather. There raged around the toes a turmoil comparable to the chaos of the deluge; comparable to the disorder of the underworld, where a storm of ordinary proportions would be regarded as a lull. In their ragged clothes the three companions had a thin time of it. O'Scullion wanted to get away from the God-forsaken spot as soon as possible.

They stayed in their room the next evening. Pill said even the bugs were queueing up to leave. 'What a depressing hole,' he said.

'We'll have to do something,' O'Scullion said.

'Shall we climb to the club?' Gombold said.

Nobody answered. The next morning, they hired ropes and boots and climbed the club. The ascent offered no particular problems. Occasionally a steep pitch of wood necessitated slow going; but the hand and footholds were good. They rested at long intervals, but their muscles and lungs felt less strain than anticipated. It was not long before they were within a hundred feet of the summit; they stood together on a platform just below where the ogre gripped the handle.

'I'm going no further,' O'Scullion said.

'What's the point?' Pill said.

They sat down, viewing the landscape and eating their luncheon. Then they began the descent.

'What are we going to do?' O'Scullion said. He had asked this so often that Gombold had given up answering. 'We must think of something. We can't stay here for ever.'

Gombold was listening to O'Scullion's voice; then it stopped; he heard yells. There was a pull on the rope; the knot cut into the flesh of his stomach. He heard the strands creaking. He heard O'Scullion's voice. In the instant during which he fell, he clung on to the side of the club, panting.

O'Scullion's voice came up from below, 'I'm hanging.'

'Are you all right?'

There was a silence. Then he called, 'Yes.'

Gombold craned his head forward as far as he could.

Below them the rope stretched into space, its end was hidden beneath the projecting knotches of the club. Gombold and Pill pulled at the rope. Foot by foot it came over the edge. Finally O'Scullion's head and shoulders appeared on the rim, and in a moment he had pulled himself alongside.

Nobody spoke. After a few minutes they continued the descent; the going was not difficult. They came to the smooth columna rib and crept home without further mishap.

The long climb had imposed a strain; the consequence of their exertion made itself felt; they were irritable, disconcerted, put out easily. They stayed in their room for sixteen hours. During that time voices came from the room next door. The wall was a thin coating of plaster, supported by laths. Gombold, nosing around, noticed just near the ceiling a gap in the plaster. By standing on the chest of drawers he could see through the hole into the other room. He spent a long time staring through. It was a dirty place.

'It stinks enough to kill the cats,' Pill said when he looked.

Around the fireplace was a line of hooks and hanging on them were chafing dishes, pots, broken planks, rags, a birdcage, a bag of ashes, and two legs from a shop window dummy. The room was larger than the one in which the three companions slept; it had angles, nooks, black holes under the ceiling, bays and promontories. Spiders as large as fists, wood-lice as large as a foot, and other nauseating creatures ran to and fro.

One of the beds was near the door, the other near the window, but the ends of both ran down to the fireplace, and faced Gombold. In a corner near the hole through which he peeped was a coloured engraving, under which was written 'We thank Thee, O Almighty Presence for giving us tranquillity, tenderness and a will to succeed.' Below the picture was a sort of panel placed on the ground, leaning against the wall. It was the signboard of an inn, representing three or four women dancing on a man's face. At the table, on which Gombold noticed seven pens, twenty-seven pieces of paper, seventy-seven different kinds of ink and a piece of indiarubber, a man sat. He had three days growth of beard, and wore a woman's nightdress, which allowed his chest and arms, bristling with hair, to be seen. Under the nightdress Gombold noticed a pair of muddy trousers and boots. He had a fag-end stuck in the corner of his mouth. He was scribbling on a piece of paper, talking aloud.

'What are they doing?' O'Scullion said.

'Nothing,' Gombold said.

He put his eye back to the hole.

The man at the table had stopped talking. In the furthest corner Gombold caught a glimpse of a youth, sitting on a cushion, who did not seem to hear, see or live. He had frightful hair of reddish colour, which he thrust back every now and then. By his side, on the ground, lay an open book.

'I suppose you think your conversation is?' The man said, replying to a statement Gombold had missed. 'I suppose you think he'll be delighted to listen to you?' His tones were vicious.

'You're the talk of the neighbourhood. Like when you were nearly drowned. And that fat bloke had to rescue you? You clung on to him so hard he nearly passed out. He said the water was two foot deep. You cried all the way home.'

The youth did not speak; the pen could be heard squeaking across the paper; the man muttered, without ceasing to write.

He said, 'You seem to imagine a briar pipe and tweeds are gay deceivers. You'll be growing a beard

next. If you begin to develop secondary sexual charac-
teristics, I'm getting out.'

'You're giving me a headache,' the youth said.

The man ignored him. 'I'm ashamed to be seen about
with you. You get yourself up like a carnival.' A pause,
then he said, 'Are you listening?'

The youth picked up the book and started to flick
through it.

Gombold stepped down from the chest of drawers
and O'Scullion took his place. Pill got into bed and
pulled the clothes over his head. O'Scullion pressed his
eye to the hole and said:

'There's a woman come into the room. She's the
mother of the kid with the hair ... '

After another hour of watching, nothing had happened and O'Scullion became bored. Pill was asleep.
Gombold stood on the chest of drawers and watched for
a bit. The man was having a bath in front of the fire.
The woman had gone and the red haired youth was still
reading.

'I want to smarten him up,' the man said. Gombold
could only hear his voice; the steam from the bath filled
the room. 'I'll give him the brown suit; the shoes you
were going to throw away; the white linen shirt; the tie
with the stripe; and the green woolly.'

The youth put down his book. 'How dare you! How
dare you act so cavalier with my wardrobe?'

The violence with which he said this was unexpected.
He had shown no sign of listening.

The man said, 'You looked like a male model in it.'

The youth relapsed into silence again. The man
finished his bath and dried himself on a length of cloth
which he took from one of the hooks. Gombold went to
bed. The next day when he tried to see into the room he
found something blocking the view.

On Sunday morning the weather was showery.

128

O'Scullion came into the room where Gombold sat reading a paper. Pill was asleep.

O'Scullion said, 'How much money have you got?'

Gombold continued to read for a few moments. Then he said, 'Two pounds.'

O'Scullion went away. When he got back, Gombold and Pill were sitting on the sofa with a paper between them.

O'Scullion said, 'Let's get away from here.'

Gombold didn't answer. He had just noticed that a man had been arrested for poisoning carp. Next to this was a photograph of Beatrice. Underneath it said:

There were 3,000,000 people at the ball given by Lord and Lady Beersheba at their house in the country. Among the guests, many of whom had been hunting that day with the Tong foxhounds, were Sir Shelumiel and Lady Cush – they are even richer this year; Lady Joan Legs, still a keen partygoer at the age of eighty-two; Air Commodore 'Sweetie' Crisham – mistaken for a woman recently, we hear; Major and Mrs Ede came over from Weasle, a house built by a madman palmed off on the family sixty years ago. Also there were Miss Sarah Bigflea, who is engaged to be married and Father Forcebougre, padre to the 44th Fighter Station. Mrs John Molner, who was celebrating the publication of her book 'Many Changes,' recalled eighteen thousand separate occasions on which she was bored silly between the wars. Others moving about the room – which provided an amusing contrast between spring and autumn with daffodils in one corner and chrysanthemums at the other – were Miss Jean Strang, who had a fetching little sequined veil over her eyes (she was blinded in a motor crash recently) and Peter Harrow, M.P. Our impressions were that black was the chief colour. Nice people enjoyed themselves: there was a cabaret arranged by Mrs Avril Hump, who wore a full-skirted dress of pink satin brightly pinned with diamonds, pretty and attractive with her silvery hair. We noticed she had effectively disguised her usual stench with 'Palms' the very latest . . . .

'What did you say?' Gombold asked.

'It doesn't matter,' O'Scullion said.

Gombold said he thought of going for a walk.

He went downstairs. When he approached the front door a cloudburst was in progress. He shuffled into the rain. For a long time he tramped along. Then it rained harder, so he walked back. He approached the house by a different route and found a gate leading to the back door. It had a high wall on either side. He was shutting it behind him when someone passed quickly round the corner of the house and he heard a voice saying, 'They'll be at each other's throats in six months.'

When he turned the corner he saw Corporal Squall standing by a dustbin. No one else was in sight. Gombold introduced himself. Squall's manner was encouraging.

'When did you get out?'

'I escaped,' Gombold said.

'Did you?'

As they went together towards the house Pill leaned out of the window.

'I've got a car,' he said. 'We can clear out this afternoon.'

'Good,' said Gombold.

Corporal Squall said, 'Why don't you join up?'

Pill closed the window. Gombold thought the idea quite good.

'Give me a few hours to get my kit packed,' Squall said. 'I'll come with you.'

Soon after this the sun came out. In the afternoon Squall brought a lot of kit, packed it into the car, and they set off.

Nothing of interest happened during the next three weeks. They crossed over to the left leg and drove the car up the flank to the knee. Corporal Squall told them to join his mob before the war broke out. They sold the car and lived for a few days on the money. After this, having nothing better to do, they joined the army. They didn't like it much: it was very dirty and uncomfortable and dull. Squall said it would liven up when the war broke out. They waited for six more months and then the war did break out.

No one knew why the war was being fought, though several imagined it was to prevent the enemy raping their wives, and others said it was to preserve free-speech. For a time Gombold didn't see any action. He was stationed at home. Then he had an embarkation leave (which wasn't enjoyable because it rained) and the whole regiment set off for the front.

Everyone agreed that the front was even more boring than the metropolitan barracks; Gombold became awfully depressed. He talked to Pill and O'Scullion and they said nothing could be done. O'Scullion said Squall had misled them. He said the Leftbuttocks were a dreary lot. They talked of duty a good deal. They also said they had the tide of history on their side. There were no brothels, which depressed Squall. Apewit seemed to be some kind of king pin in the organisation. Gombold had no idea how much weight his authority carried, but he kept ordering people about. He gave a lecture on service that had to be attended. O'Scullion said he thought they ought to change sides; the Rightbuttocks, he had heard, were a better mob.

'Squall says the tide of history is on the Right-buttocks' side and we ought to be over there with them.'

So they deserted to the enemy.

The Rightbuttocks had more facilities, they talked a lot about women, they had a few horrible brothels, and they received food parcels from home. Apart from this there didn't seem much difference. Gombold couldn't be sure whether they were better than the Leftbuttocks. Neither could he be sure that the tide of history was on their side.

One day O'Scullion said the Crotchmen, allies to the Rightbuttocks, had discovered the tide of history was flowing in their direction. Everybody laughed because the Crotchmen were so very unimportant.

The Leftbuttocks captured an Ordnance depot and held it for a few months, and then the Rightbuttocks by brilliant military strategy (which Gombold didn't understand) retook it. The Leftbuttocks retired. And then, one night, they recaptured it; no one knew how. It was a big disgrace. The Rightbuttocks retired and waited for reinforcements; these took a long while coming – someone had given the wrong instructions. When the reinforcements arrived there weren't enough weapons to go round. They had to wait on the defensive for several weeks until a supply column arrived.

On the day the column was expected Gombold stood under the shelter of a tree and looked across the fields. The camp, tucked into a hollow, was floored with mud which the wheels of lorries had crossed with water-logged furrows; the huts did not keep out the rain, the cooks' fires had to be protected by tarpaulins. Gombold walked in the direction of the troop office. The officers and senior N.C.O.s filled the draughty hut to capacity. Gombold, in his position near the door, judged what was coming.

The C.O. looked pleased. He finished filling his pipe

and lit it. 'Men,' he said, 'we move up tomorrow. Good news, eh? Very good news for me, I can tell you.'

'What are our orders, sir?' said an officer who was reputed to have a pretty wife.

'The front is in a fluid state, so we've no definite orders as to where we'll take up our position. The rendezvous will be at reference 429.'

The C.O. swung round and prodded the map behind him.

'We move at 0.800 hours tomorrow morning.'

All the men saluted smartly. The Colonel prodded the map once more. Then he ruffled through a drawer in the desk and found a blue flag which he pinned to the map with a pleased expression.

'This is going to be a tough fight,' he said. 'It's a hard and gruelling task we have ahead of us. Any questions?'

'What about rations?' said a sergeant who had the ugliest wife in the army.

'Haversack rations. We can't be sure whether we'll have a chance to get a proper meal.'

'Shall we start packing now or in the morning, sir?'

'Start now. It would be as well to have as little to do tomorrow as possible.'

Everybody shuffled from the hut.

The morning dawned clear and cold. In the distance guns were firing; not heavy sustained fire heralding a large-scale attack, but sporadic bursts of one or two rounds at a time. The Colonel came up for the final inspection before moving. As he passed on, Gombold glanced at his watch and saw that it was five minutes to zero. Behind him Pill hummed a tune which repeated every few lines that a girl had lost her maidenhead and wasn't it a shame?

Gombold stepped into the jeep. A minute later the Colonel arrived and swung himself on to the seat beside him. The drone of engines followed on the order to start up. Another burst of gunfire ahead, and the Colonel looked up.

'Might be just in time for the show,' he said.

They drove at forty miles an hour down a road blackened by shellbursts. They rounded a bend. The place was deserted.

'Dismount,' the Colonel said, 'we're going to establish an O.P. over to the left.'

As they plunged into the scrub the noise of firing became louder. Brenguns chattered from a dozen different points. Sandwiched between came the thud of infantry mortars.

'Heads down!'

A shower of bullets fell across the path, and everyone ducked by instinct.

Gombold felt sick.

They dug themselves in and that night the food was so putrid even the Colonel raised an eyebrow when he tasted it. All their blankets were found to be soaking wet when they went to bed; nobody said anything. A species of louse caused eighty men to report sick next morning. The M.O. had them stripped naked and sprayed with a new kind of drug which brought forty out in a virulent rash and proved fatal to another eighteen. The others endured the lice.

'They'll need a hell of a lot of replacements now,' Pill said. 'And what is it for? That's what I ask. All this marching and digging-in and firing?'

A man with a broken nose said, 'All I want is a bloody good fuck, yes, in a clean bed.'

'Pick 'em up there!' Corporal Squall said. 'You look like a string of old tarts coming back from a funeral.'

The enemy put on a counteroffensive and the position was retaken.

The Colonel said, 'This is where we're digging in tomorrow.'

134

He stuck a red flag in the map and retired to make a note in his diary, which he hoped would be a great success after the war.

'Dig, dig, dig, and bleeding well dig,' said the man with the broken nose, 'The only one who isn't digging is him (that one over there) the crafty sod. He's pitched in with the infantry; he's sitting pretty.'

The Colonel stuck four red and three blue flags in an octagonal shape on the map. He poked his baton in the centre.

'The attack is scheduled for tomorrow. 0.130 hours. You're getting the lion's share of fire power; two batteries of twenty-fives, one of three point sevens and four tanks are coming up in the afternoon. Oh, and there's a six-pounder anti-tank.'

'What about air support?' asked the sergeant with the ugly wife.

'Not much air support, I'm afraid.'

The allies retook the position and they dug in again.

Gombold found it impossible to think clearly. His mouth was dry and foul and there was a burning behind his eyes. To the muggy heat of the air was added the fumes of cordite and shell smoke. The earth shook as with a muscular twitch. At the maintenance post, he crouched in the trench and listened.

'Well, what I want is the sight of a fanny,' said the man with the broken nose.

A man with a pair of binoculars pressed to his eyes said, 'Remember that pub where they kept the big dog? Where they had a cross-eyed barmaid?'

He lowered his binoculars.

'What are you thinking of doing after the war?'

'When it's over I'm going to open a pub. Just me and the missus. Perfect.'

'I'm going to fuck the first thing I see,' said the man with the broken nose.

That night the lice were bigger than ever and the M.O. ordered everyone to cut their hair. This proved impossible; the camp possessed three pairs of scissors and no razor blades. The M.O. insisted. The Colonel appeared next day with his hair cropped. O'Scullion said the war wasn't preserving free-speech and wasn't preventing the enemy raping their wives (or, since they had no wives, the wives of the other men). He said he personally had no particular quarrel with the Left-buttocks; and Pill remembered an aunt who had given him sixpence once – she married a Leftbuttock and she said he was a good husband. O'Scullion said they ought to desert. Corporal Squall said if he heard them mention desertion again he'd see they were court-martialled.

Nobody knew what the enemy's next move would be. The Colonel studied a great pile of reports which came in. The map became studded with flags – a new box had been sent from G.H.Q. There were rumours of a secret weapon. One day Corporal Squall went round the camp searching for men whose names were on a list he had been given. The Colonel thought these men should volunteer for special duties. The next day a hundred men were assembled in front of the Officer's Mess. At 0.100 hours the Colonel strode out accompanied by his aide.

'Now, men, I want twenty volunteers for special duties.'

The men who had been on the list stepped forward. The Colonel smiled.

'Well done,' he said.

He turned and disappeared into the Officer's Mess. The twenty men, including Pill, O'Scullion and Gombold were told to report to the troop office at 0.150 hours.

O'Scullion said, 'What are the duties?'

'The old man will tell you,' Squall said. 'Just wait and see.'

At 0.150 hours they crowded into the troop office. The Colonel had got a brand new map from G.H.Q. It was of a totally unfamiliar area coloured green. He prodded it and stuck a triangular white flag into the centre.

'Remember, we shall be depending on you men,' he said. Corporal Squall, who was to be in charge of the party, asked one or two questions which the Colonel let his aide answer. He listened and refilled his pipe.

'The outcome of your little venture may affect the ultimate course of the war.' He prodded the map again. 'Here,' he said, 'is a depression situated over the posterior superior spine. I want radio-contact made when it is reached.'

He took a red pencil from his desk and drew horizontal lines through the 1st, 3rd, and 5th lumbar spines. This was the area he wished surveyed. It was extremely important that the allies receive information of enemy troop movements in the area. It would be a dangerous mission. Gombold sank on his bed in the billet with a sigh.

'Start packing,' Squall said.

The next morning the party set out shrouded in raincoats against the weather. They met the Left-buttock army on the second day. It was in a more southerly position than their information had led them to expect. From the scrub came a hail of rifle and machinegun fire. The party ran into the undergrowth. When Squall counted his men he found seven were missing.

'I'm not surprised,' he said. 'We must have come through enemy lines twice.'

They reached the posterior superior depression and made radio contact. It seemed the enemy had attacked and driven the allies beyond the gluteus maximus. No enemy troop movements could be observed as far north as they had reached. Over the radio came the message that there had been an unforeseen error: the depression over the Great Trochanter was meant, not the posterior superior spinal depression. So they altered course and marched south-west for three days.

Radio contact was lost and they were unable to receive instructions from base. That night, after posting sentries, they slept among the trees. They decided to stay where they were for a few days. O'Scullion said they ought to escape across to the left antecubital fossa. But Squall was against it.

'For Christ's sake don't be bloody silly,' he said. 'How do we get across? I'm not a bleeding bird.'

The next night, while they sat hunched up under the trees discussing their chances of survival, the noise of lorries rumbling by was heard. For a few minutes no one spoke; each putting his own interpretation on the noise. After some discussion it was decided to stay where they were overnight, and next morning to split up into parties, who would act independently. The enemy had invaded the whole area; the mission was at an end.

The next morning found Gombold, O'Scullion, Pill and Corporal Squall walking through the trees, jumping for cover whenever they spotted enemy soldiers, and avoiding the main roads which were crowded with transport.

'Hold it,' Squall said.

Approaching down a side road at a smart pace was a company of some twenty Leftbuttock soldiers, headed by an officer and a woman in civilian clothes. Pill cocked his gun. They were puzzled by the civilian. She was well dressed, with a hat shielding her eyes from the sun, and she was talking authoritatively to the officer beside her.

A spray of bullets made them crouch lower in the undergrowth. Pill's finger was curled round the trigger of his tommy-gun and he squeezed. Three of the soldiers fell.

'Chuck it,' said Squall. 'We haven't got a chance.' He dropped his gun, raised his hands, and stepped into the roadway. Pill threw his gun into the bushes and followed.

The enemy broke ranks and surrounded them. They were prisoners of war.

Eleven

They were marched to a place where allied prisoners were kept in cages; four men to a cage. A few civilians wandered about. Occasionally they put a bun or a piece of orange on a stick and poked it through the bars. In the distance Gombold could hear the click of turnstiles. He flopped down on his haunches, exhausted. After a while a girl cautiously pushed a tin of condensed milk towards him; her eyes fixed in hope as he dipped his fingers in and licked them. He passed the tin to Pill. The girl squealed with delight. She ran away and came back with her mother.

Just before dark, there was a stirring and shouting outside the cage, and a keeper, together with a woman civilian, opened the trap door an inch or two and filled the trough with water. They also pushed several pieces of horseflesh between the bars. While a crowd watched, Gombold and his friends ate their supper.

All the next day visitors poured through the turnstiles. An old woman sold bananas and popcorn near Gombold's cage. At midday and in the evening the inmates of the zoo were fed. Gombold didn't know if they were in a permanent POW camp or in transit, for none had been interrogated.

The keepers were unapproachable. With the idea of getting information out of the woman, Gombold bartered his wrist-watch for two bananas and a packet of raisins. She had the best of the bargain and knew Gombold's motive for the exchange, but she told him nothing.

One day she said, 'They're moving a lot of your chaps to the aquarium.'

'Why?' said O'Scullion.

'Don't ask me. It'll be nice, though. You'll be able to have a wash.' Later she said, 'I see you're classified as members of the genus Canis (wolves and Hyaenas) C.lupus C.pallipes, H.striata, and H.brunnea. They shouldn't be feeding you fruit.'

Gombold said, 'Can't we be transferred?'

A keeper came up and hurried the peanut seller away.

'Can't we get a change of species?' Gombold asked.

'You'll have to see the Head Keeper.'

O'Scullion said they should make a complaint; they'd been classified wrong. Pill said he wouldn't mind being something that ate decently. Corporal Squall thought the aquarium ideal in the hot weather.

The peanut seller edged back. 'That's a cruel thing to do.'

'But this is a zoo,' Pill said.

'There's a mineral section.'

She went back to her pitch. The turnstiles clicked louder. In the afternoon a dozen or so prisoners passed on their way to the mineral house – a sergeant labelled 'agate geode lined with quartz crystals,' three privates who were 'native sulphur, a non-metallic element occurring as yellow orthorhombic crystals', and a general holding a card showing him to be 'serpentine asbestos which rubs down to a silky fibre'. The peanut seller brought them a bunch of bananas. She told them of the record crowd expected on the bank holiday.

The cage became unbearable as the summer wore on. After making numerous applications they were brought before a committee from the department of Zoology and re-classified as apes. This had a dietary advantage. They wished at first to be re-classified as Otariidae. But Gombold said Otariidae were sea-lions and lived on a diet of raw herrings. In their new quarters they had a tea-party every afternoon. It was disturbing to notice, after a few weeks as *Pongidae,* that they were growing thick hair on their bodies and found it difficult to walk erect.

A man who sold raisins and oranges near the cage said to Pill one day, 'You're the gibbon, aren't you?'

'Am I?' said Pill.

'They said there was one dubious anthropoid among the apes.'

Pill went inside the sleeping quarters and refused to come out for several hours.

It was a bright morning and there was the promise of a record crowd. Gombold lay on a bench at the back of the cage, Corporal Squall picked his ears and O'Scullion had got hold of a tattered copy of an evening paper and was reading it upside down. Two keepers entered the cage, seized Gombold, wrapped him in a net, and bundled him into a van. They took him over to a square pen and left him.

After an hour two Zoological Society officials came to the bars and looked through intently.

The elder of the two men glanced at a form in front of him.

The younger man said, 'Can you use that swing?' He pointed to a rope trailing from the roof. Gombold nodded. 'Let us see you use it.'

Gombold leapt at the rope and swung from it. The two men put their heads together.

'Clearly not a type of arboreal monkey,' the elder said.

Over a loudspeaker Gombold heard a great noise of chattering; the sound of trees whispering together. The elder official came close to the bars of the cage.

143

'The prefrontal lobes of the brain are highly developed,' he said. 'On the other hand the occipital poles are much enlarged too. An arboreal ape, perhaps?'

The younger said, 'He certainly has good balance, sir. Has he a correspondingly complex development of the cerebellum and the cerebral areas of the brain?'

The elder man shook his head. He regarded Gombold with caution. The younger man put on a pair of leather gloves and entered the cage. Gombold backed away. His jaws were forced open and the man stared into his mouth.

'Thirty-two teeth,' he said. 'The lower incisors are inclined slightly forward.'

He removed the gloves and left the cage. Gombold grunted. The elder man began writing in a book he carried. The young man reached through the bars and patted Gombold's head and scratched his ear with a forefinger.

'Hearing is acute and the temporal lobes are large.' said the elder man. 'Dentition adapted for a mixed diet?'

The younger man nodded. He turned to the shelf behind him, piled high with junk. He seized a field telephone box, army type, and banged it down in front of Gombold.

'What use is this?'

Gombold tried to smile. He picked up the telephone and rattled it. Then he licked it. The elder man leaned forward and snipped a lock of Gombold's hair; he pinned it to the report he was making. Gombold threw the telephone into the furthest corner of the cage.

'Pan troglodytes. A sub-species undoubtedly,' said the elder man as they went away.

Gombold sat in a corner of the pen. The keepers came for him. As they drove away in the van he caught sight of his face in the glass. It was strangely unfamiliar.

144

They reached the cage; the door was opened and he was shoved inside. The tea-party was in progress. O'Scullion grabbed a cup and forced some tea between Gombold's lips. Gombold struck him in the face and shuffled into the sleeping quarter oblivious of the delighted shrieks of the crowd.

Corporal Squall came up to him and gave him a kick. Gombold stirred and blinked through sticky, half-closed eyes.

'Stand up,' Squall said.

Gombold shuffled to his feet; his fingertips dragged in the dust.

'Straight!' Squall said. He gave Gombold a blow across the mouth; the blood came oozing through the cut. 'You're on parade.'

With difficulty Gombold straightened up.

'What happened?' Squall said.

Gombold grunted; then he jabbered. Squall dealt him a back-hander. Gombold mumbled. Squall picked up a piece of wood and cracked Gombold over the shoulders with it.

Abruptly Gombold said, 'Don't do that.'

'What happened?' Squall said again.

Gombold told him about the examination the zoological officials had carried out, of the swing and the telephone.

Squall said, 'We'll be in bed with female chimpanzees soon.'

Gombold was surprised not to find the idea disgusting. He loped forward from the hips. 'Don't walk like that,' Squall said.

After a while he said:

'Suppose the four of us escaped.'

'Where would we make for?'

'Anywhere is better than here.'

During the day, choosing his time carefully when the

visitors weren't watching. Squall sounded Pill and O'Scullion. He had to beat Pill in order to bring him to his senses. O'Scullion was easier. Gombold noticed the man who sold raisins and oranges watching them. He'd seen him somewhere before. Whenever the keepers approached he darted away from the cage. But when they turned their backs, he fed the prisoners oranges without expecting payment. Early that afternoon he gave Gombold a cigarette.

He said, 'You don't remember me?'

'Can't say I do. Should I?'

'Apewit.'

'Of course, Apewit, I remember you now.'

'Careful,' he said, and strolled back to his pitch.

He soon came back and they went on talking. He said hostilities had spread over the whole area between groin and vertebrae. The Rightbuttocks had occupied 700 towns and the Leftbuttocks had raped 23,000,000 women since the outbreak of the fighting.

'Why don't you try and get away?' he said.

Gombold looked at him curiously.

'I've thought of it,' he said.

Apewit hesitated, looked at a crowd of visitors, who were out of earshot, then said: 'I could fix a boat for you.'

'What about a key to the cage?'

'I can give you one. You can't do it during the day. I have a wife and children to think of. At night no suspicion will fall on me.

'If you get away tomorrow night, come to my house.'

He told them his address. He gave Gombold full details of how to find the house. As he was leaving he passed them an orange. Inside was a key.

The next day passed slowly. In the morning Pill was taken away in the van. He returned making a series of unearthly cries and walking with his hands above his head. Squall took him to the sleeping quarters and beat him up. O'Scullion read his newspaper. Gombold tried to brush his hair. Pill returned and sat down.

They made a great effort to behave like apes. No suspicion of their plan must leak out. When the visitors had gone and the turnstiles ceased clicking the four gathered at the back of the cage. Squall had the key. It was badly made. He put it into the lock and turned it. Gombold heard the hissing intake of his breath.

'It won't work,' he said.

He grunted, the sweat trickling down the side of his face. Squall shook the cage door.

'Hold it up a bit,' he said.

Pill lifted the door a fraction of an inch. Squall tried the key again. This time it worked. The door swung open. For a second they stood rooted to the spot.

'Now!' said Squall, and they ran towards the turnstiles. It was nearly dark. The keepers were out of sight. Gombold climbed the wire fence. Looking over his shoulder he saw Pill; he was struggling with the woman from the ticket office.

'Come on,' Squall said. Behind them the keepers came running from the staff office. Gombold dared not stop. He was going now through tangled undergrowth, dodging from one bush to another. He came into the open. On and on he ran until he could go no further. Behind him he heard a crashing. He stopped in a hollow, and crouching waited until Squall almost fell over him. The zoo was now a quarter of a mile behind.

Squall squatted gasping for breath. 'My wind's gone.'

Pill joined them. He was breathing heavily.

'What were you doing?' Gombold said.

'That old bird from the tickets. She came out like a maniac. I had to throttle her.'

After half an hour they ran into a clump of trees. It

was cool. They moved through an endless succession of symmetrically growing hairs, crouching low, turning at every sound, diving for cover until satisfied there was no cause for alarm. The journey of eight miles took six hours.

'Where's O'Scullion?' said Gombold.

'I can't make it out,' said Pill. 'He was in front of me.'

It was close on midnight when they came to Apewit's house. Sitting beside the track they discussed their next move. After twenty minutes they heard a rustling behind them; the noises grew more distinct, and from beneath the heavy leaves O'Scullion emerged.

Apewit came out to see them. He said, 'I can't go with you. I'm a family man.'

'Where's the boat?'

Apewit's wife came out of the house. She said, 'We've got a family to think of, see.'

Apewit told them where to find the boat. The prisoners made their way to the Straits. Bending low, they edged forward across the mudflats. A little above the water's edge was a boat. They climbed in and pushed off into the gloom. As they paddled Gombold remarked on the extraordinary colour of the water, and said he understood from the keepers at the zoo that the river was supposed to be fathoms deep, and to have a hole through which it disappeared with startling suddenness. O'Scullion pointed out that what he had heard was folk-myth, a legend arising from a tradition of the end of the world which was to vanish into a big hole.

It was cold in the boat and none of them were wearing more than the remnants of their uniform. The sun rose. Gombold's tongue was thick and furry and his lips were dry. They took turns on the paddle; little progress was made.

'There's a breeze,' Squall said. 'Let's tie our shirts

together and rig up a sail.'

They had started to slip them off when Pill pointed towards the horizon where two dots were becoming larger. Presently they heard a buzzing. An enormous insect came into view. Another followed. The air was thick with them. They had narrow transparent wings, a long abdomen, and appeared to possess six legs. Many were brilliantly spotted with blue and green. The eyes occupied half the head surface. They flew directly towards the prisoners.

'Overboard!' said O'Scullion.

He dived across the gunwale. Gombold followed. The insects hovered a few feet above the boat. Two pairs of jaws could be seen with needle-like teeth. Gombold noted that the six legs were placed far forward on the body and formed a spiny basket in which the victims were caught.

Pill had his flesh torn as one of them grazed his arm. Gombold dived beneath the boat. He held his breath for as long as he could bear and then surfaced. Behind him the air was churned by the insects' wings. He saw three heads bobbing nearby.

'Look out, here they come again!'

Gombold dived. Twice more the insects swept over the water. Their abdomens were composed of bamboo-like segments. On the second or third segment was an organ used for attack or copulation. Finally they headed away up river. Gombold made sure they were out of sight before he swam back to the boat. It was upside down but still floating. Squall reached it before him, and they clung on, looking round for the others. Two heads appeared; Pill and O'Scullion sought a grip on the wood.

The four trod water and heaved until the boat rolled over. They climbed in and started to bale. After ten minutes they raised a sail. At midday the river brought them to a vast perpendicular wall, which seemed to halt the course of the waters. Paddling parallel with this precipice, at a distance of a hundred yards from it, they passed a considerable accumulation of rubbish, brought to the spot, Gombold supposed, by the intestinal tides. Before him, rising above the river, was an arch; it reminded him of a railway tunnel. Suddenly, the boat was sucked towards the arch. In another second they were propelled through it.

The walls inside were close together. They could distinguish the roof rising ten feet above. Squall estimated the speed of the current at three knots; paddling was difficult in the constricted space. Gombold judged it to be about nine a.m. O'Scullion said the position was not altogether hopeless. He had a small knowledge of anatomy and gave as his opinion that they were now in the region of the pelvic colon or sigmoid flexure. After the first shock had passed, the idea of making a journey through the giant's bowels did not seem a bad one. Gombold was struck by the freshness of the air, but no explanation could be found for it. The light was dim; not unpleasant after the glare of the sun. Several hours later the river petered out into marshland. They ditched the boat and climbed ashore. In the half-light they searched for human habitation and came to a village. As they approached, an old man, obviously a person of some authority, stepped forward and greeted them. Bald and toothless, he was dressed in a long coat of leather. He motioned the travellers to come with him. They followed him through the grass to a house set at a distance from the rest.

'What are you doing here?' he said, as they sat down to a meal he had prepared.

'We are surveying the area,' Gombold said.

'Where are your instruments?'

'We lost them.'

150

The old man nodded. He had taken off his long coat and wore a white suit under it.

'I myself was something of an explorer when I was younger.' He settled himself into a bamboo chair and sighed. 'I had high hopes in my youth. What exactly are you looking for?'

'Radishes,' said Pill.

The old man raised his eyebrows. Gombold was not sure what to say. He nudged Pill under the table.

The old man said, 'When I was about your age I had an idea copper might be found in the Zouchfanberg.' He pushed a box of cigars towards Corporal Squall who selected one and lit it.

The old man rang a bell and a servant appeared carrying a tray.

'I always have a drink at this time in the evening,' he said. 'Won't you join me?'

Everybody was delighted. After a few drinks they settled down to listen to the old man's reminiscences.

'I had an idea copper was there,' he said, nodding his head 'I crossed the two Labarbas to the Pufforee river. Every night we built a shurm for our mules. We had eight of them. Eight shurms to be built each night. What a task.'

He fixed his eyes on Pill.

Pill said, 'You found the copper all right?'

'Wait, my boy. Wait.' The old man curled his lip in a smile.

'He's impatient, isn't he?' he said, addressing nobody in particular. 'As we caught sight of the Lubambean hills, M'pani bushes and ba'o babs appeared. The place was much broken up by Chloofs, and the ground completely covered by yellowids, stinkwids and moolies. The natives of those parts live entirely on lorikeets, a kind of radish.'

As he said the last words he stared hard at Pill with a

twinkle in his eye. Pill shuffled uncomfortably.

'They grew the lorikeets in accordance with Lord Lyndhurst's Act. Flinders Matthew had been in the parts before me so the natives were friendly. What really interested me, though, was when I caught sight of a Rhondavel.'

He paused.

Gombold said, 'A Rhondavel?'

Corporal Squall said, 'Might I trouble you for the ash tray?'

O'Scullion said, 'Rhondavels?'

Pill said, 'I didn't mean what I said about the radishes.'

The old man passed the ash tray across to Squall.

'I had no idea Rhondavels inhabited the area. When I tried to crossexamine one of our Shangans, he refused to say a word. We tried a spot of hunting, but found nothing except old spoor of Kudu and a Paauw. No sign of Rhondavel. I stalked a klipspingiel but missed him. We came to a thick wall of wait-a-bit thorns which refused to yield to our sjamboks. The head shangan (or *Mlasp*) proposed a detour. But I wouldn't hear of it. We got through somehow ....'

Corporal Squall leaned back in his chair. 'We had a C.O. once,' he said. 'Who always ... '

' ... on the other side we found a whole herd of Rhondavel.'

Squall cleared his throat.

' ... imagine it. A whole herd. The natives had been up to something.' He squirted soda into his glass. 'We came to a river they called Ylemenoba. I believe it means "Swift." We left the mules with a *M lasp* and bought a log canoe, presenting him with three empty egg-boxes by way of payment ....'

The old man nodded. Squall cleared his throat again. Pill sat rigid in his chair. The old man fixed his eyes on him.

'Radishes, eh?' he said. He snuffled as he lifted his glass to his lips.

He went on to tell them how he slaughtered several thousand animals, adding that the natives had been converted by a man with a criminal record.

'It's not every day that a minister has 12 imprisonments and more than 400 days behind bars to his credit,' he said.

'What happened to the copper?' said Gombold.

'The copper . . . ?'

For a minute he puffed his cigar in silence. The servant entered and drew the blinds. The old man's breathing could be heard in the gloom. Gombold thought he was asleep.

'We were led a devil of a dance . . . ' he said at last.

He stood up. They followed him up the stairs to a room with four beds. With a parting smile, he left them. Gombold heard the soft pad of his feet descending the stairs.

Sitting on the beds they tried to work out exactly what to do. O'Scullion said they were between the larger and smaller intestine – the ileum was to the north. To the south lay the caecum, an uninhabited area. Between them and freedom was a distance of more than a thousand miles.

'If we head north to the pylorus,' he said, 'we might link up with the guerrillas.'

The old man appeared at breakfast wearing his long coat. Gombold put his cards on the table and told him that they were escaping from the Leftbuttocks. The old man produced a circular which the enemy had distributed among the occupied peoples.

Gombold glanced at it. ' "People, whatever their calling," ' he read, ' "are equal. The soldiers have been sent to help overcome inequality." '

A servant took the circular and put it away in a

drawer. A gong sounded and thirteen men entered carrying urns and dishes. A short grace was said.

Gombold began to eat something that tasted of fish.

'So you are not prospecting?' said the old man. He shook his head and smiled at Pill. 'After breakfast I shall show you my collection of stamps. In the afternoon we'll take a stroll to visit a friend of mine. He'll put you on the right track.'

Gombold thanked him. He waved his hand. A servant helped him from the table. He disappeared into another room and returned wearing a hat and carrying a stick.

'Back in an hour,' he said. 'Treat the house as your own.'

While he was away O'Scullion glanced through a book. Pill had a bath. Corporal Squall went to look at the birds in the old man's aviary, and Gombold did nothing. Corporal Squall came back from the aviary and O'Scullion put his book down.

'We ought to do something about our boots,' he said, and went upstairs to shave.

Corporal Squall went to see if the servants had any spare boots. Gombold was left alone. The old man returned and took him into a room fitted up with glass-fronted cases. Inside were hundreds of stamps, each arranged on a square of white or black card. The old man said:

'I've collected these for many years now. I'm told they're worth a tidy sum.'

He left Gombold and returned with Pill. Gombold sat on the terrace until luncheon. Before dusk the old man handed each of them a parcel of food, and wished them good luck, good health and a good journey. He explained the road they should follow. His servants stayed with them for a mile or so and then said goodbye.

The track curved away in front of them, in and out of

enormous trees. They padded along at five-yard intervals, keeping an eye on the track ahead. About ten miles from the village Squall called a halt. The others came panting up behind.

'We might as well stay here for a bit.'

They sat down and O'Scullion said it was a pity they ever escaped from the zoo. Nobody replied. Gombold went to sleep. When he woke Corporal Squall was telling a story about a deaf-mute who married a blind woman. Pill said he knew a better one about a man called Louis. They unwrapped their food and ate a third. A little while later they had trouble with a kind of ant and had to move. They came to a swamp. A swirl in the water, only a few yards away, made them turn.

'Look,' said O'Scullion. 'A crocodile.'

Suddenly, having seen one, they noticed others; thousands of them lolling in the water.

'Let's get out of here,' said Squall.

They took a rough bearing and decided to head north-west, parallel to the swamp. To the left the country was open, with tall grass. There was little cover. They tramped on.

On the twelfth day they came to a river – a wide stretch of motionless water. They sat and looked at it.

'Why not float a raft up it?' said Pill.

'Some hope,' said Squall.

It was hardly moving. They threw in a branch, and it lay motionless. Gombold decided to swim across. Fully dressed he slid into the slime and swam across. He waded out onto the opposite bank spluttering and pulling away the weeds that had twined themselves round his legs. The others joined him. Later in the afternoon they smelt burning wood. They stopped. Then carefully pushed forward until at last they spotted the tops of a cluster of houses. It was decided not to enter the village. Enemy troops might be in the area. For safety's sake they by-passed it. Early next morning O'Scullion began to crack up.

'I can't go on,' he said. 'I just can't.'

'Hold up,' Gombold said.

O'Scullion stumbled and fell face downwards on the cool, spongy earth.

'Water,' he said. 'Water, for God's sake; water.' His fingers curled and uncurled on the parched grass.

They propped him against a tree trunk and went in search of a stream. There was no sign of one. They found a family of orang-outangs and a grove of fruit which had no sap and a deep pit filled with snailshells, but no water. Then they saw a tarmac road, and running beside it a belt of trees. As they came nearer they saw water cascading between boulders.

They also found a wild pear tree and a patch of fungus which tasted like mushrooms. While searching for a suitable spot to camp, they came to a clump of trees and saw a number of houses with tiled roofs.

'We'd better risk it this time,' Gombold said.

He crawled through the bushes to the edge of the village. He was ready to run away if anybody looked hostile. No one showed any interest in him as he walked down the street. He walked up the path of the first house which had a doorbell. He rang the bell hard. No one answered. As he waited a woman leaned over the wall and said:

'She's gone away.'

Gombold thought quickly. 'Has she?'

Gombold rang the bell again.

The woman, who was standing on a step-ladder, said: 'It's no use your ringing that bell.'

Gombold turned to go. He said, 'How long will she be away?'

The woman's face disappeared as she stepped down. Her voice came over the wall. 'She's on her holidays.'

Gombold walked back to the wood. O'Scullion, Pill and Squall were so well hidden that it took him some time to find them.

They waited until nightfall and made their way to the house. Pill went round the back and after a minute or two opened the front door. They trooped inside. O'Scullion sat on a settee. Squall disappeared in search of the kitchen.

Pill said, 'How long can we stay here?'

Gombold said he thought a week at least. The shutters were closed. He switched on the light. On the mantelpiece was a photograph of a man and woman with a dog. A wrought-iron firescreen stood in front of the empty grate. Gombold began taking the dust covers from the furniture. Squall came back with a tin of ham, a packet of cornflakes, eight tins of bitter lemon, a tin of creamed rice and a packet of dried fruit.

Upstairs they found a bedroom with a double bed. On the dressing table was a collection of bottles and a powder bowl. Another room had a single bed. In a linen cupboard Pill discovered several pairs of silk pyjamas and a collection of shirts. They spent the evening watching a television programme in which the panel tried to guess what day it was. Ater this they saw a play about a young couple's domestic worries; then they watched the news. After this they went to bed.

In the early part of the morning a knock came at the front door. They peered from behind the shutters. Three feet away stood a man wearing a cardigan and carrying a parcel. They stood and waited. At last they heard the sound of the man's footsteps receding down the path and an engine starting. A few minutes later Gombold found a note pushed through the letter box. It said, 'Your garden gnome has been cleaned and awaits collection.' The heading on the paper said, 'Gnomes Hospital. A. and E. Scholfield'.

That night they watched a programme in which a panel listened to pins dropping. After this they saw a play about the problems of a girl brought up to believe her legs were attached to her body by coloured ribbons; then they watched the news. After this they went for a walk. When they came back the house was on fire. Flames leapt from the roof. Gombold remembered he had left the electric fire switched on. Pill remembered Squall throwing a newspaper down as they left the room.

'We can't stay here,' O'Scullion said.

They walked away from the blazing house and came to a place where a man was bending over an ancient lorry; there was hardly a speck of paint on it. They persuaded him to give them a lift as far as the next town. They piled into the back. The engine roared into life; the man smacked in his gear and the lorry lurched forward. For the greater part of the night they travelled over rough roads. They stopped at a café and had a cup of tea. O'Scullion said they were prospecting. Gombold said Pill had information that copper was to be found in the district. After thinking this over for a minute the driver asked Pill where he had received his information? Pill said he knew an old man who had once prospected for copper. Corporal Squall took the driver aside and told him the truth. It was the right thing to do because he was a guerrilla. They climbed into the lorry once more. At the next stop the driver said:

'I'm fetching petrol from an enemy post two miles away. Want to come?

Gombold shook his head. The driver climbed into the lorry; it coughed and moved down the road.

'What do you make of him?' O'Scullion said, as the lorry disappeared.

'He's in with the enemy,' said Pill. 'I expect he's off to tell them where we are.'

158

'He could have done that miles back.'

As they stood talking, a man approached them wearing a pair of downtrodden slippers.

'I shouldn't worry,' he said. 'My son is a good man. We cannot yet beat our enemies in open warfare, but all of us wait for the day when our people come; then we shall fight.'

They walked to a house, outside which stood a trestle-table; on it they found sheets of newspaper and bowls of soup.

'All the peoples will be free one day,' said the old man.

Gombold took a drink from a jug; the liquid tasted exactly like water. Their host informed them that this was not the case; the jug contained a rare wine. The food the man's wife brought tasted like bread. Once again the man corrected them; it was not bread; the meal they were eating was made from an old gourmet's recipe.

'The people of the gut will fight with us,' said the old man. 'The people of the gullet too.'

'And the people of the belly,' Gombold said. 'What of them?'

'They don't care who rules them. They think only of their day-to-day existence, and provided no one maltreats them, they are content.'

Corporal Squall put down his glass. 'Who exactly are you fighting for?'

The driver, who had returned, sat down beside him. 'For the independence of the body's members,' he said.

They went into the house which had a kind of coarse matting on the floor. The old woman made them change their boots for slippers before walking across it.

'She's proud of her Aubusson,' said the old man.

The driver suggested they lodged in the house for a few days; his sister was about to be married, he said, and they could join in the celebrations. O'Scullion wanted to turn down the invitation for he feared they would find themselves involved in a political intrigue. But Squall said that he had been talking to the driver's father and gathered that many prisoners had been helped to escape.

'Sit on the terrace if you want,' said the driver's mother. 'I'll bring you a cool drink in a bit.'

They went into the back yard and sat on the deckchairs. After a few minutes a girl came out of the house with four mugfuls of water. She placed them on a box beside Squall.

'Are you the bride?' Pill said.

The girl nodded and went indoors.

'Not before time I should think,' Squall said.

In the afternoon the wedding presents were laid out in the drawing-room; Gombold was not surprised to find himself being led into a cupboard under the stairs. An electric light had been fixed over a shelf. On the shelf, resting on pieces of matting were the wedding presents. He glanced at one or two: a vase with a crack in the handle, a mouse egg, a map of Skaill, three pairs of single sheets, a double bolster, a fish peeler and a glass for holding glue.

'If your Mary's coming I'm not,' said a voice outside.

'We can't not invite her.'

'You never told me.' It was the driver's mother. 'I superintended the invites. I never asked her.'

'Well she's coming.'

The driver's father opened the door. Gombold said: 'I've been looking at the presents.' The couple resumed their argument as he left.

'Look at the way she carried on at Eddie's wedding. I'm not going through that again.'

Gombold walked away. A lot of relations had arrived and he was introduced to eight aunts called Betty and a girl with golden hair called Beryl. O'Scullion was talking to a girl called Brenda and Pill had spilled a glass of water down the dress of a woman called Alice. In the church a little boy caused a scene and had to be smacked. A little girl wet herself. All the aunts cried. The wedding bouquet was of lilies and fern. The bridegroom wore a blue suit and had a gardenia in his buttonhole; his best man thought the vicar had insulted them by rushing the service. The photographs were taken on the church steps.

'You want to put a better expression on your face than that,' said an aunt. 'It'll come out horrible in the photo.'

The bride's mother said: 'What's the matter with you, Dorrie?'

'Can we have the happy couple alone now?' the photographer said.

The reception was held in a pub nearby. There was a row later on because the men went downstairs to the bar. The bride came back having changed her dress. Squall and Gombold asked for glasses of water and were given double whiskies.

'Are you Albert's mates?' said an uncle of the groom.

'Yes,' said Squall.

'He should never have married her,' said another uncle.

'She was engaged to a bloke called Bill,' said the first uncle. 'Why didn't he marry her?'

The first uncle went away. Another uncle and a cousin joined Gombold and Squall.

'Her father's an old sod,' said the cousin. 'Quite a problem for the refuse disposal people he'll be when he kicks it. Sixteen stone and a wing collar.'

The first uncle came back. 'He should never have consented to it,' he said.

'Everything will turn out for the best,' said the second uncle.

Gombold went to the bar and paid for a round. When he came back the cousin had taken off his coat and given Squall a fag.

He was saying, 'Her mother is an old tart. I've had a cut off the bacon times before now. Any port in a storm. And what a port.'

'It does no harm,' said the second uncle. 'What harm does it do?'

The third uncle, who hadn't spoken, opened a packet of crisps. Gombold went to the lavatory. When he came back the third uncle had loosened his collar and given Pill a fag; Squall was talking to the girl with golden hair.

The third uncle said: 'What do you think of that for news? A smack in the eye for some people. The smile faded from her face when I told her. I acted, you see, on a sudden impulse and when Johnson came I asked what it'd fetch. I had a feeling she wouldn't be so delighted when she heard.'

Gombold pushed his chair back. There was a scream. Beer spilled down his neck. A woman began to laugh.

Gombold stretched his legs.

'She owned it at one time. Well, it's a long story that has no turning and I won't bore you with it; but all she ever did was piss in it as far as I could see.'

The cousin said something Gombold couldn't hear. Then he said, 'There's no doubt she's looking better with her new teeth.'

The second uncle said: 'Everybody's happy enough. I'm happy, so is she, after her fashion.'

'Which isn't saying much,' the third uncle said.

Gombold went to the lavatory again. When he came back the aunts had joined the party and Squall had disappeared.

'What you want to come down here for?' said the bride's mother.

An aunt said to Gombold, 'Are you a friend of Dorrie's?'

'Yes,' said Gombold.

He stood up and went outside into the yard. O'Scullion was sitting on a wall.

He said, 'I've just been having a talk with the groom.'

He thought the vicar had insulted them. Gombold went back inside. The best man had borrowed a scarf from one of the aunts and was dancing on the table; he had stuffed two oranges up his shirt. The aunts were shrieking with laughter. Gombold sat beside the bride. Someone had just been sick.

'He never knows where to stop,' said the bride sourly as the best man finished his dance.

Next morning they sat in the back of the lorry as it bumped over the country roads. In the afternoon they ran into a populated area, passing groups of bungalows and a few houses. The driver slowed down and edged the lorry into a narrow defile just off the road. He told them to wait. He disappeared and came back with a man who spoke ten languages. He was the first in the line of underground contacts. The driver shook hands. They were, he told them, to do exactly as the man ordered, for they had reached the Pylorus and the enemy were all around. He said goodbye.

For two days they rested with the man who spoke ten languages, sleeping on the floor of the conservatory and smelling the incense which burnt near an image in the corner. On the third day a milkman called at the house and brought with him a woman with no roof to her mouth. She was the second contact. They stayed with her for a week. She kept dogs. They made a railway journey of a hundred or so miles and she handed them on to the third contact, a man who lived in a bombed warehouse. He kept them in barrels. The barrels were large and had originally held a kind of salted fish; they smelt appallingly. Each barrel had a bung hole through which a tiny section of the outside world could be seen.

In the early hours of the morning Gombold woke drenched in sweat. His eyes throbbed. Around him were the curving walls of the barrel. He saw the warehouse cat tearing at a rat. He was on the point of raising the lid on the barrel when he heard voices. He crouched motionless, holding his breath. The lid of the barrel was jerked off and a quantity of fish offal thrown on top of him. He heard the sound of hammering and realised the lid had been nailed down.

He had the sensation of falling. His head bumped against the lid; fish heads covered him; he was suffocating. After a silence he felt a tumbling under him. The barrel was on a train. Scraping the fish from the bung he tried to see outside. He saw nothing. His thoughts turned to the others. Were they in the same situation? He had no means of contacting them. Later he fainted. When he recovered he heard noises; wheels moving, vibrating thwangs, the sound of voices. He realised that the barrels had been off-loaded. He pushed at the bung and it moved. Exerting all his strength he managed to dislodge it. It rattled into the darkness.

A voice said, 'Are you throwing things at me?'

And a minute later: 'Well, somebody is.'

Gombold saw a section of a gaudily furnished room. The barrel must be standing on a staircase or balcony: he could see a man and a woman.

'Not very lively tonight is it?' the man said. 'We shan't get rich at this rate.' The woman shrugged.

'This'll never pay for my bit of fur,' she said.

She disappeared from view. A moment later a voice close to the barrel said, 'I don't know, 'strewth I don't!'

The man picked up a megaphone and bawled, 'Come

to the old firm, lads. All tastes catered for. No reasonable request refused.'

The view was blotted out by a leg; someone stood in front of the barrel. A minute later there came a scratching at the lid, then it was thrown back and Gombold was exposed, blinking in the light. Three women were looking down at him.

Later Pill said, 'This is a knock shop, I reckon.'

Squall said, 'I could do with something to eat.'

They were sitting in a room furnished with eight or nine couches waiting for their contact to arrive. The owner of the place came in.

'Must have a breather,' he said. 'Had a nice journey?'

'No,' O'Scullion said.

The man said, 'Can I think of anything to keep you amused while you're waiting?'

'No,' O'Scullion said.

'Well this is a nice room to wait in,' the man said. 'We've had a lot of decorating done lately.'

'Are you the owner of this place?' Gombold asked.

'No I'm the manager.'

O'Scullion asked when their contact would arrive. The manager said he didn't know.

He offered to show them round; Pill accepted before anyone could reply. They were led down a long corridor and up two flights of stairs and down another corridor until they came to a doorway. The manager unlocked it and they descended a flight of stairs.

The manager said to O'Scullion, 'We understand everyone at the Consummatum est. Can I suggest a good belting?' They had stopped before an open door. 'Are you fond of a clip around the ear? Or is it a tanned bottie you'd like?'

'I'm not ready for that yet,' O'Scullion said.

'We'll make you ready. Nell in there is a real brute; she'll make you see stars as soon as look at you.'

A woman put her face round the door and stared at them.

'Come on, dearie, be a sport,' she said.

'You might hurt me,' O'Scullion said.

The manager ushered them further down the corridor.

'What you want to go and offend her for?' he said. 'It's not often Nell takes a fancy to a man. She'd have beaten you black and blue if you'd only asked.'

'What's up out there?' called Nell. 'Are they dead?'

The manager shot back and went inside. Gombold heard him shouting, 'Business is slack! Can I help it?' He came back.

He said to O'Scullion, 'Go on, tell her you've changed your mind. Look at her fingering the whip. Can't you feel it whistling down onto your bare –'

'I couldn't fancy her,' said O'Scullion.

'Keep your voice down then, or she'll lay about you for free,' said the man, leading them to another door. 'What about Milly?' he said.

Nobody said anthing as he opened the door of the room. Squall looked inside.

'A bit young,' he said.

The manager said, 'That's the beauty of it. She doesn't look a day over ten, does she? And yet she's getting on for thirty. You can have her with or without the school satchel.'

The girl came to the door and said, 'Hallo mister, can you tell me the way to the playing fields? I've lost my way.'

The manager winked. 'How old are you, my dear?' he said, patting her head.

'I'm eight next birthday.'

'Use a bit of common, Milly!' he said, straightening up. 'You'll never get away with that any more.'

She shrugged. 'I'm sitting for my eleven plus next week.'

'And while you're about it get yourself a new pair of socks, will you?'

'If you say so.'

'Socks like that – it's enough to put anybody off. You're supposed to look fresh.' He turned to Squall. 'How about it, sir? Interested?'

Squall shrugged and looked at Milly. The manager turned away.

'What is it? Tired after your journey? You're hard to please. There's a school desk, and a blackboard. Milly's good at giving an impression.'

He led them further down the corridor.

'You don't know what you want and that's a fact,' he said. 'How about Flo – a real treat she is; or Fan – she'll make you think you're in heaven; or Ivy – she's something to write home about she is.'

They climbed twenty-four steps and O'Scullion said he thought they ought to sit down. The manager led them to a couch under a picture of waving palms. Squall said he could do with a meal.

The manager said, 'Don't you like women, gents? Is that it?'

Pill said, 'Look we've had a long journey – '

The manager said, 'Don't apologise. Don't apologise. We have a lot in here with exactly the same taste as yourself. It's nothing to be ashamed of. I don't mind telling you, I get a bit tired myself. When you've seen one you've seen them all.'

He stood up and hammered on a door.

'Johnie!'

After a pause they heard a cough behind the door; a youth wearing a filthy pullover and smoking a fag put his head round.

'What you want, you bleeding old creep?'

The manager clucked his tongue against his teeth and said, 'See what I have to put up with?' He said to the youth, 'Cut it out will you? You're getting too big for your boots.'

Johnie began to cough. 'These fags you dish out are murder,' he said. He looked at Squall. 'Any kink you got? Like baseball boots or bell-bottoms?'

He slouched off; his cough could be heard from inside the room. The manager beamed.

'He's got a lovely pair of leather jeans, gents. We charge for the extras, but it's worth it. You should see him in his little vest, with the motor oil on his face – it's not just sex it's poetry, pure poetry. And that's what we aim at. Anybody can give you sex but the Consummatum est gives you the poetry of sex at no extra charge.'

Squall said, 'We've no money. You should know that.'

They were shown through a doorway into the main hall.

The manager said, 'Well any time you do feel like a bit of relaxation, don't forget us.' He stopped as a man approached. 'What can we do for you , sir?' he said, waving the four men aside.

Gombold remembered the man who died hoisting the flag of the revolution.

'It's quite likely,' said Offjenkin. 'We're a large and turbulent family.'

He led the way towards a group of men. They worked for him under the strictest possible discipline; though exactly what they were working for was not at first apparent.

'We are against fragments, wonderful ventures, allegorical dramas, sentences more than eight words long, second chances, old men with green eyes, chinese-white, murder without crime, miracles, textbooks on Hygiene, muscle re-education and all forms of stammering,' said Offjenkin.

168

A man nearby cleaning a machine gun said, 'And phonology.'

'And young men with four shirts and choice silver wedding presents,' said another.

Offjenkin presented Gombold and Squall with a pamphlet each . He sat down in the middle of his men.

'We are in favour of walls,' he said, 'and Norse folk tales, "I love you," dream houses, spider's webs, village greens, cuckoldry within reason, psychoanalytical studies of Hamlet, domestic bliss, first-hand information and cross-stitching.'

The man nearby cleaning the machine gun said, 'And Beginner's luck.'

'And clowns, wisdom teeth, dead roses and mousetraps,' said another.

Offjenkin said, 'You'll be all right. Ask no questions, do as you're told, and' – his face twisted into a smile – 'you may in time come to identify yourself with our views.'

For several weeks the organised and purposeful band climbed the tunnel, keeping to little used paths. One morning Offjenkin's scouts told him that the mouth had been reached. A concave roof stretched above them; pale red light washed round the landscape. Ringing the plain were the teeth; numerous caves housed communities of troglodytes. Searching for a place to pitch a tent one of the men stuck the peg into a cleft of rock and hit a sinew or nerve of the jaw. The plain rose and shook, and a distant roaring was heard. Gombold lay flat behind a blackened rock and prayed to be delivered alive from the situation. A river of liquid poured down upon them. Men rushed up the mountainside and clung to rocks as the flood passed. After the disturbance had subsided several were missing.

For five days they marched in a long straggling line weighed down with equipment. They travelled fast, sometimes by day, sometimes by night, heading for the distant mountains; often they covered fifty miles at a stretch. They followed Offjenkin blindly knowing nothing, asking no questions. On the afternoon of the fifth day they made a temporary camp, but erected no tents. Offjenkin left them, taking eight of their number with him; the remainder set out in a different direction under Offjenkin's second-in-command. They camped beside an oval lake. They lit fires, piling on dead branches and making a noise; one of the men rang a bell.

Then everybody went back to the camp; Offjenkin seemed pleased.

He said, 'That was a good day's work.'

'We don't want to provoke a counterattack,' said the second-in-command.

Offjenkin laughed. 'I do,' he said.

The next day they entered one of the largest caves near the front teeth and in the darkness piled leaves over a hole in the ground; at the same time two of their number recited the alphabet in an effeminate voice. The atmosphere was tense with excitement.

Offjenkin said, 'That should worry them.'

'You must be careful,' said the second-in-command.

'I'll show them,' said Offjenkin, striding round the camp tearing a photograph of a bishop to pieces. 'I mean what I say.'

A few days later Gombold found himself lying on a slope overlooking a village. He saw a profusion of rock, plants and flowers; grains of sand created sparkling refractions of light. The sweep of the vaulting above spread an even, homogenous glow across a landscape very different from the darkness from which they had come. A band played in the distance. A fête was in progress.

'The enemy are in that tent,' Offjenkin said, pointing

to a striped marquee.

'Are they armed?' Gombold asked.

Offjenkin said nothing. He moved off with his escort. Gombold listened to the distant music. A burst of applause came from the tent. A few minutes later he heard a rustling in the undergrowth and Offjenkin and his men filtered back: with much satisfaction telling how the whole village, every man, woman and child, had been stared at. Such incidents, Offjenkin declared, were liable to rock the status quo and tumble any Government from power.

'They must be made to realise we mean business,' he said. He sat on a cushion which had a crown painted on it. 'I think we have them worried.'

'Undoubtedly,' said the second-in-command.

'What are they doing in that tent?' asked Pill.

'I don't know, said Offjenkin, 'We weren't allowed in.'

'Why didn't you cut the guy ropes or something?' said Squall.

Offjenkin frowned. 'We don't want to go too far,' he said.

'They might mount a counter attack.'

'I wish they would,' said Offjenkin with a toss of his head. 'I'd like to come to blows with them. I expect they're worried. They gave us one or two anxious looks down there.' He laughed. 'Wait till our next move.'

Before this could be accomplished they had many days' journey through the chasms which separated the plain from the outside world. Standing at last on the edge of the forest, contemplating the confusion of forms, the composition of trunks, Gombold took pleasure in seeing avenues of glistening foliage.

Squall said, 'We ought to get some kind of medal.'

'Why?' asked Gombold.

'The way we escaped.'

171

Gombold thought nothing more of this until they reached the outskirts of a city. Squall, his uniform brushed, appeared in the doorway of Gombold's tent.

'Now,' he said, 'I was i/c of the expedition, remember?'

'Yes,' said Gombold.

'Well officially I still am. So get yourself smartened up.'

Struggling to his feet Gombold saluted. O'Scullion and Pill were polishing the remnants of their kit when he approached them.

O'Scullion thought they ought to strike out on their own, Pill said he didn't see why they shouldn't find out what Squall had in mind first.

When they had smartened themselves up they reported to Squall who inspected them. Then he marched them at a stiff pace down the road into the city. As they approached a cart passed them with six girls in it. The roads were lined with people waving flags. A company of Leftbuttock soldiers stood in front of the town hall; a military band played a rousing march. In front of the cathedral a company of Rightbuttocks soldiers wheeled among an enormous number of coloured standards. A woman on horseback was tossing flowers into the crowd. Lining the main thoroughfare were triumphal arches decorated with roses. Gombold and his comrades wandered among the crowd until they came to a raised platform upon which Major-General Vulp, Sir Shelumiel Cush, Beatrice, Mrs Vulp and a number of other people, of whom Gombold had no knowledge, sat with eight or nine men in grey suits.

They watched while a lot of speeches were made; some kind of rapprochement between the Left and Right-buttocks had clearly been arranged. Major-General Vulp spoke for half an hour and then handed the microphone to Sir Shelumiel Cush who announced that a new world was about to be born. Everybody cheered. A lot of medals were handed out. After this the celebrities drove away and everybody began to scream with laughter and pat each other on the back.

Squall said, 'I don't think we can do much.'

So they crept back to the forest and told Offjenkin the news. 'I thought you realised,' he said.

They stayed in the forests for a long while. Whenever they ventured into the town they found a band playing, or a carnival in progress. Offjenkin staged one or two futile attacks – he circulated among a crowd of women in a restaurant and told them the proprietor was mad; he organised a march into the city centre wearing a mask and carrying a banner on which nothing was written, and then he sat on the steps of the law courts dressed in a sack and wearing a cap. A lot of newspapers printed his picture the next day, which pleased him. Then he arranged for a play to be translated and performed.

'There'll be some long faces,' he said. 'I'm expecting to be attacked for it.'

When the day came the play proved a great success and he was asked to dine by Sir Shelumiel Cush and Major-General Vulp. He met Beatrice and said she was charming. After this he wrote two or three other plays, but took to missing out the third acts which were too controversial. Each time he had a success he was seen less and less in the camp. One day a unanimous vote elected Squall head of the force. Offjenkin was away having dinner with the modernest woman in the world. She wore a placard on her back saying, 'I am the modernest woman in the world.' When Offjenkin returned and was told of Squall's election he became angry.

He said, 'We were about to open a children's section.' The next day he left the force for ever. He lived with the modernest woman in the world who eventually married him. There was a big wedding and everybody said how modern the modernest woman was in marrying such an outrageous person. She said she thought startling people ought to be encouraged. In the newspaper Gombold read of a new play by Offjenkin which was the most daring thing ever written. It was about a man and woman who got married. The modernest woman in the world was quoted as saying she hardly knew how to live with such a wild, rough person as Offjenkin.

O'Scullion became second-in-command to Squall. Offjenkin's second-in-command resigned. When they heard that Squall was head of the force and that O'Scullion was second-in-command the papers asked why a deserter like Squall and an escaped convict like O'Scullion were tolerated. The police came with dogs and the force retreated further and further into the forest.

Gombold realised that the tactics they were using had proved useless. Words were more effective than actions; in the right hands verbs and nouns could create panic. Offjenkin had made an attempt to design a sentence which would speak for itself, but had abandoned the idea as too destructive. Gombold bought a dictionary and began to study the construction of the sentence.

The blast of a long sentence was curiously local, and a lot of shorter sentences seemed better. And then there was the problem of gathering enough of the enemy together in order that they might listen. He started wondering where and how he could hit the enemy most. Perhaps there were key points. He started calculating and found some sentences were puny against large targets. Then perhaps a new type of sentence. But Gombold did not know enough about sentences and the logic stopped short. The war was a few weeks old when he started to construct the perfect sentence. Squall allowed him a tent to himself, and he studied the chemistry and behaviour of words, phrase design, the forging, casting and milling, the theories of paraphrase and periphrase, the fusing and the aiming.

In a library he unearthed accounts of the damage words had done in the past. His figures showed that when a particularly dangerous collection of words exploded the shock waves were capable of killing centuries afterwards. He thought of a book. But that was no use. It would vibrate the structure, but not enough. To be destructive, words had to be irrefutable. And then the book might not be read. He was aware that words and sentences often buried themselves into readers' minds before exploding and then went off harmlessly. Print was less effective and the spoken word because the blast was greater; eyes could ignore, slide past, dangerous verbs or nouns. But if you could lock the enemy into a room somewhere and fire the sentence at them you would get a sort of seismic disturbance . . . .

The idea shaped in his mind while he was sitting in a chair in the tent. He looked up more books, studied the propagation of idiom, the effect of adjectives, and found pages on the penetrative power of faulty grammar. There was a piece about a sentence which caused a revolution. Gombold pulled out a pad and pencil and worked for a week, covering sheets with calculations, equations, formulae – accelerations, resistances – and came up with a preliminary theoretical answer. A sentence no more than six words long, with no adjectives and in the second person plural, should result in the complete collapse of the enemy power.

The next problem was to get Squall and O'Scullion to listen to his theory, to believe and accept it. He spent three weeks setting it out on paper and took it to his superiors.

175

'But,' said O'Scullion, 'how do you get them together?'

'Couldn't we try having it printed and distributed?' said Pill.

'No,' Gombold said.

Squall said, 'You'd better have some tests done.'

Over the next few months O'Scullion helped with designs. They went into the city and used it in a shop.

'Not so good,' Gombold said, as they came away.

'Perhaps they didn't hear,' O'Scullion said.

'It takes too long to say.'

Later he went into the city on his own to test another sentence; it was a failure. On the way back he saw an elderly woman in front of him. As she passed a group of children playing in the road a small boy said something to her. The reaction was immediate. She turned a bright pink; cracks appeared across her face, patches of skin flaked and chipped. She crumbled before his eyes. Gombold questioned the boy and found the sentence he had used was quite simple in construction.

A great party to be held at Money-box Lodge seemed the perfect time for attack. A list of guests was published and most of the enemy had been invited. Squall told the force what he wanted them to do, but not what the sentence was. Only he, Gombold and a few others knew that. Hidden in the forest they studied photographs of Money-box Lodge to check the defences. Gombold remembered the monstrous hound kept by the Major. Reports came in of another dog recently bought by the Major; it resembled a wolf in size, the breed was uncertain. It seemed as though extra precautions ought to be taken against these animals. Security was increased. If the secret leaked out the raid would have to be called off. It was going to be suicidal enough as it was. There were at least three exits from the dining-room; these would have to be sealed off once the

176

saboteurs were inside.

One morning Squall said, 'Start briefing your crew this afternoon and see that security is foolproof.'

After lunch a little aeroplane landed and a man climbed out; two minutes later he was in Squall's tent with a guard outside. He had brought with him a tin box lined with foil, inside were square cakes which were to be given to the hound. The man left again immediately. In the mess a message came through: 'Report for briefing immediately.' At three o'clock twelve men sat on benches opposite Squall. They eyed the familiar maps and posters on the walls, waiting. Squall walked down the centre to the dais. The tent was still.

Squall faced them feet braced apart, flushed a little. He had a ruler in one hand, the other in his pocket. He cleared his throat and said:

'You're going to have a chance to clobber the enemy harder than a small force has ever done.' Outside there was no sound. 'Very soon we are going to attack the major stronghold.'

Squall turned to the map and pointed with his ruler. He went on to explain the tactics, told each man what his duty would be. O'Scullion took over and described the house and what was supposed to happen, how success would cripple the enemy.

Squall stood up. 'Any questions?'

A man stood up. 'What are the defences like, sir?'

'We've had extensive photo-recces,' Squall said, 'and the defences seem to be confined to a dog guarding the entrance. You'll be shown how to deal with that.' He was uneasily wondering about the mysterious wolf.

He crossed the room to a trestle table where a dust cover was hiding something, pulled the cover off, and revealed a model of Money-box Lodge.

'Come over and have a look at it,' he said.

There was a scraping of forms as the men got up and

crowded round.

'Look at it and when you've got every detail photographed in your minds, go away and draw them from memory, come back and check your drawings, correct them, then go away and draw them again until you're perfect.'

As the sun set across the forest the men gathered in Squall's tent for supper.

Squall said, 'I don't know what this horrible muck is we're drinking.'

Pill said, 'Do you mind passing the salt?'

O'Scullion said, 'Is this fish we're eating? I'd have brought sandwiches if I'd known.'

Squall crumbled a slice of bread into small pieces.

'The most lousy meal I've ever had in my life,' he said. He filled each glass with a muddy wine. 'If we're successful we'll make an annual event of this.'

'There's a bottle of scotch in the Red Cross box,' said a man with a hooked nose.

'Why didn't you bring it then?' Squall said.

'It's locked.'

Squall searched in his pocket for the keys and threw them over. The man with the hooked nose shuffled out.

Gombold went for a walk among the huge motionless trees. For some time the woods had been exhibiting a noticeable grey shade. The open spaces had increased until in some parts of the forest great glades of pink flesh were laid bare. He strolled down a path, kicking the fallen hairs; the giant was growing old; a parasitic existence would not be possible for much longer.

The journey to Money-box Lodge was accomplished with no difficulty. They stood beside the walls and watched the guests driving up in their cars. All the women were covered in diamonds. The modernest woman in the world arrived with Offjenkin. Hogg

178

came with a woman detective. In a flurry of newspaper men, the photographers' flashlights and gasps from the crowd, Beatrice and her husband arrived. Eighty-eight cabinet ministers, thirty-three trade unionists, seven hundred and six university professors and two elderly publishers arrived one after the other. The wife of a left-wing politician, dressed entirely in blue, drove through the gates in a blue car. Her husband sat in the back seat smoking a cigar. The blare of trumpets echoed across the woods; the party had begun.

Gombold slid over the wall. The night was hot and he was in his shirtsleeves. They came to the entrance and threw a sop to the dog who, upon devouring it, fell into a deep sleep. They climbed the stairs. Inside the house they saw one or two servants; no one spoke. The leading four came to the dining-room. They stood in an alcove, a little nervous because this was the treacherous part; they were about to open the door. The room came suddenly to life, angry voices raised, women screaming, as the tommy-guns were trained upon them. After a while Squall said, 'Well, boys, I suppose we'd better start the ball rolling.' It was the end of waiting and the start of action. For one moment the enemy was at bay; Gombold saw with satisfaction the terror in their eyes. And then he realised that they had been betrayed. The conspirators pressed the triggers of their guns but the bullets were blanks. Gombold turned and ran down the stairs. He was among a crowd of men and women in a room lined with pictures; a row was going on above.

'This is a private party,' said a woman.

'What do you mean?' Gombold said. 'I'm a member. I've been invited. I know Vulp very well.'

The woman turned to a man who was playing a game with circles on a board. Gombold moved into the crowd. The Major came in and made an announcement. At the window Gombold saw O'Scullion, Pill and Squall led away. They were handcuffed. In the corner he saw Offjenkin and attemped to avoid him but this proved impossible.

'Weren't you one of them?' Offjenkin said.

'No, no,' Gombold said.

Offjenkin introduced his wife. Gombold shook hands and went away feeling ashamed.

In the forest he was alone. He curled up beneath a tree and went to sleep. But his sleep was interrupted by dreams. In the darkness he thought of rescue and dismissed each evolving plan. More and more impressed by a feeling of helplessness, he fell asleep once more. And dreamed. Dreamed of men fishing in rivers for fish which had long been extinct. Examined the properties of drugs and minerals, motions of the stars, the mysteries of life. Turned again to images he had abandoned. In the morning he made the journey back to the camp. He saw three men in the branches of a tree; one drumming with a kettle; the second knocking two pieces of metal together causing sparks to fly; and the third pouring water from an earthenware vessel. Higher up in the treetop he discerned a gigantic jug lashed to a branch. Inside an old man was writing at a rough table. Evidently this was his home. All trace of the camp had disappeared. A man working nearby asked him if he knew the rebels. Gombold shook his head and went away.

A few weeks later Squall and the others were brought to trial. Vulp presided. The jury consisted of six dumb men, three deaf women and three lay figures made of branches, grass and flowers. The public galleries were crowded. The court-room had been wired for sound and vision. The prosecution opened their case. Gombold was surprised to find the counsel to be the fattest man in the world. He was a well-known figure; his size endeared him. On the second day he said, 'Are you fond of bananas?'

Squall said, 'Moderately.'

The prosecuting counsel eyed him. 'Answer my question,' he said.

'I'm not overfond of them,' Squall said.

'Define overfond.'

'I don't know how to.'

Here the judge intervened and said, 'You must answer counsel's question.'

'I am fond of bananas,' said Squall.

The prosecuting counsel rustled his gown and tilted his wig further back. 'Do you often buy bananas?'

'Not often.'

'About how many times a week do you buy a banana?'

'Four or five times,' Squall cleared his throat nervously.

The prosecuting counsel paused and addressed the jury.

'I regard four or five bananas a *week* an excessive amount of fruit to consume.'

A titter went round the court. The fans blew a breeze onto the lay figures.

The prosecuting counsel said, 'Are you fond of carrots?'

'Yes,' said Squall.

'And cucumbers?'

Squall nodded his head. The prosecuting counsel smiled.

'You admit it, do you?'

'What is wrong with it?' Squall said.

The counsel frowned. The judge leaned forward.

'You must let counsel ask the questions,' he said.

Counsel nodded. He consulted his papers. 'What length are these – bananas, or carrots, or cucumbers?'

'Average.'

'Average? I don't know what average is.' The court was hushed. 'How long are they?'

'I don't measure them.'

The judge said, 'If you persist in your attitude to counsel you will jeopardise your case.'

'What length are they?' counsel said.

'About nine inches long.'

A gasp went up from the body of the court. Counsel smiled.

'You are asking the court to believe you regularly purchase bananas of such a length?'

'Yes,' said Squall. Prosecuting counsel smiled around the court. A long pause followed.

'I rest my case,' he said at last.

The court was adjourned for two days. When it resumed hearing the case for the defence the courtroom was empty. The judge ordered the defending counsel to use no words of more than three letters long and to remember to address his words to the ceiling. The witnesses for the defence were surrounded by the utmost secrecy and were not allowed to appear in the courtroom during the trial. On the fifth day the judge summed up. He said the case had caused grave public concern and right-thinking people were shocked by it. The jury retired for two hours and brought in a verdict of guilty.

The execution was to be carried out on the following day.

At three o'clock Gombold stood among the crowd waiting for the prisoners to be brought from the gaol. The place of execution was guarded. All along the route were men selling souvenirs; photographs, bits of hair, a vest said to have been worn by Pill, a tooth lost by Squall in the struggle, and the mess furniture used before the attack. Even the keys to the Red Cross box and the half-empty bottle of wine seemed to have

182

assumed great importance. When the prisoners came out a cheer went up from the crowd. They walked the few yards to the place of execution in silence. Squall made a speech and the crowd cheered. Pill and O'Scullion were silent. It was a very impressive occasion. The soldiers standing around the scaffold took off their hats and bowed their heads. A crowd of women fainted. And then, after a short prayer, the execution took place and everybody went home.

It was a sad moment for Gombold as he viewed the bodies of his former companions. An old man wiped the drips from his aged nose and asked if Gombold could buy him a drink. Gombold led the way to a pub where the old man introduced a blousy woman as Squall's mother.

'It's a sad moment for her,' he said, sniffing. 'She thought the world of him.'

'He was led astray,' said the woman. She was small and blonde and had obviously been a beauty in her youth. The dye in her hair was wearing thin; grey streaks could clearly be seen.

The man said, 'Have another?'

'I might as well,' said the woman.

The barmaid leaned across to Gombold and said: 'She had a lot of trouble with him. Didn't you, dear?'

Squall's mother swallowed her drink and burst into tears. A little while later she became so drunk she had to be helped out of the pub.

The barmaid said, 'She'll take it out of the old man tonight.'

Gombold left the pub and went back into the forest. It was six o'clock when he reached the place where the force had last pitched camp.

A woman who picked rags beside the road outside the city was reputed to have noticed the first signs of approaching disaster. She was trundling her barrow down a side-turning when she felt a spasm in the earth beneath her feet. She said nothing to anyone until she read in the newspapers that the giant was dying. A short while later, while walking in the forest, Gombold heard a noise of roaring in the air; a rushing wind, an intake of gigantic breath. As he walked Gombold noticed once again the denuded forest about him; saw bare patches where once the gleaming vistas had seemed impenetrable. He passed the spot where once the beasts had quarrelled and saw only the marks of paw and hoof; a whisker, the mitre upended in mud. In the end his wanderings brought him to the crown of the head. He was in this spot when a gigantic shudder shook the whole surface of the forest. The trees waved violently, a storm raged above. At this moment the creature on whose body he had led a precarious existence for so long, who supported the towns, lakes, canals, spires, buildings with no merit and railways, unaccountably and for a reason no one could guess at, died.

The prospect of living on a corpse did not affect many people. Indeed there were those who maintained the giant was not dead. Presented with the rotting flesh and the presence of maggots where once had been pleasant acres, they spoke in terms of temporary phenomena.

'I expect it'll blow-over,' said a woman pushing a pram.

As the days passed and the hairs shrivelled up, the skin peeled from the bones and signs of decay began to be all too apparent, a meeting was called by Vulp. Gombold saw the familiar figure stride on to the platform, the dog at his heels; he seemed more sure of himself than ever.

He opened the meeting by remarking that the Government had the situation well in hand. A man with a long muffler moved among the crowd distributing leaflets.

184

'We're very worried,' a woman said, 'the whole area round our house has caved in.'

Vulp touched his moustache. 'The situation raises very understandable anxieties,' he said. 'In my view – and I've stated as much before – there is no real ground for anxiety.'

'What is going to happen to us?' said a man wearing a grey overcoat.

'The establishment of a new system must inevitably involve many changes,' said Vulp, 'and individuals will naturally wonder how they themselves will be affected.'

'What are you going to do?' said a woman in a grey dress.

Vulp did not speak for a minute. He took a sip of water from a carafe and smiled around the room; many people took confidence from his smile.

'It will be understood that the Government cannot guarantee that some individuals may not suffer temporary upset. But a number of definite assurances can be given ....'

The man in the grey overcoat shouted something in a hoarse voice. The crowd cheered. Vulp paused.

'Why don't you resign?' said a woman.

A number of police entered the hall and removed the demonstrators.

Vulp said, 'It is the Government's intention to establish a special Commission to consider and keep the problems posed by situation under constant review. The scope of the Commission will not, of course, supplant the existing committees nor derogate from the management responsibilities of local authorities.'

'What about the area round my house?' called a woman.

Vulp stepped to the edge of the platform.

'Will you kindly let me continue my speech?' he said in a firm voice.

185

A stone was thrown through a window; flying glass narrowly missed a number of Vulp's supporters. He was about to speak again when a whistle was blown and clouds of smoke filled the building. An uproar ensued.

'What a disgraceful exhibition,' said a woman, as Gombold pushed past her.

Outside leaning against a wall Gombold found a number of pieces of timber. They appeared to be part of the platform upon which Vulp had made his speech; the whole building seemed in danger of collapsing. Gombold walked away.

In his memory the rest of the day always remained clear and distinct. The death of the giant could no longer be concealed; the Government had left the city; the countryside was considered unsafe. Most of the reports were a nightmare – grotesque, circumstantial, and untrue. When Vulp's speech was reported there was nobody to read or listen to it. The rotting flesh had caused widespread chaos. The forests, dry as tinder, had been set on fire; a thick pall of acrid smoke hung across the land. Gombold found himself sitting beside the hole from which he had once rescued the fattest man on earth. At first he had been surprised and confused; then, as he sat there, hardly breathing or speaking, hour after hour, he realised that to hope for any kind of relief was pointless. The smoke drifted nearer. Through it could be seen the bones, white and terrifying, the charred flesh hanging in strips from them. He walked away from the hole and stepped jauntily down the path to Vulp's house. It seemed empty, the whole place was deserted; all life had left. He broke open a window and climbed into one of the downstairs rooms.

The pictures were hanging on the walls, the carpets stretched endlessly through room after room and the clock ticked in the hall. But there was nobody to observe the time, nobody to admire the opulence, nobody to see the end. Gombold climbed the stairs and glanced into one or two rooms; Vulp's study looked out over the countryside; the greens and yellows of putrescence could be seen stretching mile upon mile until it reached the line of burning. On the next floor Gombold found a vase of dead flowers; on the next a shattered looking-glass; on the next a photograph of a litter of puppies. Quietly he descended the stairs.

There was one thing he had to do, an awkward, unpleasant thing that perhaps had better have been left alone. But he wanted to do it and not just trust the indifferent flames to sweep the house away. He searched and found a tin of petrol which he dripped about on the carpets and over the furniture. At the end of half an hour he had finished his task and, standing by an open window, he tossed matches into the room. The flames lapped the carpet in a wave of light; the light grew brighter, more intense. Heat escaping from the room caused him to retreat further and further, watching as he did so the flames climbing. Glass shattered, he heard the rumble of floors collapsing , the splinter of wood as the houses succumbed to the devouring flame. And as the time passed and the climax had been reached, his eyes began to blink, and he glanced several times at his watch as though he expected someone to come to aid the house. But it wasn't any use. Nobody came.

About five o'clock he climbed back into the wood and stopped to look back at the house, black, skeletal against the sky. Then he entered the forest for the last time and, finding the hole, climbed down into it.

Up Against It

A SCREENPLAY FOR THE BEATLES

Introduction

'Well, the sound and the fury is over', Orton wrote to an American friend in October 1966. 'LOOT and JOE ORTON (as you can see from the reviews) a great success. I feel exhausted. 18 months of struggling to vindicate the honour of my play (my own is beyond vindication) have left me weak at the knees.'

By January 1967, Orton's sense of exhauston had given way to exhilaration. He had just turned 34. His reputation had been secured. The grind of *Loot's* rewrites had paid off not only in acclaim but in craft. And Orton knew it. He was riding high and entering the most fecund period of his literary life. His career had acquired a new velocity. By the second week of January, the first draft of his farce masterpiece *What the Butler Saw* was completed and tucked away in the drawer beneath his divan bed to 'mature' for six months. A TV production of *The Good and Faithful Servant* with Donald Pleasance was in rehearsal. *Entertaining Mr Sloane*, after being scuttled by ITV, was rescheduled. *Loot* had been bought for Broadway. And on January 11, Orton stepped up to the podium at Quaglino's in a large flowered tie and a wide grin to accept the *Evening Standard* Award for the Best Play of the Year.

'I was on the front of the Evening Standard receiving the award,' Orton wrote in the diary he'd begun a few weeks earlier and puckishly called *Diary of a Somebody*, 'I'm very happy.' The word 'happy' is so rare in Orton's diaries as to be startling. He distrusted happiness; and in this case, it didn't last long. The TV programme that broadcast the ceremony ran its credits over Orton receiving the award. 'The whole had the effect of the man with the bladder hitting the Emperor on the head as he rode in triumph. Just to take him down a peg and remind him that he wasn't a god.'

But Orton was in a weird state of grace, and even this minor disappointment was quickly forgotten the next day when Orton was contacted to work on a film script for the Beatles. In the aristocracy of success, Orton was learning fast, there were no strangers.

Orton had never written a film script. In 1964, he worked up a nineteen page treatment for Lindsay Anderson who wanted to make a modern movie version of *The Bacchae*. The film never got off the ground; and Orton turned his notion into *The Erpingham Camp*. Funny as Orton's treatment was, his arch style didn't seem to suit the camera. 'Not film dialogue, is it?' was Lindsay Anderson's verdict. But since then, Orton's understanding of plot and tone had become more sophisticated. In his rewrites of *Loot* and the first draft of *What the Butler Saw* he worked hard to make his stage pictures as startling as his words. His comedy was becoming more visual. To match the Beatles' high jinks with his own wicked fun was an irresistible challenge. Always the tease, Orton tried to hide his enthusiasm when Walter Shenson called him. Shenson, who had produced *A Hard Day's Night* and *Help*, wanted Orton to 'punch-up' a dull script the Beatles had already commissioned. Orton recorded the conversation in his diary:

'Would you like to see it with a view to working on the film script?' I was very impressed by this, but I put on a nonchalant manner. 'Well, I'm frightfully up to my eyes in it at the moment', I said. 'I'm writing my third play'. 'I'd certainly love to have you take a look at this draft', he said. 'I've discussed it with the boys. I mean I mentioned your name to them. They've heard of you. They didn't react too much, I must say. But I think I can persuade them to have you.' By this time I was feeling foolish and not at all nonchalant. 'Yes', I said. 'Please send the script over and I'll read it.'

Orton read the Beatles' script on January 15, the day he re-read the first draft of *What the Butler Saw* ('Pleased, but still work to be done'). After such hard and inspired writing, he needed a change of pace; and the Beatles' script promised to be more a romp than a slog. He was full of fun and ideas. And, besides, the script had possibilities.

Like the idea. Basically it is that there aren't four young men. Just four aspects of one man. Sounds dreary, but as I thought about it I realised what wonderful opportunities it would give. The end in the present script is the girl advancing on the four to accept a proposal of marriage from one of them (which, the script coyly says, we shall never know). Already have the idea that the end should be a church with four bridegrooms and one bride. THE HOMECOMING in fact, but alibied in such a way that no one could object. Lots of opportunities for sexual ambiguities — a woman's bedroom at night, her husband outside and four men inside. I also would like to incorporate a lot of material from the first novel Kenneth [Halliwell] and I wrote called THE SILVER BUCKET. In it a young girl is expelled from her native village for some unnamed offence. Already see how it could be one boy expelled from some great industrial metropolis by a ceremony of mammoth proportions. Could be funny. As long as I wasn't expected to write a naturalistic script. Rang Walter Shenson . . . Arranged to meet him tomorrow.

Basically the Beatles are getting fed up with the Dick Lester type of direction. They want dialogue to speak. Also they are tired of actors like Leon McKern [sic] stealing scenes. Difficult this as I don't think any of the Beatles can act in any accepted sense. As Marilyn Monroe couldn't act. Hope to discuss this problem in detail tomorrow.

Before seeing Shenson, Orton met with his agent Peggy Ramsay. It was nearly three years to the week since she'd summoned him to her office in St Martin's Lane and agreed to represent *Entertaining Mr Sloane*. As Orton was getting up to leave from that first meeting, she'd asked him what he lived on while he wrote. Orton explained that he was on the dole and surviving on £3.10s. a week. She immediately marshalled her forces and found him a producer within three weeks. Orton's advance on the play had been £100. Now Peggy Ramsay was telling him, 'We'll ask ten thousand. Not a hope of getting it, of course. But we'll allow ourselves to be beaten down.'

'The class of my characters has gone up over the years', Orton observed in 1967. Success had widened his social horizons. Unaccustomed to power and a stranger to abundance, Orton eyed movie moguls like Shenson with a combination of wonder and suspicion. Since 1953, he'd lived a hermetic existence with Kenneth Halliwell in a succession of North London bedsitters. They'd met when both were students at RADA. Halliwell was twenty-four; and Orton was eighteen. Halliwell, who was well-educated, presented himself as a sophisticate; and Orton, then only a provincial lad from Leicester who hadn't even passed his Eleven-plus, saw in him a mentor and a friend. They abandoned acting as a bad bet. and set out to make their fame and fortune in literature. Writing had been Halliwell's idea. He educated Orton to be his constant companion and intellectual equal. They studied and often wrote together. They were inseparable; and only with Orton's success in 1964, did he begin to move outside Halliwell's orbit. 'I'm from the gutter and don't you forget it,' Orton told the producer Oscar Lewenstein, because I won't.' Orton was an outsider; and it was precisely his rejection of the bourgeois world which made his laughter dangerous. Nonetheless, he relished infiltrating alien territory. Any association with the Beatles would put him at the hot centre of pop culture. In meeting Shenson, Orton was taking his first steps down the corridors of commercial power. His diary shows how carefully he watched every move.

> I went into a door with a sheet of paper pinned onto it saying 'With the compliments of Walter Shenson (films) Inc.' Inside was a small office. Empty. I looked into a further office. In it was a man about thirty-five, pinkish face, rather a bright, cringing air. 'Are you for Walter?' he said. 'Yes,' I said. 'My name is Joe Orton'. I said this in a bold, confident tone. He squeezed past me in the doorway. 'Walter!' he gave a quick, sharp call. A man appeared in a far doorway. Middle-aged. Short hair going to grey. A bald patch. He started towards me, his hand outstretched. In fact he'd begun the motion of shaking hands before his hand touched mine. 'Come into my office', he said. 'That's the wrong door'. 'I thought it was a bit crummy,' I said. 'For a film producer.' 'Heh, heh, heh,' laughed Walter Shenson. 'Throw your coat over here, heh, heh, heh.' I put down my coat and he disappeared into another office. . . While he was gone I looked around. It was a big, long room. On the shelf over the fireplace was a cube with the faces of the four Beatles on each side of the cube. I picked it up and opened the lid, inside was a card saying 'Horse shit'. 'Heh, heh, heh,' said Walter Shenson, appearing behind me, 'That's a joke thing some guy sent me from back home. They're quite a thing over there, now, heh, heh, heh.'

> We talked for a while about the script. I gave away a few of my ideas. Enough to whet his appetite . . . Over lunch he said that one of the ideas for a new Beatles' film was *The Three Musketeers*. 'Oh, no!' I said. 'That's been done to death.' 'Brigitte Bardot wanted to paly Lady de-Winter,' he said. 'She's been done to death as well,' I said. 'Oh, heh, heh, heh, boy!' he said. 'You certainly are quick' . . .

By the end of the day, Orton had a title for his original film script: *Up Against It*, and had written the first two pages. 'Miss Drumgoole and Father Brodie have come to life as interesting characters. Which should delight the Beatles,' he wrote. 'I'm not bothering to write characters for them. I shall just do all my box of tricks — Sloane and Hal on them. After all if I repeat myself in this film it doesn't matter. Nobody who sees the film will have seen *Sloane* or *Loot*.'

The film was a lark, and Orton never invested it with the care or passion he gave his plays. His instructions to Peggy Ramsay on January 25, reflected his insouciance:

'We should ask £15,000', I said, 'and then if they beat us down, remember no lower than 10,000. After all, whether I do it or not is a matter of indifference to me.' Peggy agreed. 'If they won't pay us 10 they can fuck themselves,' I said. 'Of course, darling', Peggy said.

Shenson had promised to arrange a meeting between Orton and the Beatles. In his talk Orton heard the first seductive stroke of the movie rubdown, the slap and tickle of famous names and big paydays:

'You'll be hearing either from Brian Epstein or Paul McCartney [Shenson told Orton on January 17]. So don't be surprised if a Beatle rings you up.' 'What an experience', I said. 'I shall feel as nervous as I would if St Michael, or God was on the line.' 'Oh, there's not any need to be worried, Joe', Shenson said. 'I can say, from my heart that the boys are very respectful of talent. I mean, most respectful of anyone they feel has talent. I can really say that, Joe.'

The Call finally came at dinner time a week later on January 23. 'Epstein's adviser rang while I was eating a meal of mashed potatoes, tinned salmon and beetroot', Orton noted wryly.

Orton arrived promptly the next day at Epstein's office to be faced with the screenwriter's first debilitating hazard: waiting. 'After about five minutes or so a youngish man with a hair-style which was way out in 1958, short, college-boy came up and said, ". . . I'm Brian Epstein's personal assistant" ' Orton wrote in his diary on January 24.

It crossed my mind to wonder why the English have never got around to finding a perfectly respectable word for 'boy-friend'. 'I'm afraid there's been a most awful mix-up. And all the boys' appointments have been put back an hour and a half'. I was a bit chilly in my manner after that. 'Do you want me to come back at six?' I said. 'Well, no. Could we make another appointment? 'What guarantee is there that you won't break that?' I said. 'I think you better find yourself a different writer.' This said with indifferent success, though the effect was startling. He asked me to wait a minute and went away to return with Brian Epstein himself. Somehow I'd expected something like Michael Codron. I'd imagined Epstein to be florid, Jewish, dark-haired and overbearing. Instead I was face to face with a mousey-haired, slight young man. Washed-out in a way. He had a suburban accent. I went into his office. 'Could you meet Paul and me for dinner tonight?' he said. 'We do want to have the pleasure of talking to you.' 'I've a theatre engagement tonight' I replied, by now sulky and unhelpful. 'Could I send the car to fetch you after the show?' I didn't much relish this flim-flammery, left almost tripping over the carpet and crashing into the secretary who gave a squeal of surprise as I hurtled past her. This I never mention when re-telling the story. I always end on a note of hurt dignity.

Orton's first glimpse of the Beatles' world caught the ludicrous contradiction in these cultural supermen: playing rebel and living posh.

Arrived in Belgravia at ten minutes to eight . . . I found Chapel Street easily. I didn't want to get there too early so I walked around for a while and came back through a nearby mews. When I got back to the house it was nearly eight o'clock. I rang the bell and an old man entered. He seemed surprised to see me. 'Is this Brian Epstein's house?' I said. 'Yes, sir,' he said, and led the way to the hall. I suddenly realised that the man was the butler. I've never seen one before . . . He took me into a room and said in a loud voice 'Mr Orton'. Everybody looked up and stood to their feet. I was introduced to one or two people. And Paul McCartney. He was just as the photographs. Only he'd grown a moustache. His hair was shorter too. He was playing the latest Beatles record 'Penny Lane'. I like it very much. Then he played the other side — Strawberry something. I didn't like this as much. We talked intermittently. Before we went out to dinner we agreed to throw out the idea of setting the film in the thirties. We went down to dinner. The trusted old retainer — looking too much like a butler to be good casting — busied himself in the corner. 'The only thing I get from the theatre,' Paul M. said, 'is a sore arse.' He said *Loot* was the only play he hadn't wanted to leave before the end. 'I'd've liked a bit more,' he said. We talked of the theatre. I said that compared with the pop-scene the theatre was square. 'The theatre started going down hill when Queen Victoria knighted Henry Irving,' I said. 'Too fucking respectable'. We

talked of drugs, of mushrooms which give hallucinations — like
L.S.D. 'The drug not the money,' I said. We talked of tattoos.
And after one or two veiled references, marijuana. I said I'd
smoked it in Morocco. The atmosphere relaxed a little. Dinner
ended and we went upstairs agains. We watched a programme
on TV; it had phrases in it like 'the in crowd' and 'swinging
London'. There was a little scratching at the door. I thought
it was the old retainer, but someone got up to open the door
and about five very young and pretty boys trouped in. I
rather hoped this was the evening's entertainment. It wasn't,
though. It was a pop group called The Easybeats. I'd seen
them on TV. I liked them very much . . . A French photographer arrived . . . He'd taken a set of new photographs of
The Beatles. They wanted one to use on the record sleeve.
Excellent photographs. The four Beatles look different in
their moustaches. Like anarchists in the early years of the
century. After a while . . . I talked to the leading Easybeat.
Feeling slightly like an Edwardian masher with a Gaiety girl.
And then I came over tired and decided to go home. I had a
last word with Paul M. 'Well,' I said, 'I'd like to do the film.
There's only one thing we've got to fix up.' 'You mean the
bread?' 'Yes'. We smiled and parted. I got a cab home. Told
Kenneth about it. Then he got up to make a cup of tea. And
we talked a little more. And went to sleep.

While the contract was being negotiated (£5,000 for the first
draft with the right to buy the script back if unacceptable to the
Beatles), Orton grew a moustache and blithely got to work. 'I
shall enjoy writing the film,' he wrote in his diary.

Orton worked fast, aided by the discovery — 'inspiration' was
his word for it — of an old novel which provided the backbone of
the scenario. 'I'd already written the beginning of the script up to
where McTurk is thrown out of town,' he wrote on January 29.
'And then I remembered that in the cupboard somewhere was
the manuscript of a novel I'd written in 1959 called THE VISION
OF GOMBOLD PROVAL [posthumously published as *Head To
Toe*]. It had always been my intention some day to rewrite it.
I decided to get it down and see if there was anything I could use.
I found, to my surprise, that it was excellent. It has great faults as
a novel, but as the basis for a film it was more than adequate. So
I'm rewriting the whole thing. Miraculously towards the middle
of the novel four young men appear.' By February 11, when
Orton was summoned to Shenson's office for one final pep talk
before the contract was signed, the script was almost completed.

Shenson 'was most concerned to impress me that "the boys" shouldn't be made to do anything in the film that would reflect badly on them,' Orton wrote, getting his first dose of the screenwriter's second debilitating hazard: the commercial compromise. 'You see, he said, 'the kids will all imitate whatever the boys do.' I hadn't the heart to tell him that the boys, in my script, have been caught in flagrante, become involved in dubious political activity, dressed as women, committed murder, been put in prison and committed adultery. And the script isn't finished yet. I thought it best to say nothing of my plans for the Beatles until he had a chance of reading the script. We parted at five o'clock amicably. With the contract, according to him, as good as signed. And on my part, the film almost written.'

Even in its title, *Up Against It* announced the rambunctious sexuality of Orton's trickster temperament. Phallic fun was part of his comic revenge on society. In his life and his work, Orton displayed a trickster's ruthless sexual rapacity. He wanted to goose an audience and take it for a tumble. He was a hostile sharpshooter loudly proclaiming his innocence. But his diaries leave no doubt about the anarchic prupose behind his outrageousness:

> Kenneth, who reads the *Observer*, tells me of the latest group thing in America — complete sexual licence. 'It's the only way to smash the wretched civilisation', I said, making a mental note to hot-up *What the Butler Saw* when I rewrite . . . Sex is the only way to infuriate them. Much more fucking and they'll be screaming hysterics in next to no time.

Orton had learned how to corrupt an audience with pleasure. It was a rare gift, and one that had not come easy. 'Cleanse my heart, give me the ability to rage correctly,' prays Gombold, Orton's spokesman in *Head to Toe*. But it took a six month prison term for the comic defacement of public library books in 1962 to bring a saving detachment to his writing. He had dreamed of a cauterising verbal power that would create a 'seismic disturbance'. In time, he found a way to make language stir things up. His lethal wit conjured up the same wicked and faithless world that had always enraged him, but with a difference. It made his anger irresistible. *Up Against It* signals the new playfulness that came with Orton's liberation from anonymity and self-doubt. Bitterness had evaporated from his writing to be replaced by a detached gaiety at the murderous vanity of mankind.

LOW. I'm hungry, I need help.
MRS O'SCULLION. I'm not interested in your private life.

Always the enemy of boundaries, Orton played havoc not only
with society's notions of normality but the literary genres that
codified it. *Up Against It* attempts to do to movie romance what
Loot had done to detective fiction and *What the Butler Saw*
would do to classical farce. The film uses romantic imagery while
the dialogue takes pot-shots at the assumptions beneath it.

LOW. Is there any woman you wouldn't wait in the rain for?
McTURK. The Statue of Liberty.

All the romantic ideals — devotion, loyalty, monogamy — are
turned upside down as Orton attempts to invent a new form
while satirising the old one. *Up Against It* teases the cosy, lustless
screen version of romance. 'Anything worth doing, is worth doing
in public', McTurk observes. In their outrageousness, the
characters are always commenting on the courtly romantic setting.
'I must go,' Rowena says to McTurk, shafting him yet again in
the last minutes of the film. 'Love seems out of place in a garden
in the moonlight.' McTurk finds solace in the arms of a second
woman who has unsuccessfully pursued him throughout the film.
'My heart is broken', he tells Patricia Drumgoole, about to propose
marriage as Orton lampoons the romantic equation of suffering
with satisfaction. 'But everything else is in working order.' After
their adventures, the characters are more pragmatic about life.
The marriage takes place — a happy ending in which romantic
propaganda is mischievously inverted so that the bride can have
three bridegrooms. 'Just the happy quartette', coos the photographer snapping the new marriage of Love, Money and Lust
on the steps of the church. The third husband is a rebel leader
who sees marriage as a radical act. 'Getting married and having
children is the most rebellious thing a man can do', says Jack
Ramsay. 'It shows a disregard for the conventional bourgeois
status quo and a fine, careless anarchic sense of the absurd.'
Marriage, which institutionalises the sexual scarcity romance
promotes, gives way in the film's final image to a vision of sexual
abundance:

The young men kiss her. There is a struggle. MISS DRUM-
GOOLE squeals with delight and disappears under the
coverlet with her husbands.

THE END

'Oscar Lewenstein read *Up Against It* and liked it very much', Orton wrote on February 25, a day after he'd handed in his first draft. 'He thought it had a poetic quality. This is because I used all the romantic clichés — moonlight, roses, unrequited love and the Cinderella figure of the poor girl who loves him and is finally rewarded by his love in the last reel. O.L. said he liked least the scenes in the Albert Hall (with the shooting of the woman Prime Minister Lillian Corbett). This clearly because of the parody of the Kennedy assassination he doesn't think that Epstein, The Beatles, or W. Shenson will opt for it.'

But it was panic, not poetry, that the script explored. *Up Against It* is part of Orton's experiment in farce method, his search for a way to marry terror and elation. 'I'm Princess of the Church', says the Archbishop of Canterbury who turns out to be a woman in Orton's parody of the Sidney Street Siege. 'Let me pass. I've some hard praying to do.' Violating social and familial pieties, the upheavals of farce created the shock Orton wanted in laughter. In its pandemonium, farce provided him with the perfect anarchist apocalypse. Orton tried to show this in his battle scene where McTurk, Low and Ramsay run their ambulance into an enemy truck and start a chain reaction of destruction from which no one emerges victorious. Nothing can diminish the panorama of suffering. Every heroic gesture turns into a fiasco. 'The victims and the helpers struggle together in the mud of the battlefield'. Orton even produces the final abyss which engulfs everyone.

Mayhem is Orton's metaphor for history: a tableau of viciousness in which to be saved from one disaster is only to be eligible for greater violence. 'Seeing what has happened before. [McTurk, Low and Ramsay] decline to be helped and fight off the stretcher bearers.' The victims become victimisers in a struggle to cling to life and remain intact.

When a priest and choir boys appear on the scene, the promise of salvation in the midst of carnage floors the rebels. Low, 'struck dumb, kneels'. McTurk, overcome by despair, 'bursts into tears and fits of sobbing'. But Ramsay 'shrieks with maniacal laughter and begins to leap about in a kind of glee'. Orton would choose the latter course. His grotesque laughter rejected the impotence of despair.

'I've just got McTurk in prison', Orton wrote on February 26, and realise, of course, the whole script is about schizophrenia'. Like Orton, the characters teeter between optimism and disenchantment, rebellion and acceptance, male and female roles.

Farce becomes a paradigm for the tumult of consciousness. 'Back! Back to the women! Our only hope!' pleads one character, grabbing the steering wheel of a car as McTurk and Low try to change allegiance from the all-female goverment troops to the male rebels. The driver replies: 'No! The men! We must go on.'

Orton had written *Up Against It* so fast that he asked Peggy Ramsay to wait three weeks before submitting it. She found the script 'splendid', although, as Orton noted in his diary, 'she was worried by the way what she called my "dubious morality" showed through. Especially the killing of the Prime Minister.' The script was sent to Shenson on March 6. 'Peggy feels it will be too much for him,' Orton wrote in his diary. She was right. He called the next day, saying he was 'fascinated' but worried whether it should be four boys or four aspects of one person.

'. . . As you know, Joe, we're all different people. And we have to learn to live with those aspects. I understand that the original idea was to show how a man can live with himself.' Which is pretentious shit. I can't write that, or, what is more important, alter my script to fit that idea. I'd much rather have it about four boys anyway. Shenson is going to speak to Epstein from Los Angeles tonight. He has suggested Antonioni to direct. Rubbish!

By March 29, Orton had still heard nothing from the Beatles. He fixed on Brian Epstein as the culprit: 'An amateur and a fool. He isn't equipped to judge the quality of a script. Probably he will never say "yes" equally hasn't got the courage to say "no". A thoroughly weak, flaccid type.' And then on April 4, *Up Against It* was returned. 'No explanation why. No criticism of the script. And apparently, Brian Epstein has no comment to make either. Fuck them.'

But Orton's luck was still holding. On April 10, the day the *Evening Standard* reported 'the shock of Joe Orton's pride', he was revising *Up Against It* for Oscar Lewenstein. 'I've turned the four Beatles into three young men. It's a much better script without the weight of stars hanging on it.' [It is this revised script which is printed here.] Two days later, Lewenstein bought it for £10,000 and 10% of the production company's net profits — an altogether better deal than the Beatles had offered. Lewenstein, who as director of Woodfall Productions had been associated with *Tom Jones, A Taste of Honey, The Loneliness of the Long Distance Runner* and many other high quality productions in the short-lived British cinema renaissance, thought *Up Against It* 'probably the best first draft of a screen-play I have ever read.' For his part, Orton was delighted. He had just sold *Loot* to the movies for a reported £100,000 and was re-writing *The Erpingham Camp* and *The Ruffian on the Stair* for a double bill called *Crimes of Passion* at the Royal Court in June. He had every reason to feel merry and to swagger to an American friend: 'I'm now engaged on a film for which I'm being paid the equivalent of $30,000. I'm going up, up, up.'

'To be young, good-looking, healthy, famous, comparatively rich *and* happy is surely going against nature,' Orton wrote in his diary on May 22. He and Halliwell were talking about how happy they were in Morocco and worrying that perhaps they were too happy and 'would be struck down from afar by disaster.' On that day Orton wrote: 'I hope no doom strikes'. Ten weeks later, they were dead. On August 9, 1967, a chauffeur sent to drive Orton to Twickenham Studios to discuss *Up Against It* with Richard Lester, discovered the bodies in their Islington bedsitter. Halliwell had battered in Orton's head with a hammer, and then swallowed twenty-two Nembutals to kill himself. In their writing together, Orton and Halliwell had imagined everything about their relationship except success. And Orton's success only magnified Halliwell's punishing sense of failure and put Orton out of touch with his friend's suffering. Through murder, Halliwell achieved the public association with Joe Orton's career that he'd been denied in life.

Oscar Lewenstein put other playwrights to work on *Up Against It*. Charles Wood, James Saunders, Roger McGough, and Christopher Logue all tinkered with the script. But the wicked fun Orton poked at the world was inimitable; and the film was finally abandoned. The script remains a tantalising remnant of what might have been, the last comic fragment of a voluptuary of fiasco.

John Lahr

John Lahr is the author of *Prick Up Your Ears*: The Biography of Joe Orton.

CAST LIST

(Main characters only)

IAN McTURK

CHRISTOPHER LOW

JACK RAMSAY

FATHER BRODIE

THE MAYOR

MISS DRUMGOOLE

CONNIE

ROWENA TORRENCE

MRS O'SCULLION

BERNARD COATES

RAMSAY'S FATHER

1. Exterior. A city. *Unreal in the light of the setting sun. Smoke drifts from a chimney. A bell is heard from a church tower. Children call. A sudden silence.*

2. Exterior. A deserted street. Evening. *A church against the sky. Next to the church a large house standing in an unweeded garden. Laurels and rhododendrons in the watery light.*

3. Exterior. The roof of the house. Evening. *A cat crosses the tiles to the edge of a skylight. A bedroom is seen through the skylight. A bed with a candlewick bedspread. On the bed a GIRL is lying. She has her face buried in the pillow. She is sobbing.*

4. Interior. The bedroom. *On a table beside the bed is a photograph of a young man (IAN McTURK). The girl, (ROWENA TORRENCE) sits up. She wipes her eyes, lifts the photograph from the table. Stares at it. Kisses it. Weeps.*

5. Interior. A stairwell from above. *At the bottom of the well, in the hall, IAN McTURK and CHRISTOPHER LOW are sitting. Their arms are folded across their chests. They are wearing dark suits and ties.*

6. Interior. Father Brodie's study. *Brown leather chairs. Bookcases full of musty books. A faded carpet on the floor. A large desk. A green-shaded lamp.* FATHER BRODIE *is sitting at his desk. A man (the MAYOR) and a woman (CONNIE) are in the room with* FATHER BRODIE. CONNIE *wears a police uniform.* FATHER BRODIE *pours a whisky.* MISS DRUMGOOLE *enters from the hall. She is a kind, rather plain girl. She wears a starched apron.*

MISS DRUMGOOLE. The young men are outside, sir. They're in a repentant mood. Don't be too hard on them.

FATHER BRODIE. The matter is out of my hands, Miss Drumgoole. Such wickedness cannot be tolerated. Ask them to step this way.

MISS DRUMGOOLE *shakes her head. She goes out.*
FATHER BRODIE *lifts a figure of a praying saint. It is hollow.*
He fits it over, and conceals the whisky bottle.

7. Interior. The corridor. McTURK *and* LOW *are waiting. Their*
arms are folded. MISS DRUMGOOLE *appears in the doorway.*

MISS DRUMGOOLE. Father Brodie will see you now. He's been
wrestling all afternoon with his conscience.

McTURK. Who won?

MISS DRUMGOOLE. You must ask him yourself. It's not a
question a girl like me can put to a priest.

She leads the way into the study.

8. Interior. Father Brodie's study. McTURK *and* LOW *are shown*
in by MISS DRUMGOOLE.

FATHER BRODIE. Come in. Close the door quietly. My choirboys
are asleep.

LOW *shuts the door. He and* McTURK *stand before the desk.*
MISS DRUMGOOLE *folds her hands together by the bookcase.*
The others in the room regard the two young men with a sour
expression.

MAYOR (*standing to his feet*). We've been deputed to act as
spokesmen for the citizens of this town. I believe you've
already met Father Brodie, priest of this Parish and one-time
heckler at Orange rallies?

FATHER BRODIE *acknowledges the compliment with a*
gracious smile. The MAYOR *turns to* CONNIE.

MAYOR. And this is Police Superintendant Constance Boon —
to rhyme, most appropriately with Loon. As you know I am
Terence O'Scullion, Lord Mayor and prominent right-wing
politician. I also hold strong views on sexual promiscuity
and the taking of drugs.

FATHER BRODIE. Do you object to Miss Drumgoole being
present at this interview?

McTURK. No. She's been a real friend to us. Through all the
troubles we've endured since we came to this town.

MISS DRUMGOOLE *weeps silently. The* MAYOR *turns to the young men and speaks in a cold, unemotional tone.*

MAYOR. The townsfolk won't tolerate any longer your indiscretions. They have recently, with the destruction of the Memorial to the Fallen of two world wars, reached monumental proportions.

LOW. We weren't responsible for blowing up the War Memorial, sir. I've always been against such pointless anarchy.

MAYOR. Who then d'you suggest damaged a monument which cost ten thousand pounds?

FATHER BRODIE. In 1919.

MAYOR. It would be worth considerably more today. Why, the allegorical figure of Peace, even without her left arm, must be quite valuable. And you say that you weren't responsible?

McTURK. No.

CONNIE. You were seen by a constable to place a large wreath at the foot of the monument. Shortly afterwards the wreath exploded. Do you deny that you mined the Flanders poppies in that wreath?

LOW. I met a man by the Corn Exchange. He said he was a World War Two veteran. He pressed the wreath into my hands, begging me to place it under the bronze plaque to his fallen comrades. This I did. Shortly afterwards the Memorial was shaken by a violent explosion. I had nothing whatever to do with the outrage. I placed the wreath there in order to help a sick man.

CONNIE. Never, in the whole of my life, have I heard anything so lame and stupid!

FATHER BRODIE. I shall add insolence to the list of misdemeanours for which you're to be punished. (*He makes a note in a folder on his desk.*) Sit down.

McTURK *lowers himself into a chair.*

FATHER BRODIE. Not on that chair. It has a broken leg.

McTURK. Have you sent for a doctor?

FATHER BRODIE. Doctors can do nothing for it. It's incurable.

LOW. What about faith healing?

FATHER BRODIE. I've no faith in faith healing.

The two young men sit on an ottoman.

FATHER BRODIE. I won't waste more time discussing your
  conduct. I'll come straight to the point. At four a.m. this
  morning my own niece, Rowena Torrence, was seen to enter
  your room in an advanced state of nudity. What excuse had
  she for being with you at that hour?

McTURK. She'd come to borrow a cup of sugar.

CONNIE. But she's on a diet.

McTURK. I didn't give in to her demands.

MAYOR. Was she provocative?

McTURK. Nobody is provocative at four in the morning.

FATHER BRODIE. A woman's wiles are in operation at any
  hour of the day or night. (*With a cough.*) So I've heard.

LOW. Well, Father, I've had less experience of women than
  you. I've always led a decent life.

McTURK. It wasn't me who let your niece into the room,
  Father.

FATHER BRODIE. That isn't true. I saw the incident with my
  own eyes. (*To* CONNIE.) Do you confirm that, Superintendant?

CONNIE. I handed you the binoculars myself, Father.

MAYOR. And you left the blind up as well, McTurk. The last
  indulgence of a sensualist.

FATHER BRODIE. It's my painful duty to have to inform you,
  McTurk, that my niece, upon careful scrutiny, appears to be
  as much in need of repair as the Memorial to the Fallen.
  For your outrage upon the living and for your friend's outrage
  upon the dead the City Fathers have decided to expel you
  both from this fair city.

  MISS DRUMGOOLE *gives a cry.*

MISS DRUMGOOLE (*to the young men*). What's to become
  of you both now?

FATHER BRODIE. You'll meet the Lord Mayor and the
  Aldermen tomorrow morning. They will escort you to the
  city limits.

McTURK. Can't I see Rowena? To say goodbye. I love her very
  much.

LOW. It seems a pity not to return her cup of sugar.

FATHER BRODIE. My niece is confined to her room. I've forbidden her to communicate with anybody. (*To* MISS DRUMGOOLE.) Show them the door. I've business to discuss with the Lord Mayor.

MISS DRUMGOOLE *opens the door.* McTURK *and* LOW *follow her.* FATHER BRODIE *lifts the praying saint from the whisky bottle.*

9. Interior. The corridor. MISS DRUMGOOLE *enters followed by the two young men.* MISS DRUMGOOLE *leads the way to the door.*

MISS DRUMGOOLE. I shall miss our evening walks to the public library. Who will carry my books now?

LOW. We're innocent of everything. I feel like crying when I think of all I've had to endure.

McTURK (*to* MISS DRUMGOOLE). Will you give a message to Miss Torrence?

MISS DRUMGOOLE *turns quickly. Stares at him in horror.*

MISS DRUMGOOLE. Father Brodie would be dreadfully upset if he knew I'd betrayed his trust.

McTURK. I'll be in the garden.

MISS DRUMGOOLE *shakes her head. Opens the front door.*

MISS DRUMGOOLE. There was a time when I thought you loved me, Ian McTurk. You brought me flowers and boxes of inexpensive chocolates. Now all you can think of is the lovely Rowena Torrence. She has stolen you from me.

It is raining outside. The sun has set. A cold wind is blowing.

MISS DRUMGOOLE. I should hate her, but I can't. She's so beautiful. (*With a wistful sigh.*) I'll tell her you're in the garden.

McTURK *kisses her ardently. He releases her.* McTURK *and* LOW *go into the garden.* MISS DRUMGOOLE *shuts the door.*

MISS DRUMGOOLE (*with an ecstatic shiver*). Ian McTurk gives a most charming sensation when he kisses. I understand how he sets all hearts aflame!

10. Exterior. The shrubbery at the back of the house. Night.
The boys push their way through dank and dripping rhododen-
drons. Rain streams down their faces.

LOW. Oh, if only I hadn't offered to help that El Alamein
veteran carry his wreath, I'd've been home in time to prevent
you taking the virginity of Father Brodie's niece. My kind
heart has undone us both.

McTURK. Yes, you must learn to control your generous
impulses.

LOW. If we're caught speaking to Miss Torrence we'll be in
trouble. Let's leave this place at once.

McTURK. I must say goodbye. Rowena is the most beautiful
and the most cultured girl I've ever met. She speaks three
languages and she's an expert conjuror. She's worth waiting
in the rain for.

LOW. Is there any woman you wouldn't wait in the rain for?

McTURK. The Statue of Liberty.

They push on through the shrubs. The rain streams down
their faces.

11. Exterior. A balcony overlooking the shrubbery. ROWENA
TORRENCE *comes onto the balcony carrying an umbrella. She*
is wearing a nightgown. MISS DRUMGOOLE *appears behind her*
in the lighted window.

MISS DRUMGOOLE. Hurry with your last goodbyes, Miss
Rowena. Your uncle wishes to speak to you.

ROWENA. What for?

MISS DRUMGOOLE. He's sending you to a convent. You'll be
in safe hands there, he says. All the nuns are women.

ROWENA (*looking about her into the rain*). Oh, my darling,
where are you?

She comes forward onto the balcony with the umbrella.
Speaks her words to the night and the sighing branches.

ROWENA. My heart is breaking. I'll never see him again!

The rain is lashed to a fury by the wind. McTURK *and* LOW
*appear through the bushes. Their clothes are sticking to them
with rain. They wave.*

McTURK. We've been ordered to leave the town. Will you be
there to see us off?

ROWENA. No.

McTURK. Why not?

ROWENA. I'm being sent away too.

MISS DRUMGOOLE (*appearing on the balcony*). Your uncle is
coming. Hurry unless you want him to catch you.

ROWENA. There's no pain like the pain of first love. (*With a
cry of anguish.*) I shall remember the heartbreak of this
moment for ever!

She leans over the balcony. McTURK *climbs onto* LOW'*s
shoulders.* McTURK *kisses* ROWENA. MISS DRUMGOOLE
pulls her away. ROWENA *hurries into the house.*

MISS DRUMGOOLE. Away with you, Ian McTurk. Your wild
ways will bring nothing but harm.

McTURK (*urgently*). Can I write to her? What's her address?

MISS DRUMGOOLE. She can be reached c/o Mrs O'Scullion,
The Convent of La Dulcinella, 42 Millfield Street, Bradford.

She hurries indoors. McTURK *and* LOW *push their way into
the shrubbery.* MISS DRUMGOOLE *reappears on the
balcony.*

MISS DRUMGOOLE (*calling*). And kindly mark your letters
'Secular'.

12. Exterior. The shrubbery. McTURK *and* LOW *pushing through
the dripping bushes.*

McTURK. I feel numb at the thought of losing her.

LOW. She didn't do any conjuring tricks.

They push on.

LOW. She leans well over a balcony, though. For a woman.

13. Exterior. The front of the house. Night. *The two young men approach the edge of the shrubbery and step onto the drive.* FATHER BRODIE *opens the front door and shouts to them.*

FATHER BRODIE. Unless you leave these premises at once, I'll set the dog onto you!

They stuff their hands into their pockets and hurry away from the house.

14. Exterior. A main thoroughfare of the city. Early morning. *Weak sunlight. A light breeze blowing. A procession of citizens. Slow march. Music. Drum and cymbals.*

At the head of the procession is FATHER BRODIE. *Six* CHORISTERS *surround him. They swing censers and chant a solemn dirge.*

The MAYOR (TERENCE O'SCULLION) *and the* LADY MAYORESS (MRS O'SCULLION) *in their robes of office, lead the* ALDERMEN *and* CIVIC DIGNITARIES.

McTURK *and* LOW *are escorted by* CONNIE *and a number of* MOUNTED POLICEMEN *and* WOMEN.

Banners, billowing in the early breeze, are carried by WOMEN. 'I fell under his fatal spell', 'I was happy till I met Ian McTurk', 'He ruined my life'.

Members of the BRITISH LEGION *and ex-Servicemen's associations carry banners:* 'Hands off public monuments', 'Hang him!' 'Hooligans out!' *and* 'Did we die for this?'.

The procession passes, leaving MISS DRUMGOOLE *alone in the street. She watches the procession disappear and dabs her eyes.*

MISS DRUMGOOLE. What's to become of them now? (*Puts away her handkerchief.*) Whatever they've done they have kind hearts. I love them both, but Ian McTurk is my special favourite.

She gives way to a fresh burst of tears.

MISS DRUMGOOLE. How shall I ever bear not seeing his cheery smile every morning?

She blows her nose and makes her way up the street.

15. Exterior. Scrubland. Distant houses. *The sun has risen higher. The procession approaches. The music stops. The procession halts. Silence.*

The MOUNTED POLICEWOMEN *lead* McTURK *and* LOW *forward.* FATHER BRODIE, CONNIE *and the* MAYOR *follow them to a signpost which says* 'You are now entering the city limits. We hope your stay will be pleasant'.

The POLICEWOMEN, *the* PRISONERS, CONNIE, FATHER BRODIE *and the* MAYOR *stop by the signpost.* FATHER BRODIE *takes a book from his pocket.*

FATHER BRODIE. Here is a copy of the scriptures. I've marked the relevant passages on Charity, Brotherly Love and the consuming of unlawful meat. Take them to your heart and your future lives will be blameless.

LOW (*accepting the book*). It was me who dropped the hair lacquer into the font, Father, I can't leave without making a clean breast of it.

FATHER BRODIE. Don't mention breasts in my presence. I'm a celibate.

He steps back. The MAYOR *steps forward.*

MAYOR. In order that you shan't be able to claim that we cast you adrift without means, the citizens present you with this wallet. (*Applause from the crowd.*) In it is twenty pounds and a photograph of the new wing of the Maternity Home.

McTURK *accepts the wallet.*

McTURK. I'm rather surprised that you should consider building a new wing to the Maternity Home now, sir. It'll be empty when I've gone.

MAYOR. I think you'd better leave that particular problem to me, McTurk. I'm not a man to see a Maternity Home empty for long.

He steps back. CONNIE *steps forward.*

CONNIE. You've heard what Father Brodie and the Lord Mayor have to say to you. And now, get out of the town! We never wish to see you again.

The citizens boo loudly, and wave their banners. McTURK *and* LOW *turn and walk away. The gap between the citizens and the two boys widens.*

16. Exterior. A piece of rising ground. *The citizens dwarfed on the horizon. The boys top the ridge. They turn back to look. The procession dips its banners and melts away.*

A vast and chequered plain lies ahead. In the distance is a dark forest. McTURK *and* LOW *loosen their collars and strike out into the unknown world that lies waiting.*

McTURK. We're free!

LOW. On our own!

McTURK. The world's our oyster!

LOW. The bad times have gone. Happiness lies ahead!

17. Exterior. A dark forest. Evening. *Silence. The two young men, footsore and weary, push their way through the undergrowth. A* MAN's *voice is heard calling for help.* LOW *stops.*

LOW. What's that?

McTURK (*without stopping*). Someone's calling for help. Haven't you heard the sound of a fellow human being in distress before?

LOW. No.

McTURK. It's replaced 'Sweet Lavender' as a street cry.

LOW. Let's see what's the matter?

He turns back. McTURK *seizes him by the hand.*

McTURK. Remember the old soldier and his wreath? Curb this insatiable desire to offer a helping hand. It'll bring you nothing but unhappiness.

LOW. I must see what they want.

He shrugs McTURK *away. He starts off into the undergrowth in the direction of the cries for help.*

McTURK (*shouting after him*). Remember what happened when you helped the old lady across the road? She beat you senseless with her umbrella.

LOW *stops. Half turns.*

LOW (*to himself*). She'd just come out of hospital.

McTURK (*catching up with him*). You occupied the bed she'd just left for a month.

LOW *moves off again.* McTURK *catches his arm.*

McTURK. What about the blind man who you gave your last shilling to? He nearly bit your finger off.

LOW. He had a nervous nature.

He pushes on through the undergrowth. McTURK *shrugs. Turns back to the path. Leaves* LOW. LOW *goes on alone.*

18. Exterior. Another part of the forest. Night. McTURK *is nowhere in sight.* LOW *pushes his way through the thick undergrowth. The cries for help are near at hand. He stops before a hole in the ground. He stares. By the rim of the hole in the ground is a pie dish. A half-empty jar of pickles. A cheese, a fork and asparagus tongs, a coffee pot, a box of biscuits and a decanter.* LOW *looks down the hole.*

19. Interior. Down the hole. *A* MAN *is standing at the bottom of the hole. He is fat. He has a bald head. He stares up at* LOW.

LOW. D'you want any help?

FAT MAN. Have you got a rope?

LOW. No.

FAT MAN. You'll find one on the path. I'd be grateful if you'd hurry. There isn't much time.

20. Exterior. The forest. A few yards from the hole. LOW *is looking for a rope. A man is seen approaching on a white horse. He has a kindly expression on his face. He is shabbily dressed. He is about forty years of age. His name is* BERNARD COATES. *As the horse approaches* LOW *runs up to* BERNARD COATES.

LOW (*politely*). You don't happen to have a rope on you, sir?

Without a moment's thought BERNARD COATES *slashes at* LOW *with his riding crop and continues his journey.* LOW *gives a cry of pain and fright. He puts a hand to his cheek which is bleeding. He stumbles off the path and, in doing so, discovers a rope lying at the foot of a tree.*

21. Exterior. The hole. LOW *is pulling the* FAT MAN *from the hole. The man's face appears over the rim. His body appears. Finally he crawls from his prison.* LOW *blows on his hands which are cut and scraped by the rope.*

LOW (*with a pleasant smile*). Have you been down there long?

> *The man says nothing. He seizes* LOW *by the throat with one hand and pummels him with the other.* LOW *is too surprised to resist. The* FAT MAN *drags him, nearly senseless, to the rim of the hole.* LOW *cries out in anguish.*
> *On the edge of the hole the* FAT MAN *pauses. He is about to fling* LOW *down into the prison when the bushes in front of them part and* BERNARD COATES *appears. He is on foot. Seeing the struggle taking place by the hole he runs forward and separates the combatants. As* LOW *draws back from his attacker,* BERNARD COATES *begins to beat the* FAT MAN *about the face and body. Ignoring the man's cries of distress, he hurls him back into the hole.* LOW, *nursing his wounds, is too surprised by what has taken place to say anything.*
> BERNARD COATES *collects the food lying beside the hole. He puts it into a bag which he has with him. As he does so, he addresses* LOW, *over his shoulder.*

COATES. What are you doing in this forest? It isn't common land, you know.

LOW. I heard someone calling for help and came to their rescue.

> BERNARD COATES *stops. Stares hard at* LOW.

COATES. What right had you to do such a thing? Are you a member of the Women's Voluntary Service?

LOW. No.

COATES. Then your action was misguided and uncalled-for.

> *He picks up his bag and walks away. As he does so* LOW *calls after him.*

LOW. How do I get out of this forest? I'm lost.

> *Without turning round or stopping* BERNARD COATES *answers him.*

COATES. You can come with me if you wish. I own vast tracts of the land around here. I'm a millionaire.

LOW (*following him*). Why was that man down the hole? Is he a prisoner?

COATES. Of course he's a prisoner. I should've thought that was obvious.

LOW. What've you done with your horse?

COATES. It threw me as I was crossing a stream. I shall have it destroyed. I've no time to waste on dumb animals. Yet I've a kindly nature. You'd be surprised how generous I can be. You can carry my bag if you like. I'm a man with a charitable nature.

He hands his bag to LOW *who shoulders it.*

22. Exterior. A clearing in the forest. LOW *and* BERNARD COATES *are sitting under a tree. They are eating food from* BERNARD's *bag.*

COATES. My name is Bernard Coates. I'm very rich and I'm engaged to be married. You probably find that hard to believe?

LOW. No

COATES. I suppose you think I couldn't be rich because I have such bad teeth?

LOW. If you're so rich why can't you afford a shilling for a toothbrush?

COATES. I have bad teeth because if you're rich it doesn't matter whether you disgust people or not. In fact I'll go as far as to say that the poor prefer the rich to be disgusting.

He crams a piece of pie into his mouth. He almost chokes. LOW *pats him on the back.*

COATES (*wiping his mouth*). Are you rich? I'd be surprised if you were.

LOW. I haven't got a penny to bless myself with.

COATES. That must be most inconvenient for you. Would you like to go to a party?

LOW. Yes.

COATES. Let me just bury the remains of this food and I'll take you to one.

He gets up and is soon lost among the trees.

23. Exterior. The same spot. Later. *An owl hoots.* LOW *wanders in search of* BERNARD COATES.

LOW (*calling, anxious*). Bernard! Bernard Coates! (*Pause.*) Where are you?

No reply. He stumbles along the path. He is soon lost among the trees.

24. Exterior. Another part of the forest. McTURK *is sitting wrapped in his overcoat. A chill mist has fallen over the forest.* LOW *approaches across the clearing. He is weary, his face is stained with blood. He whistles tunelessly between his teeth.*

McTURK. Who roughed you up?

LOW. A man I tried to help. (*He limps toward* McTURK.) I'll never do another generous act as long as I live.

McTURK. You've said that before. You always revert.

25. Exterior. A stone gateway leading into the drive of a small manor house. Early morning. *A ornamental iron plaque swings over the gate. It says:* 'MONEY-BOX LODGE'.
McTURK *and* LOW *approach the gate.*

LOW. This house looks promising. Let's ask for food.

McTURK. No. I'm too proud to beg.

LOW. We could pay with the money that the Lord Mayor gave us.

McTURK *takes the wallet from his pocket. He opens it. He realises with surprise and misgiving, that it is empty.*

LOW. What's happened to the money?

McTURK. There never was any money. The Mayor's speech was made with half an eye to the local elections. I'd rather starve than enter a house like this.

He trudges away, proud and lonely. LOW shrugs, walks up the drive.

26. Exterior. LOW *approaches the front door of Money-Box Lodge. He searches for a bell. He can't find one. He pushes the door open. He goes inside.*

27. Interior. The hall of Money-Box Lodge. *A balcony runs the length of one wall. A wide staircase leads from it. LOW finds his feet sinking into the rich pile of the carpet. He stops. Silence. A door on the landing opens and BERNARD COATES appears dressed in his underclothes. He carries a folded newspaper.*

LOW (*calling to* BERNARD COATES). Might I have a word with you, sir.

> BERNARD COATES *stops, sees who is calling him, is extremely agitated. He comes down the stairs and puts a jaunty expression on his face in order to conceal his real feelings.*

COATES (*waving the newspaper*). The election results are through. (*With a breezy smile.*) Had you heard the news?

LOW. I'm too tired to bother with them.

COATES. Well you can borrow my paper. I've finished with it now.

> *He pushes the newspaper into* LOW's *hand and hurries away with a nervous smile.* LOW *is left alone. He opens the newspaper.*

28. Front page of the paper. *A photograph of a smiling woman, microphones before her. A man lifting her hand in victory. Caption says:* 'LILLY CORBETT IT IS!'

29. LOW *opens the newspaper at an inside page.*

30. Close-up of inside page. *Headline:* 'A DELIGHTFULLY FEMININE PRIME MINISTER!'

31. Interior. The hall. LOW *folds up the newspaper. A tall, well-built* WOMAN *appears in a doorway opposite him.* LOW *smiles.*

LOW. Are you the owner of the house?

The woman (MRS O'SCULLION) *points a gun at him.*

MRS O'SCULLION. Stay where you are! Don't attempt to escape or I shall have no hesitation in shooting you.

LOW. I'm hungry and thirsty. I need help.

MRS O'SCULLION. I'm not interested in your private life. What are you doing here?

LOW. I found the door open. I meant no harm.

MRS O'SCULLION. Who gave you permission to read that paper? It's private property, you know. Put it down.

LOW *puts the newspaper onto a table.* BERNARD COATES *appears in the doorway.*

LOW (*seeing* BERNARD *with relief*). I met you last night, sir. Don't you remember? You promised to take me to a party.

BERNARD COATES *glances at* MRS O'SCULLION *with apprehension. Looks back at* LOW. *Gives a little cough of apology.*

COATES. There's no party here. You'll have to go somewhere else.

MRS O'SCULLION (*to* COATES). Why are you talking to strange young men without your trousers?

COATES. I was dressing for dinner. This fellow came and asked me to take him to a party.

MRS O'SCULLION *casts a withering glance at* BERNARD COATES.

MRS O'SCULLION. It was premature to take your clothes off. He's obviously a burglar.

BERNARD COATES *nods to* LOW *and shambles away up the stairs.* MRS O'SCULLION *calls into another room.*

MRS O'SCULLION. Con! Where are you! Give us a hand.

CONNIE *appears. She has on a pair of men's pyjamas and a plaid dressing-gown. She stands for a moment taking in the situation.*

MRS O'SCULLION. This kid forced his way in here and wants Bernie to take him to a party.

CONNIE *turns to* LOW. *There is an ironical contempt for him in the way she looks him up and down. She waves* MRS O'SCULLION *aside.* MRS O'SCULLION *puts the gun away.*

CONNIE (*to* LOW). Where's your friend?

LOW. He's gone ahead. I came in here for help.

CONNIE (*coming closer*). You're an attractive little thing, aren't you? (*She puts a hand under his chin.*) You're not frightened of me, are you?

LOW. Yes.

CONNIE (*to* MRS O'SCULLION). Give him a room.

MRS O'SCULLION'*s mouth drops open in amazement.*

MRS O'SCULLION. A room? But he may be dangerous. He looks as though he is.

CONNIE. Nonsense! He's just a little tart. Give him a room. Make sure it's a good one. With a double bed. I may be working late tonight.

32. Exterior. A pathway near the house. *A hedge. Beyond the hedge a rose garden. Further off a rose arbour.* McTURK, *travel-stained and woebegone, walks down the pathway. The silvery mists of early morning hang on the distant trees.*
 Suddenly, at the end of the arbour, ROWENA TORRENCE *is seen wearing a filmy négligée.*

33. Exterior. The Rose Arbour. McTURK *is running across the garden and down the arbour to greet* ROWENA. *He calls to her across the silent, dew-drenched garden.*

McTURK. Rowena! Rowena!

34. Exterior. The Rose Arbour. ROWENA TORRENCE *turns to greet* McTURK. *They embrace in the centre of the arbour. He kisses her. Rose petals, each one touched with a pearl of dew, fall slowly upon them.*

ROWENA (*caressing him*). Oh, my darling, what a state you're in. You're muddy and dirty, but I still love you.

McTURK. What are you doing here?

ROWENA. I'm staying here until the convent is ready to receive me. There are one or two minor technicalities like the loss of my virginity which are holding things up.

The arbour swings away from McTURK. The colours dissolve. The shadows reach out to him. He clings to ROWENA.

McTURK. Can you get me something to eat. I'm ready to faint. I've had nothing since yesterday.

ROWENA. You'll have to go to the kitchen. It's much nicer for you there than in the dining-room. I'm sure they'll make you comfy.

She leads him from the arbour. He puts an arm round her waist.

McTURK. I never want to leave you again. We'll be together forever.

ROWENA (*with a tinkly laugh*). Of course we will. Only this morning I'm playing tennis. So you will excuse me, won't you?

She gently pushes his hand away from her waist and smiles.

35. Interior. A large and luxuriously appointed bedroom.
CONNIE *and* LOW *enter.*

CONNIE. I'm just across the hall. If you want me. (*She gives a coarse emphasis to her remarks.*) You've got a shower — (*She pulls back the shower curtain.*) See?

LOW. How much will all this cost?

CONNIE *comes close to him. Puts an arm round his waist and squeezes him hard.*

CONNIE. Nothing that you can't well afford. (*Seeing his alarm she pinches his cheek.*) A little sweetie, aren't you?

Suddenly he finds her in his arms. They fall onto the bed.

CONNIE. You want someone to look after you. I think I can fit you into my place.

She is unable to restrain herself. She mauls him in a most unexpected manner. His teeth shake. He struggles for breath. A faint yell escapes him before she envelops him completely.

36. Interior. The kitchen of Money-Box Lodge. MISS
DRUMGOOLE *is washing dishes at the sink.* McTURK *is eating
a meal.*

McTURK. What are you doing here? It's a long way to Father
Brodie's pantry.

MISS DRUMGOOLE. I'm accompanying Miss Rowena and
Mrs O'Scullion to the convent. We're only stopping here a
night or two. Naturally I must earn my keep. And so I
opted to help in the kitchen.

She dries her hands. She sits opposite McTURK *and pours
herself a cup of tea.*

MISS DRUMGOOLE (*with a sigh*). I could sit opposite you
forever, Ian McTurk. Has any woman ever said that to you
before?

McTURK. A bus conductress hinted as much once. She gave me
a free ride.

MISS DRUMGOOLE (*with a sentimental smile*). And so would I,
Ian McTurk. If you'd only ask. (*She lifts the cup to her lips.*)
Your mother must've been a lucky woman.

McTURK. No. She was dogged by bad luck. She threw herself
over the balcony of a cinema during a Mario Lanza film.

MISS DRUMGOOLE. And what about your father?

McTURK. He was strangled during a political disturbance.

MISS DRUMGOOLE. Was he demonstrating against the
Government?

McTURK. No. He was selling fruit to passing tourists.

MISS DRUMGOOLE. Life hasn't been kind to you, has it? I'm
afraid it has many more shocks in store for you. Miss Rowena
asked me to see you left the house immediately you'd
finished breakfast.

McTURK *stares.*

McTURK (*pause*). But I love her. She's going to marry me.

MISS DRUMGOOLE *gives a bitter laugh.*

MISS DRUMGOOLE. She's destined for richer hands than
yours.

She takes him to the window. She lifts the cup with one hand. Points through the window with the other.

MISS DRUMGOOLE. That's the man she's going to marry.

37. Exterior. Seen through the kitchen window. ROWENA, *carrying a tennis racket is walking with* BERNARD COATES. *They are deep in conversation.* MISS DRUMGOOLE'*s voice is heard over the picture.*

MISS DRUMGOOLE. He's made a fortune in the catering trade. The engagement is to be announced at the Hoteliers' dinner on Friday.

38. Interior. The kitchen. McTURK *turns to* MISS DRUMGOOLE, *angry.*

McTURK. I don't believe you!

MISS DRUMGOOLE. She was afraid that would be your reaction. She left this letter for you. (*She takes a letter from her bosom.*) It explains how she fell in love with Bernard Coates quite suddenly after accidentally seeing his trading figures for last year.

She gives McTURK *the letter. He opens it. Reads. Tears the letter to pieces, on the verge of tears.*

McTURK (*pause, bitterly*). I'll never trust a woman again as long as I live.

He goes to the door.

MISS DRUMGOOLE (*shaking her head*). Another man's heart Miss Rowena has broken!

39. Interior. A car on a road winding between trees. LOW *is sitting beside* CONNIE *who is driving. She smiles and squeezes his leg above the knee. He knocks her hand away, sullen.*

40. Exterior. A country road lined with trees. Early afternoon. McTURK *walking alone. Rounding a bend in the road he comes upon a number of* MEN *sitting among the trees. They are* *unshaven and wear old clothes. Two or three tents are pitched nearby. A fire has been lit. McTURK walks over to them.*

McTURK. Good afternoon. I hope you don't mind my introducing myself to you. My name is Ian McTurk.

A young man who appears to be the leader stands up. He wears a torn army jerkin. His name is JACK RAMSAY.

RAMSAY. My name is John Ramsay. I'm the leader of a semi-political organisation. I call myself Jack and I encourage other people to do the same.

McTURK. I'd like to join your organisation.

RAMSAY. Why?

McTURK. A woman has broken my heart.

RAMSAY. Well, that's as good a reason as any to enter politics. We're planning a series of outrages against society. You're just in time to see the fun. Go and give your name to somebody and report back to me immediately.

41. Exterior. Morning. McTURK and RAMSAY in a large city. *They pass a hoarding. On it is a picture of Lillian Corbett. The poster says:* 'IF YOU THINK LIKE A WOMAN, VOTE LIKE A WOMAN'.

RAMSAY. We're going to assassinate Mrs Corbett. She's played the fool long enough. I'm putting the finishing touches to my plan. (*He takes a pamphlet from his pocket.*) Read that. It's fresh from the printers.

McTURK. What is it?

RAMSAY. Spicy gossip about people in authority. You see, when we try to undermine people's confidence in the Government of the day we use a variety of tactics: the smear, the lie and, in extreme cases, even the truth.

McTURK *opens the pamphlet.*

42. Close-up of the pamphlet. *It is crudely printed and meant to appeal to the emotions of the lowest level. It shows a flashlight picture of Christopher Low in a bubble bath. A caption says:* 'LATEST ADDITION TO POLICE CHIEF'S HAREM'.

43. Exterior. A public square. *A large crowd of* MEN. RAMSAY *pushes his way to the platform. He mounts the steps. Loud cheers.* RAMSAY *holds up his hands.*

RAMSAY. We all know why we're here! (*The crowd answers with a roar.*) We're here because there's nothing on the telly! Isn't that so?

The crowd answers 'Yes', 'You've never said a truer word', 'Good old Jackie'.

RAMSAY. And what better reason can there be for demonstrating against a Government that has consistently flouted the will of the people!

Several flags are produced and waved. An OLD MAN *next to* McTURK *begins to shout violently.*

OLD MAN. Freedom from tyranny!

McTURK (*with interest*). Are you oppressed?

OLD MAN. No.

McTURK. Then why are you calling for freedom?

OLD MAN. I always do at these meetings. I've been coming to them all my life. (*He waves a flag.*) Death to the oppressors!

RAMSAY (*appealing to the crowd*). I'm one of the fortunate ones. I don't need an excuse to be against the Government. It is in my blood. (*He waves his flag.*) My mum and dad were demonstrating against the import of Japanese goods when I was born. They used my mum's placard as a stretcher. And I'm not ashamed to own it!

The crowd cheers. The OLD MAN *clambers onto the platform.*

OLD MAN. I'm Jackie's dad and I can vouch for every word he says!

RAMSAY *helps the* OLD MAN *up beside him.*

OLD MAN (*addressing the crowd*). I want to speak to you today about the Archbishop of Canterbury. I know, and Jackie here knows (*He smiles and nods to* JACK RAMSAY.) and many of you know, that a month ago she was caught in compromising circumstances. It was hushed up, of course.

Crowd shouts 'Typical!', 'They always get away with it, don't they?' *and* 'What a way for a princess of the Church to behave'. *The* OLD MAN *nods to the crowd.*

OLD MAN. She'd just finished officiating at a ceremony attended by high-ranking ecclesiastics!

He nods and winks. The crowd roars its understanding.

OLD MAN. If you or me had done that sort of thing we'd be in trouble. Owing to her exalted rank the Archbishop got off scot free! (*He turns and speaks off mike to* RAMSAY.) Pass round those scandalous snaps of the Archbishop, Jackie. I've got them going now.

McTURK, RAMSAY *and their helpers hand pamphlets around in the crowd. The* OLD MAN *is heard shouting.*

OLD MAN. This state of affairs is a disgrace! It cannot be allowed to continue! We must fight to the death for our rights!

The crowd cheers. Hats are thrown into the air. Suddenly police whistles are heard. Uniformed POLICEWOMEN *converge onto the square. At the same time* MOUNTED POLICEWOMEN *ride down the panic-stricken crowd.*

McTURK. Is that old man really your father?

RAMSAY. No. But I allow him to think he is.

McTURK. Why?

RAMSAY. There's no time to explain. We must get away from here. Follow me!

They push their way through a chaos of young men and POLICEWOMEN.

44. Exterior. Side streets leading from the square. RAMSAY *and* McTURK *running. Outside a tall, imposing building several* MEN *have chained themselves to the railings.* RAMSAY *gives them an encouraging nod and hurries on.*

RAMSAY (*to* McTURK). These are some of the ways we demonstrate our opposition to the present regime. Later this afternoon my father intends to commit an appalling act in the National Gallery.

45. Interior. The National Gallery. *A painting of a naked Adonis. The* OLD MAN *enters bent nearly double. He takes an axe from*

*under his coat and slashes at the picture. Cries of horror from the
black* LADY ATTENDANTS *who rush upon him.*

OLD MAN (*struggling in the grip of several* NEGRESSES). I'm
making a gesture of defiance! You should be interested in
the mind of Man not his body! All you think of is the
sensuousness of the male! Look at his mind, you evil beasts!

The ATTENDANTS *carry him away.*

46. Exterior. A street in a sleazy neighbourhood. *A shop-front
sign says* 'LULU CODRON — PALMIST'.
JACK RAMSAY *and* IAN McTURK *arrive at the door,
panting.* RAMSAY *knocks. The door is opened an inch or two
by the* MAYOR (TERENCE O'SCULLION). *He is poorly dressed,
in contrast to the last time* McTURK *saw him. He has a hangdog
expression. He opens the door to allow the young men in.*
RAMSAY *looks down the street to assure himself that they
haven't been followed.*

47. Interior. The back of the shop. Evening. *A dingy, depressing
place.* RAMSAY *hands his jerkin and cap to the* MAYOR *and
leads the way upstairs.*

McTURK (*dropping back as the* MAYOR *hangs* RAMSAY's
jerkin on a hook). Aren't you the Lord Mayor of the town
where I was born?

MAYOR. I was. My circumstances have been sadly reduced, I'm afraid.

McTURK. Why have you joined this dubious political organisation?

MAYOR. Like most men in positions of trust I was engaged in
illegal activities. My own wife denounced me to the authorities.
I had to flee to escape a prison sentence. I'm now a wanted
man. My only hope of regaining a place in society is by
destroying those who brought about my disgrace.

He leads the way upstairs.

48. Interior. The room above the shop. Night. *A large number of*
MEN *are gathered together talking, smoking and drinking. The*
MAYOR *leads* McTURK *to a table at which* CHRISTOPHER

LOW *is sitting. The table is littered with papers and important-looking documents.*

MAYOR. This is Christopher Low who once blew an arm from the allegorical figure of Peace on the Memorial to the Fallen. I believe you've already met.

McTURK (*to* LOW). Is it true that you're the plaything of the head of the C.I.D?

LOW. Perfectly true. I'm very ashamed of the fact. If only society had treated me better I might not now be plotting to destroy it.

McTURK *sits. The* MAYOR *sits next to him.* RAMSAY *is at the head of the table.* McTURK *is surprised to find* MISS DRUMGOOLE *sitting in the empty space on the other side of him. He gives a shocked exclamation.*

McTURK. Miss Drumgoole! What are you doing here?

MISS DRUMGOOLE. I lost my position as Father Brodie's housekeeper because I'd helped you in your romantic affair with Miss Rowena. I'm now employed as a part-time secretary by the Security Service. My love for you has led me to betray my country. (*A tear falls from her eye.*) I hope that one day you'll be able to repay me.

RAMSAY *leans across.*

RAMSAY (*to* McTURK). Miss Drumgoole is a valuable ally. She's just brought us plans of the Conference which is to be held at the Albert Hall tomorrow.

He gets to his feet. The room falls silent in anticipation. All eyes are upon him.

RAMSAY. Patricia Drumgoole has given up her godless life as housekeeper to a clergyman to join our cause. As far as I know she is the only woman in this room. I shall carry out a thorough check later on.

Everyone looks confident of being able to pass the test.

RAMSAY. Tomorrow, as many of you know, we are going to assassinate the Prime Minister. (*To* CHRISTOPHER LOW.) Make a note of that, will you? I don't want it to slip my mind. (*He turns back to the meeting.*) Our plans have had to be altered slightly. The reason for this being that only women

are allowed into the Conference Hall. This problem appeared
to be insuperable. Fortunately a solution was quickly found.

49. Exterior. Outside the Conference Hall. *A car draws up.*
RAMSAY, McTURK *and* LOW *get out. With heavily made-up
eyes, furs and smart hats, they resemble perfectly women of
authority and fashion. They enter the Conference Hall.*

50. Interior. The entrance hall. RAMSAY *opens his handbag and
shows a card to the uniformed* POLICEWOMAN.

POLICEWOMAN. What's the password?

RAMSAY. 'Irresistible'.

POLICEWOMAN. Would you like to check with Security now?

RAMSAY. Yes.

> *The* POLICEWOMAN *leads the way down a corridor.*
> RAMSAY, McTURK *and* LOW *follow.*

51. Interior. An office. MISS DRUMGOOLE *is sitting at a
typewriter.* CONNIE, *in uniform, sits behind an enormous desk.*
CHRISTOPHER LOW *tilts his hat further over, throwing his
face into shadow.* RAMSAY *wastes no time. His manner is
correct and official.*

RAMSAY (*taking three passes from his handbag*). Here are my
passes. I wish to go up immediately.

CONNIE. Where are you from?

RAMSAY. We represent the nice part of Acton.

CONNIE (*to* MISS DRUMGOOLE). See if you've anything
under Acton.

> MISS DRUMGOOLE *goes to a filing cabinet.*

RAMSAY. I don't think there's any need for this. We're perfectly
respectable girls.

McTURK. My auntie is the spiritual adviser to a baking powder firm.

LOW. And I have connections with several prominent men.
There's no need at all to check my bona-fides.

CONNIE (*with a smile*). I'm sorry to cause you inconvenience, but we cannot be too careful. There've been rumours of a plot to kill the P.M.

MISS DRUMGOOLE *goes to another filing cabinet, opens it. Leafs through.*

CONNIE (*to* RAMSAY). Is this your first Conference?

RAMSAY. Yes.

CONNIE. You needn't be worried. You'll love everybody.

RAMSAY. I was terrified my clothes would be dowdy.

CONNIE. I think you look very smart.

RAMSAY. And my hair — where do you get yours done? It's so lovely.

CONNIE (*smiles*). I'm so glad you like it. Most people think because a girl's in uniform she doesn't have to worry about her appearance. They couldn't be further from the truth.

Her manner is relaxed. She takes out a hand-mirror and studies her face.

CONNIE. I've been having my hair done at Senora Sally Warren's. She caters almost exclusively for the horse guards, but she may be able to fit you in. (*To* MISS DRUMGOOLE.) Have you got Sally's card?

MISS DRUMGOOLE *produces the card from the file. Hands it to* RAMSAY.

CONNIE (*with a smile*). Have a bon coiffeur, won't you, dear? (*To* MISS DRUMGOOLE.) I don't think there's any real need to check up. I'm not the suspicious type.

MISS DRUMGOOLE. I'll take these ladies to the Conference Hall, ma'am. Will you be good enough to sign the admittance chit?

CONNIE *scribbles her name at the bottom of a half sheet of paper.* MISS DRUMGOOLE *leads the way into the corridor.* CONNIE *suddenly focuses her attention on* CHRISTOPHER LOW.

CONNIE. I say.

LOW *stops.*

Have you got a brother? A little brunette. Rather wistful, but quite good fun?

LOW. No.

CONNIE *looks puzzled.* LOW *follows the others.* CONNIE *lights a cigarette.*

52. Interior. The Conference Hall. *Every seat is occupied by a woman. Nurses, nuns, policewomen, uniformed usherettes, representatives of the armed forces. Delegates in their fashionable dresses.* RAMSAY, McTURK *and* LOW *push their way through the throng.*

53. Interior. The Conference Hall. RAMSAY, McTURK *and* LOW. *A group of* WOMEN.

MRS O'SCULLION (*to* RAMSAY). What are you going to wear for the disarmament conference?

RAMSAY. I did think a wool two-piece, simplicity itself, yet with a sort of dash and elegance.

MRS O'SCULLION (*flinging up her hands*). Oh, how perfect!

LOW. I think it would be fun if our delegates wore matching costumes.

MRS O'SCULLION. What a perfectly marvellous idea! (*She turns to the woman beside her.*) We must tell Lillian about this wonderful idea!

54. Interior. The Conference Hall. *A flurry as the* PRIME MINISTER *arrives. She is beautifully dressed.*

A burst of applause. Several hundred WOMEN *sway with excitement.*

The PRIME MINISTER *takes her place at a table on the platform. Flashlight photographs are taken.*

55. Interior. A box overlooking the conference platform. RAMSAY, McTURK *and* LOW *open their handbags. In each is a section of a telescopic rifle.* RAMSAY *assembles the rifle.*

56. Interior. The Conference Hall. The platform. *The* PRIME MINISTER *addresses herself to the microphones in front of her.*

PRIME MINISTER. This is my first report as Prime Minister and I'd like to commence by paying to the ladies of the cabinet an immediate tribute. How they manage to run the country and remain so attractive I do not know.

She turns off the mike and speaks to a middle-aged woman.

PRIME MINISTER. I think you're looking simply splendid after your facial, Pixie.

The WOMAN *smiles modestly.*
The PRIME MINISTER *turns back to the microphones.*

PRIME MINISTER. Well, dears, we've just had the most heavenly cabinet meeting!

MRS O'SCULLION *struggles to her feet. Her face is flushed. Her lip trembles.*

MRS O'SCULLION. Oh, Lillian! And I wasn't there! How could you!

PRIME MINISTER. The very next time, darling. (*With a consolatory smile.*)

MRS O'SCULLION. No! You've betrayed my trust. I wouldn't come now if you begged me!

She stamps her foot. Bursts into tears. Dabbing her eyes she runs from the platform. The PRIME MINISTER *sighs.*

PRIME MINISTER. Georgina gets so excited by the smallest things. I sometimes wonder whether it was altogether wise to give her the Foreign Office. (*She flicks ash from her cigarette end.*) We had the meeting at Molly's house. And we've come to a decision that is sure to have far-reaching consequences.

A flutter of anticipation.

PRIME MINISTER. We're having the House of Commons redecorated in Chinese white lacquer and natural oak woodwork!

Every woman in the hall gives an exclamation of delight. A shimmer of silk, a sway of feathers, the tinkling of ten thousand pearls.

57. Interior. The box. RAMSAY *has assembled the rifle.*
LOW *and* McTURK *open their handbags. They take out lipsticks.*

*They turn up the lipsticks. In each is a bullet. They hand the
bullets to* RAMSAY *who loads the rifle.*

58. Interior. The Conference Hall. The platform. *The* PRIME
MINISTER *has just been given a standing ovation. She
consults her notes.*

PRIME MINISTER. And now, the International field — this
afternoon I shall put a stop to speculation. I shall attend
the disarmament conference in a great flowing dress in white
broderie Anglaise with heavenly flounces. The price was
simply outrageous!

59. Interior. The box. *The door is abruptly pushed open.*
RAMSAY, *holding the rifle, is pressed back against the wall.*
CONNIE *looks in.*

CONNIE (*in a whisper*). We're having trouble downstairs with
a group who say they're from Acton. Could you come and
help us sort it out?

McTURK. We must stay and hear the end of the Prime Minister's
speech.

CONNIE *smiles, looks down onto the platform. The* PRIME
MINISTER *is smiling.*

CONNIE. She has the most perfect set of teeth I've ever seen.

LOW. And all her own. So they say.

McTURK. Is it true that she's the brains behind a chain of
beauty salons?

CONNIE. Yes.

LOW. They haven't done much for her, have they?

CONNIE *giggles.*

CONNIE. Now then, we mustn't talk like that. (*With a wink.*)
Though I couldn't agree with you more. She is hideous!
(*Swings heavily on the door of the box.*) See you in a jiffy then?

She closes the door and leaves the box laughing. RAMSAY
steps from behind the door and takes aim at the platform.

60. Interior. The Conference Hall. The platform. *A WOMAN REPORTER is questioning the* PRIME MINISTER.

REPORTER. Will there be an official statement, Prime Minister?

PRIME MINISTER. Yes. Doors are closed to further negotiations. My wardrobe is complete.

REPORTER. Lillian, if you are asked to take part in a four-girl meeting in the Autumn will you go?

PRIME MINISTER. Well, it depends on the aims and terms of such a meeting. I'm in favour of direct contact with our rivals, as you know, but after the disgraceful things they said about my drawing-room curtains last time, I don't think I can make too great an effort to be polite.

She looks around the hall with a hurt expression. The entire conference is with her on this point.

61. Interior. The box. RAMSAY *takes aim at the distant figure of the* PRIME MINISTER. McTURK *and* LOW *drop back. A burst of applause.* RAMSAY *pulls the trigger. A shot is heard. He puts the rifle down. They all let themselves out of the box and enter the corridor.*

62. Interior. The Conference Hall. *Women are fainting, row by row, falling to the ground in hysterics. On the platform a number of delegates have passed out. They have dropped from their chairs and are awaiting medical treatment. The dead body of the* PRIME MINISTER *is being removed by the ambulance staff.* POLICE-WOMEN *hurry to and fro questioning witnesses.* TRAINED NURSES *attempt to give medical attention. As quickly as one woman is revived another faints.*

63. Interior. A staircase. RAMSAY, McTURK *and* LOW *hurry down.* CONNIE *appears at the bottom of the stairs with a tall woman. The three young men stop. They continue their descent in a more orderly manner.* CONNIE *meets them. Her manner is frigid.*

CONNIE. This is Tess Eliot. She runs a dyeworks in the Bridgenorth Road. She claims to represent Acton.

TESS ELIOT. I was elected by my fellow workers in Bijou garments. Do you mind telling me just what you're playing at?

The door behind them bursts open and MRS O'SCULLION *rushes in.*

MRS O'SCULLION (*waving her arms, hysterically*). Lilly's been done in! We shall all have to go into mourning!

CONNIE *turns to the young men, her suspicions confirmed. Before she can speak* RAMSAY *brings her low with a flying tackle.* McTURK *hits* TESS ELIOT *with his handbag.* LOW *shoves* MRS O'SCULLION *to one side. Hundreds of screaming women are suddenly upon them, flooding from the conference hall. The boys run down the corridor.* CONNIE *sits up, dazed, crying aloud in surprise.*

CONNIE. They were men!

64. Exterior. A street. *The boys running.* RAMSAY *stops at a news-stand to buy a paper. He opens it.*

65. Page of print. *Three 'Identikit' pictures. Headline:* 'Have you seen these men?'

66. Exterior. Another street. *The boys enter, running. Out of breath. They stop near a newsagents. They go inside.*

67. Interior. The newsagent's shop. RAMSAY'*s father is behind the counter. He looks up when the three young men enter.*

RAMSAY'S FATHER. You've struck a blow for freedom, Jackie. Your mother's face went white when she heard what you'd done. I was being forcibly fed by her. She cursed you. She said you were the type of son no mother should love. I threw my gruel at her. I've always found her a most disgusting woman, as you may have heard me say.

RAMSAY. When did you get out of prison?

RAMSAY'S FATHER. Not two hours ago. I was released on the personal say-so of the Governor of Brixton. Your mother, as a common or garden wardress, had no option but to release me.

He pulls a copy of a newspaper from a rack behind him and shoves it under RAMSAY's *face.*

RAMSAY'S FATHER. Look at that, Jackie. Lady Cudlipp has done you proud!

68. Newspaper Headline: 'A Nation Mourns!'

69. Exterior. A broad thoroughfare leading to a cathedral. *With official pomp, increased by security arrangements, the coffin containing the body of the late* PRIME MINISTER, *is carried on a gun carriage to its last resting place. Slow March.*
Mourning figures led by the ARCHBISHOP OF CANTERBURY, DR MAUD ELPHINSTONE. *Flags are much in evidence.* RAMSAY, McTURK *and* LOW *with a number of revolutionaries appear at the head of the procession. They bar the way into the cathedral.*
The ARCHBISHOP OF CANTERBURY *raises her hands in saintly horror.*

ARCHBISHOP. I'm a Princess of the Church! Let me pass. I've some hard praying to do.

RAMSAY *thrusts her aside. Cries of* 'Sacrilege' *and* 'Blasphemy' *mingled with* 'The last days are come' *from the multitude.*

RAMSAY (*addressing the crowd*). Who are your leaders? What do you know of their private lives?

The crowd are uneasy.

RAMSAY. I'm going to speak plainly. Pardon me if I give offence. Facts are often unpleasant. I was privileged recently to attend a select dinner in the home of a high-ranking member of the Government. During the meal she behaved in a way which left me in no doubt as to her intentions. Afterwards she suggested that I accompany her on a trip to ratify an international treaty. All expenses paid. I refused, knowing that what she proposed was wrong. How many other lads has she tried to intimidate in this vile way.

LOW. I was the passing fancy of the head of the C.I.D.

RAMSAY'S FATHER *is seen on the edge of the crowd.*

RAMSAY'S FATHER. She ruined his life. I've often heard him say so. Her kisses set his blood on fire!

LOW. Let's overthrow the Government. That is the solution to all our problems.

RAMSAY. We'll pass a law forbidding anyone to entertain in private. We cannot afford this stifling secrecy.

McTURK. Anything that is worth doing is worth doing in public.

Cheers. RAMSAY'S FATHER waves his handkerchief.

RAMSAY'S FATHER. Death to the oppressors! Liberty! Down with the tyrants!

Wild cheering. Fighting breaks out round the gun carriage. The ARCHBISHOP OF CANTERBURY and her fellow clerics drop to their knees in prayer.

70. Exterior. The area round the cathedral. *Police appear and make baton charges. Shots are exchanged between POLICE-WOMEN and RIOTERS. The crowd scatters in panic. The rebels fight it out with the police across the gun carriage and heads of the kneeling clerics. The representatives of the legal government cower behind the pillars of the cathedral.*

Across the picture appears a ticker-tape message which reads: 'Anarchy rumours strong denial from Whitehall'.

71. Exterior. Several streets around the cathedral. *Pitched battles between POLICE and RIOTERS. RAMSAY and his men round up a number of pro-government supporters — mostly blondes. POLICEWOMEN fire on rebel troop positions. Scenes of wild disorder.*

Across the picture appears a ticker-tape message which reads: 'Strong woman needed says "Pixie" Heath'.

72. Exterior. Street. Mid-day. RAMSAY'S FATHER *is seen selling newspapers.*

RAMSAY'S FATHER (*calling hoarsely*). 'Police chief elected President!'

He holds up a newspaper.

73. Headline from the newspaper: 'Gorgeous Connie in Downing Street'.

74. Interior. The cabinet room in Downing Street. CONNIE
is seated with a number of prominent ministers. ROWENA *is
ushered into the room.* CONNIE *rises, smiling.*

CONNIE. Ah, my dear, come in. Did you have a pleasant
  honeymoon?

ROWENA. Yes. My husband was nearly killed.

CONNIE. Good. Everything is going according to plan then. Take
  a seat.

  ROWENA *sits.*

CONNIE. You know the rest of the girls, don't you? (*The other
  women smile.*) As you've probably heard, dear, we've had a
  spot of bother since Lilly died. Everything north of the
  Humber is in male hands. Even Girl Guides and Brownies
  have tales to tell that make hardened matrons blush. We
  must do something. And quickly.

ROWENA. How can I help?

CONNIE. We've discovered the identity of one of the rebel
  leaders. His name is Ian McTurk.

ROWENA. Oh, I know him. I was going to marry him once. He
  was sent away from the town where he was born for my sake.

CONNIE (*with a smile*). I'd like you to use your influence for
  the public good. Once we have their leaders the rebellion can
  quickly be crushed.

  *She smiles around the table. The other women nod in
  agreement.*

75. Interior. The shop. *The windows are crowded with men firing
into the street.* RAMSAY *hurries up to* McTURK. *He hands him
a note.*

RAMSAY. This note has just been delivered. It's addressed to
  you in a woman's hand.

  McTURK *opens the letter. His eyes swim with tears. He reads:*

76. The letter. *It says:* 'My darling. Please forgive me for what I
did. I must see you to explain. Yours ever — Rowena Coates.'

77. Interior. The shop. McTURK *folds up the letter.*

McTURK. It's from Rowena. She still loves me.

RAMSAY. It may be a trap.

McTURK. She asks for my forgiveness. I must go to her.

He hands his rifle to RAMSAY *and hurries away.* RAMSAY *takes his place in the firing line.*

78. Exterior. The garden of a town house. *High walls and long unweeded flowerbeds. Moonlight.* McTURK *advances. At the end of the garden he sees* ROWENA. *He runs to her across the dew-laden grass. He kisses her. Buries his head on her breast.*

McTURK. I love you so. Don't ever leave me again.

Her arms are about him.

ROWENA. Oh, my poor darling, how unhappy I've made you.

She kisses him. As she does so a number of uniformed POLICEWOMEN *surround them. They drag* McTURK *away. Without looking at him* ROWENA *turns and leaves the garden. She meets* CONNIE.

CONNIE (*patting her shoulder*). You did very well. We're all proud of you.

79. Exterior. The shop. *The signal for a final assault is given. The shop is attacked on all sides by screaming women waving rifles. They batter down the door and shoot at the rebels inside.*

80. Exterior. The roof of the shop. RAMSAY *climbs across the tiles with a flag. He sticks the flag on the highest point of the roof.*

RAMSAY. Long live the glorious revolution!

A fusilade of bullets is fired from the POLICEWOMEN *below.* RAMSAY *staggers across the roof back to the skylight. He clutches his heart. He falls fainting.* CHRISTOPHER LOW *climbs from the skylight and crawls across the roof to* RAMSAY. RAMSAY *has raised himself a little. Blood pours from his wounds.* LOW *helps him up. As they reach the skylight another round of shots is fired from the police.* RAMSAY *and* LOW *sway together. Another round. Cries of horror from below as* RAMSAY *slumps forward and crashes over the edge of the roof onto the pavement taking* LOW *with him.*

81. Exterior. The shop. CONNIE *and her detectives are seen handcuffing lines of men and leading them into waiting buses.* McTURK *is put into a police van and driven away.*

82. Exterior. A wharf. Night. McTURK *is led from the car and down a flight of steps to a waiting motor launch. The launch heads for the open sea.*

83. Exterior. A landing stage. *The launch is tied up. One of the guards leaps ashore.* McTURK *is dragged up the steps. A* GUARD *follows with a rifle.*

84. Interior. A prison cell. *The door is opened and* McTURK *is shoved inside by the* GUARD.

GUARD. Here's your kip for tonight. It's late and the Governor is asleep. He might change you tomorrow.

McTURK *looks around him. The door is banged shut. He hammers on the door.*

McTURK. I haven't had a trial!

GUARD. If you're guilty a trial is a waste of public money.

McTURK. Everybody must have a trial. That's the rules.

GUARD. The rules have been changed.

McTURK. Are they allowed to do that?

GUARD. It makes no difference to you whether they're allowed to change the rules or not. (*Pause.*) You can have less food. That's allowed.

McTURK. What else is allowed?

GUARD. Books. And the occasional woman — if you care for that type of thing.

McTURK. I want to see the Governor.

GUARD. He's asleep. Make an application in the morning.

He switches out the light. McTURK *sits on his bunk. He buries his head in his hands.*

85. Interior. The Governor's room. *The* GOVERNOR (BERNARD COATES) *is seated at a table, a file before him.* McTURK *is led into the room by the* GUARD. BERNARD COATES *takes* McTURK's *hand.*

BERNARD COATES. How are you, my boy? We met once before I believe, under happier circumstances.

He shakes his head. Sits at the desk. Opens the file.

What made you decide to overthrow the Government of the country? Was it a childhood ambition?

McTURK. It would take too long to explain.

BERNARD COATES. You've been given a twenty year sentence. Isn't that time enough?

McTURK. Surely I've the right to appeal?

BERNARD COATES. Under normal circumstances a prisoner does have the right of appeal. However, in your case, the authorities have decided to waive that right.

McTURK. Why?

BERNARD COATES. I couldn't say. Would you like me to find out?

McTURK. Yes.

BERNARD COATES (*turns to the* GUARD). Why has the right of appeal been withheld from the prisoner?

GUARD (*salutes smartly*). The prisoner has been denied the right of appeal on grounds of height, sir!

BERNARD COATES (*turns back to* McTURK *with a sympathetic shake of the head*). You're too small to lodge an appeal McTurk. There's nothing I can do for you, I'm afraid. Is there anything you'd like to alleviate your condition?

McTURK. I'd like a better cell. The one I have at the moment is filthy.

BERNARD COATES. Well, that's simple enough. (*To the* GUARD.) See the prisoner is put into a better cell. (*To* McTURK.) Come and see me any time. I'm always ready to help you.

McTURK *and the* GUARD *leave the room.*

86. Interior. Another cell. *The door is opened.* McTURK *is shoved inside.* McTURK *stares about him in horror. It is worse than the first. There is no bunk. The walls are peeling. A film of grime covers everything. There is a heap of straw in the corner. The* GUARD *bangs the door.* McTURK *shouts through the door.*

McTURK. I want to see the Governor. He promised to see my quarters were better. These are much worse.

GUARD (*looking through the spy-hole*). I wish you wouldn't complain. It only makes things worse.

The sound of his feet retreating along the corridor is heard. McTURK *sits upon the floor. He buries his face in his hands in despair.*

87. Interior. The cell. *On the wall of the cell is a calendar. On the calendar is a young girl in the briefest of bikinis. She is posed with a beach ball. Leaves are torn from the calendar as the days pass. Snow falls outside the window.* McTURK, *unshaven, ragged, wild, with straws in his hair, accepts food from the* GUARD. *He eats the food on the floor. The door bangs shut.*

Green leaves show outside the window. The girl on the calendar grows older. From being a lovely seventeen-year-old she matures into a ripe twenty-seven. More leaves are torn from the calendar. It is raining outside, McTURK *lies in the straw in the corner of the cell. Half-naked, hairy, bestial. The* GUARD *opens the door, pushes the food inside, shuts the door with a bang. Ice has formed around the windows. Icicles hang from the walls. The woman on the calendar is a matron of thirty-seven. The cell grows dark.*

McTURK *sleeps, half buried in the straw. The woman on the calendar is old, grey-haired, withered. She still holds up the beach ball with a gay smile. She has no teeth. Her smile is hideous.*

The sun shines into the window. It is summer. McTURK *scratches himself. A noise is heard. A tapping and scraping.* McTURK *sits up and listens. The next instant a part of the floor gives way and he topples into a deep hole which appears under him. Finding no bones broken he stands to his feet.*

88. Interior. A roughly-hewn tunnel. *In the semi-darkness* JACK RAMSAY *leans on a shovel.*

RAMSAY. Hallo. I've come to rescue you.

McTURK. But I've been in prison for ten years. What kept you so long?

RAMSAY. I had several things to attend to. I came as quickly as I could.

McTURK. I thought you'd been killed when you fell off the roof.

RAMSAY. No. I've a strong constitution. I gave up being a revolutionary and married a woman in the diplomatic service. I've lived abroad for many years. My wife recently divorced me.

McTURK. For what reason?

RAMSAY. She found a letter from a strange woman in my wallet. I'd rather not go into details just now. I packed my bags and went back to my father. He persuaded me to join forces with his revolutionary front. My mother and he were at loggerheads again. It's quite impossible living at home these days. And so we raised a small rebellion up north somewhere. It's progressing nicely I believe.

McTURK. What happened to Christopher Low who was my best friend?

RAMSAY. He broke his neck.

McTURK. He's dead?

RAMSAY. No. He's having a wild affair with the Matron of a hospital. His temperature has never been below a hundred in ten years.

McTURK *moves along the tunnel examining* RAMSAY's *work.*

McTURK. Where does this tunnel lead?

RAMSAY. I don't know.

McTURK *moves back along the tunnel. He picks up the shovel.*

McTURK. If we dig a little further we can break into the main sewer and escape that way.

He begins to dig.

89. Interior. The cell. Evening. *The* GUARD *opens the door. Brings in a bowl of soup. Puts it on the floor. Looks around for* *the prisoner. Kicks at the straw. Sees the hole. Scratches his head. Looks down into the hole. Puzzled.*

GUARD (*calling*). What are you doing down there?

90. Interior. The tunnel. McTURK *and* RAMSAY *are digging. A large hole is made in the wall. They climb through into a sewer.*

91. Interior. The sewer. McTURK *and* RAMSAY *advance cautiously. After a while they reach a point where the tunnel divides into two. They stop. Stare. Lights are seen behind them. Moving guards. Sound of voices.*

McTURK. We're being followed!

92. Interior. Another part of the tunnel. *The* GUARD *leads a number of men. They are following* McTURK *and* RAMSAY.

GUARD. Shoot anything that moves. That's an order.

He moves. They shoot him. He collapses into the sewer and is carried away by the swiftly flowing waters.

93. Interior. The sewer. McTURK *and* RAMSAY *stumble forward to an iron-ribbed grating. The water disappears under the grating. There is no way of escape.*

McTURK. We've got to swim for it!

He kicks off his boots and wades into the water. He ducks under the grating and disappears. RAMSAY *does the same.*

94. Exterior. The open sea. Day. McTURK *and* RAMSAY *are swimming. Waves slide past, white and green, ridge upon ridge, disappearing into drifts where the horizon erases the ridges. A yacht is seen in the distance driven on by the force of the wind. The two men wave, cry out.*

95. Exterior. The side of the yacht. *The boys swim up. A rope is lowered. They are helped out of the water by deckhands.*

96. Exterior. The deck of the yacht.

McTURK (*to a deckhand*). Take us to your Captain.

The deckhand leads the way below.

97. Interior. The yacht. *The two men stand outside a door marked 'Captain'. They knock. A voice calls 'Come in'. They enter the cabin.*

98. Interior. The Captain's cabin. *The two men enter and are surprised to see* CHRISTOPHER LOW, *in a white uniform, standing at the desk.*

McTURK (*open-mouthed*). Are you the Captain?

LOW. No. I'm the cabin boy.

McTURK. What are you doing here?

LOW. Well, after I recovered from my wounds I was kept a prisoner by the Matron of the Hospital. She insisted that I was not well enough to travel. Tiring of this kind of life I rebelled at last and thumbed a lift on an ambulance that was going to the scene of a fatal accident. On the way there the ambulance was stopped at a road-block. Fearing discovery I ran into a nearby wood. In the middle of the wood I met a rich woman who was picnicking in the nude.

RAMSAY. Why was she doing a thing like that?

LOW. She said she was the most modern woman in the world and she invited me to join her in her 'with it' mode of life. (*To McTURK.*) Her name is Rowena Coates née Torrence.

McTURK *appears about to swoon.*

McTURK. I gave my heart to her and she betrayed me. I can't stay here.

RAMSAY. We can't leave. We're forty miles west of Ireland.

LOW. You can't stay. Rowena is married to Bernard Coates. He's the Governor of the prison from which you've just escaped.

The door opens and ROWENA *enters. She gives a gasp of surprise upon seeing* McTURK.

McTURK. I suppose you'll turn me over to the police.

ROWENA (*gives a tinkly laugh*). Of course not. Nobody does that kind of thing nowadays. Come and meet my husband. He'll be so pleased to hear you've escaped.

McTURK. I'd like to wash and change my clothes. I've been sleeping in them for years.

ROWENA. What a virile attitude you have to life! Would you like a shower?

McTURK. Yes.

ROWENA. Come with me then. I'll take a shower with you.

RAMSAY *looks shocked.*

RAMSAY. We can't take a shower with you. You're a woman.

ROWENA. Would you like to take one with my husband? I'll call him. He'll be delighted to oblige.

She turns and exits. She can be heard calling.

ROWENA (*outside the cabin*). Bernie! Bernie! One of your prisoners has escaped! Do come and take a shower with him!

99. Interior. The Captain's cabin. *A dinner party is in progress.* ROWENA, BERNARD COATES, *the* MAYOR *and* MRS O'SCULLION, MISS DRUMGOOLE *and a number of other guests including the fat man that* CHRISTOPHER LOW *once rescued from the hole in the forest.* BERNARD COATES *turns to* McTURK. *He puts a hand on his knee in a friendly way.*

BERNARD COATES (*with a smile*). My wife, as I expect you've already been told, is the most modern woman in the world. I'd be a real old stick-in-the-mud without her.

He laughs to himself and spoons soup from his plate.

McTURK. This soup tastes modern enough. What's it made of?

BERNARD COATES. I never ask. Our cabin boy brings us anything he fancies. He escaped from a mental home, you know?

CHRISTOPHER LOW *leans over* McTURK. *Pours soup into his plate.*

LOW. I was strapped down for a week. I thought my mind was going to give way.

ROWENA (*with a tinkly laugh*). And it did finally, didn't it? (*She turns to* MRS O'SCULLION.) He went off his head with the strain of being declared insane!

MRS O'SCULLION. Fascinating. You always meet such interesting people, Rowena.

BERNARD COATES (*to* McTURK). Rowena came home one day with this young man. I've been insulted in the woods, she said. (*He laughs and drinks a little wine.*) I suppose he'd raped her or something. What would we do without the contemporary scene!

ROWENA *looks round the table with a bright, wholesome expression.*

ROWENA. I was being 'nudies' on our country estate when this perfectly mad creature rushes upon me. He'd just crashed the ambulance which was taking him to a place of stricter confinement. I just had to offer him a job.

CHRISTOPHER LOW *splashes soup down her dress. She rises to her feet with a scream.* LOW *shuffles away.*

ROWENA (*with a fluttery laugh*). Don't worry. He's not in control of himself, you see. I'll just go and change my gown.

She hurries away. The MAYOR *leans across to* McTURK.

MAYOR. I'm the Mayor of the town where you were born. I remember your disgrace well.

McTURK. Weren't you involved in the plot to assassinate the Prime Minister?

MAYOR. How nice of you to remember.

McTURK. What are you doing here? I thought you were a wanted man.

MAYOR. My wife withdrew the charges she had made against me and I returned to normal life. I made a fortune in dishonest dealings on the Stock Exchange. I met Bernie through a mutual friend who was the idol of the bistros. He'd just sawn a woman in half.

McTURK. Any conjuror can do that.

MAYOR. Ah, but my friend wasn't a conjuror. He was a

plumber's mate. The girl was expecting his child. It was most distressing. The only solution was a number 2 saw and a trip to the left luggage office at Victoria Station.

He dabs his mouth with a napkin. MISS DRUMGOOLE *leans across to* McTURK *with a shy smile.*

MISS DRUMGOOLE. You probably don't remember me, Ian McTurk. I'm the revolutionary Patricia Drumgoole. A graduate of Father Brodie's pantry.

McTURK. How did you come to be on this yacht with a class of person you once affected to despise?

MISS DRUMGOOLE. I was sharing a room in a girls' hostel with a young socialite who was invited to this yachting party. She was too bored to accept the invitation and suggested that I go in her place.

McTURK. Are you enjoying yourself?

MISS DRUMGOOLE. No. I'd rather be married to you.

McTURK. That's impossible. My heart is broken.

CHRISTOPHER LOW *has cleared the soup plates from the table. As he is halfway across the cabin he drops them. The whole table looks up sharply and then pretends not to have noticed.* RAMSAY *hurries over and helps* LOW *pick up the broken dishes.*

RAMSAY (*in an angry whisper*). What's the matter with you? Are you on the pill again?

LOW. These people expect a mental patient to behave like a mental patient.

RAMSAY. You're not a mental patient.

LOW. They don't know that. I'm a great success as a lunatic.

They put the tray aside. LOW *opens a serving hatch. Food is passed through to him.*

RAMSAY. What was in the soup? It was disgusting.

LOW. It was tinned mushrooms. And I boiled a packet of cigars with it.

RAMSAY. I find this unashamed luxury pointless and soul destroying.

He goes back to his place at the table.

100. Exterior. The deck of the yacht. Moonlight. *The sails billow in a light breeze. Only the sound of the ocean disturbs the tranquil calm of the night.* McTURK *strolls with* ROWENA. *They stop beside a lifebelt fixed to the rail. Painted on the belt is the name of the yacht,* 'The Fairy Wish'.

McTURK. You're more beautiful than ever in the moonlight. The years have made no difference to my feelings for you. I'd like to take you in my arms and kiss you.

He moves closer. She smiles and steps away.

ROWENA. Tell me about your adventures since we last met.

McTURK. I've had no adventures. I haven't seen a woman for ten years. (*Pause.*) I can see through that dress.

ROWENA. After ten years in the company of men that in itself is an adventure.

He takes her hand. Presses her fingers to his lips.

McTURK. If you only knew how, through the long, lonely nights in my prison cell, I've yearned for the touch of your hand.

She smiles. He kisses her lips.

McTURK. Why did you marry Bernard? Was it because he's rich?

ROWENA. Yes.

McTURK. How tragic that I had to be born poor.

He folds her in his arms. The MAYOR *approaches smoking a cigar. They break from their embrace.*

MAYOR. Bernie sent me up to look for you. We're going to look at the stars through my wife's telescope. It should be fun. Won't you join us?

ROWENA *pulls her wrap about her shoulders and goes below. The* MAYOR *smiles. He raises his eyebrows in a cynical way.*

MAYOR. Be careful what you're doing. Bernie is a very jealous man.

McTURK (*haughtily*). When I want your advice I'll ask for it!

He goes below. A disagreeable expression passes over the MAYOR's *face.*

101. Interior. The lounge of the yacht. Morning. McTURK,
RAMSAY *and* LOW. LOW *serves coffee from a tray.*

LOW (*handing coffee to* RAMSAY). Miss Drumgoole was washed
overboard last night. She left a tin of biscuits in her cabin.
Do either of you want them?

RAMSAY. How did it happen?

LOW. She was crossing the desk in the dark when she mistook
the handrail for the companionway. The watch heard a cry
of 'woman overboard' but thought it was a joke.

McTURK. I refused her hand in marriage last night. I had to be
brutal with her. This persistent importuning is most
embarrassing.

RAMSAY. She took her life from disappointment. You mustn't
feel guilty. You did all you could.

McTURK. I've no intention of feeling guilty. I leave that to
Liberal politicians and clergymen. They get paid for it.

He fits a cigarette into a long holder.

McTURK. Rowena has consented to meet me in her cabin at
noon. I'm going to give her a good raping. You won't either
of you disturb me, will you?

He drinks coffee. RAMSAY *and* CHRISTOPHER LOW *look
on in disapproval.*

102. Interior. ROWENA's cabin. *A large daybed with cushions.*
ROWENA *paces the cabin. She touches her hair with a nervous
gesture. A knock at the door. She calls out in a gay voice to
conceal her apprehension.*

ROWENA. Come in!

McTURK *enters.*

McTURK (*closing the door behind him*). They're holding a
'silent ten minutes' in memory of the woman who was washed
overboard last night. We shan't be interrupted.

He seizes her in his arms. She gives a little squeak of fright.

ROWENA. We shouldn't be doing this. Think of my husband.

McTURK. I wish you wouldn't keep harping on your husband.
I took a shower with him yesterday. What more do you want?

He kisses her on the mouth. They fall among the cushions. She struggles. Pushes him away.

ROWENA. No! Please go away! (*She bursts into tears.*) I shall ring for the steward.

McTURK. What d'you want the steward for when I'm here?

He takes off his shirt. ROWENA *gives a cry of horror.*

ROWENA. What are those scars on your back? Are they the marks of the lash?

McTURK. No. I've been wearing an overtight string vest. (*Puts an arm round her.*) How would you like me? I do a very nice semi-nude.

ROWENA *stands to her feet. Her face is flushed.*

ROWENA. You must go. I can't allow you to behave in this terrible way. It's wrong and we should be ashamed of ourselves.

McTURK *stares at her. Puzzled.*

McTURK. I thought you were the most modern woman in the world.

ROWENA (*with a toss of her hair*). What's that got to do with it?

McTURK. Well, I thought modern birds lived for this kind of thing.

ROWENA (*gives a cold smile. Goes to the door*). I'm afraid you're quite wrong. Being modern has nothing to do with playing nasties. Will you kindly leave my cabin or I shall inform my husband of your disgraceful conduct.

McTURK *picks up his shirt and, shame-faced, leaves the cabin.*

103. Exterior. The deck of the yacht. *The guests are gathered in a circle. Many of them have black ribbons round their arms. They sing the hymn 'Now the labourer's task is o'er'. They bow their heads at the end of the hymn.*

MRS O'SCULLION. I've known Patty Drumgoole for years. She was a really kind, sweet girl.

MAYOR. She was rather a plain girl, I thought.

MRS O'SCULLION. She was our parlour maid, don't you remember? I lent her to Father Brodie who never returned her.

RAMSAY. The world will be a sadder place now she's gone.

The crowd stand silent. Many are weeping. The fat man who
CHRISTOPHER LOW *once rescued from the hole in the*
forest passes by.

FAT MAN (*calling gaily*). The sandpit is open!

The guests begin to drift away. RAMSAY *seizes the* FAT
MAN *by the arm, shakes him roughly.*

RAMSAY. A woman was drowned last night! Doesn't that mean
anything to you?

The FAT MAN *says nothing. Suddenly he punches* RAMSAY
in the mouth. RAMSAY *reels away, his mouth and nose*
bleeding. The FAT MAN *hurries after the others.* RAMSAY
sinks into a deckchair, mops his mouth and nose with a
handkerchief. CHRISTOPHER LOW *appears with a tray*
of iced drinks.

LOW. I once rescued that man from a hole in a forest. He was
a prisoner.

McTURK. How did he reward you?

LOW. He knocked two of my teeth out.

He puts a glass down beside RAMSAY.

RAMSAY I've just remonstrated with him over his callous
behaviour in the face of human misery.

LOW. What did he do?

RAMSAY (*spitting blood into his handkerchief*). He knocked
two of my teeth out.

McTURK *sits down beside them. He has an expression of*
complete despair on his face.

McTURK. We're going to be asked to leave the boat. I've just
had an argument with Bernie.

RAMSAY. What about?

McTURK. His wife. He saw me leaving her cabin and became
suspicious. I believe he's insanely jealous.

BERNARD COATES *stands in front of them. With him is*
the FAT MAN. *The rest of the guests are behind him, watching.*

BERNARD COATES (*to* RAMSAY). Why did you insult the
President of the Humpty-Dumpty club?

RAMSAY. I didn't.

FAT MAN (*to* BERNARD). I was on my way to the sandpit when this hooligan grabbed me by the arm and hurled abuse at me.

Everyone waits for RAMSAY's *explanation.*

RAMSAY. I wanted him to face up to the realities of human existence.

BERNARD COATES *gives an impatient sniff.*

BERNARD COATES. As I think I told you last night, my outlook is broadminded, go-ahead and thoroughly up-to-date, but I won't have people insulting my guests or making free with my wife. There's a gunboat in the immediate vicinity of this ship. I've been in radio contact. You'll be taken off my hands and sent to prison.

He turns on his heel and strides away. The guests follow, applauding him for the strong measures he has taken. RAMSAY, McTURK *and* LOW *sit in gloom.*

LOW (*standing to his feet at last*). I shall take the lifeboat and escape. Does anyone care to join me?

He walks away along the deck. The others hesitate and follow.

104. Exterior. The open sea. *A storm. The lifeboat sinks lower in the water, is tossed about by the fury of the waves. The* YOUNG MEN *attempt to row. Lose the oars. Drift helplessly. In the middle of the watery chaos a spar is seen floating towards them. A* WOMAN *is clinging to it.* CHRISTOPHER LOW *stands to his feet. The others pull him back.*

LOW. Look! It's Miss Drumgoole!

The boat rocks. Water pours in over the sides. The spar drifts nearer.

McTURK. There's no room for any more. You'll sink the boat!

RAMSAY. We can't leave her to drown. That'd be a monstrous thing to do.

LOW *and* RAMSAY *fling out a rope to* MISS DRUMGOOLE *who clings to it. The storm rages. They drag her aboard.*

MISS DRUMGOOLE. Oh, thank goodness, you saw me. I thought my last hour had come.

LOW. We couldn't leave a fellow human being to die. We had to rescue you.

The wind howls and the boat sinks beneath the added weight. They all four are thrown into the water. At the mercy of the elements and on the point of death they all cry for help. The wind howls louder and no one answers.

105. Exterior. A beach. McTURK *drags himself from the sea, exhausted, his clothes torn to shreds. A party of* YOUNG NURSES *are playing on the sands. A tall, imperious* WOMAN *is with them.* McTURK *approaches. One of the* NURSES *screams.* McTURK *stumbles forward and faints.*

106. Interior. A hospital ward. McTURK *is in bed. He stares about him, bringing the room into focus. At the end of the bed is the tall, imperious* WOMAN *in the uniform of a hospital* MATRON. *With her is* CONNIE.

McTURK. Where am I?

CONNIE. You are in St. Helena's Recovery Home. You were found naked and exhausted on the beach by the Matron. (*The* WOMAN *nods.*) She brought you back here and tended you with her own hands.

MATRON. You've been a most difficult patient. I had to give you injections to bring you up to par.

McTURK (*to* CONNIE). Don't send me back to prison. I couldn't bear it.

CONNIE. I've no intention of sending you back to prison. As long as you're sorry for what you did you'll be allowed to resume your normal life. What was your occupation?

McTURK. I have no occupation.

CONNIE. Then you'd better join the army. We're at war now, you know.

McTURK. War? How terrible. Who are we fighting?

CONNIE. The rebels, of course. Who else should we be fighting. You'll be with my regiment.

McTURK. But my sympathies lie entirely with your enemies.

CONNIE. I shall pretend I haven't heard that. (*To* MATRON.) See that he reaches the Recruitment Centre by 13.00 hours.

She marches away down the ward. The MATRON *bends over and kisses* McTURK.

MATRON. I'll be sorry to lose you, but you've a duty to do.

McTURK. Was anyone with me when I was found?

MATRON. No.

McTURK. I rescued a young woman from the sea. I wonder what became of her.

MATRON. She's dead, I expect. (*With a smile.*) I'll give you an alcohol rub before you go. As a sort of parting present.

She hurries away. McTURK *closes his eyes.*

107. Interior. A Recruitment Centre. *The hall is full of* WOMEN. *A few* MEN *are present. Recruiting posters line the walls. The main space of the room is taken up with booths in which the recruits fill up their forms. At the top of the room is a table on a platform. Sitting at the table are a number of high-ranking* ARMY OFFICERS. MRS O'SCULLION *sits with them. At the top of the table sits* CONNIE (*in uniform*). *She gets to her feet. Loud cheers.*

CONNIE (*smiling, waiting for silence*). As most of you know we are now at war. Our efforts to reach agreement with the rebels came to an abrupt end last night. Naturally there is dismay in official circles. Failure came after several hours of extra talks, optimism and the postponement of 'Pixie' Heath's trip abroad. A little note was left on my desk by 'Pixie' this morning. (*She picks up a note from in front of her.*) It reads, quite simply — (*She glances at the note.*) 'Men too much for me. Feel worn out. Personal charm a failure'. Acting on the advice of Dr Maud and the Rev Daisy Greene, I declared a state of war as existing from 13.00 hours.

Loud cheering. CONNIE *sits down. Uniformed* OFFICERS *pass round recruiting forms.* McTURK, *carrying his form, approaches one of the booths.* RAMSAY *takes the form from him.*

RAMSAY. I've already filled in your form.

McTURK. I wasn't going to fill it in. I was hoping to get rid of it.

CHRISTOPHER LOW *appears on the other side of* McTURK.

LOW. It's all been arranged. We've joined Field Marshal Boon's regiment.

RAMSAY. The tide of history is with women. You can't fight it. Their ideology is sounder.

Everyone stands to attention as CONNIE *leaves the platform. She stops beside* CHRISTOPHER LOW. *Smiles.*

CONNIE. Lovely to see you here. Are you joining the army?

LOW. Yes.

CONNIE. Good. It'll make a woman of you. (*Chucks him under the chin.*) Come and see me in my caravan. Talk over old times.

The uniformed WOMEN *allow her to pass. She sweeps from the Recruitment Centre to a burst of applause and* MARTIAL MUSIC.

108. Exterior. An Army Camp. *A little rain is falling. Tucked into a hollow the camp is floored with mud which the wheels of lorries have crossed with waterlogged furrows.* McTURK *meets* RAMSAY *on the edge of the muddy wasteland. They are both in uniform.* McTURK *shoulders a gun.*

McTURK. What happened to your patrol?

RAMSAY. It was wiped out in a skirmish two days ago.

McTURK. How did you escape?

RAMSAY. I ran away before the firing began.

McTURK. Did anybody see you?

RAMSAY. A master sergeant spotted me hiding behind an abandoned supply truck.

McTURK. What happened?

RAMSAY. I shot her. It was the first time I'd used a gun since the campaign began.

They trudge wearily towards a distant Troop Office.

109. Interior. The Troop Office. CONNIE *stands before a map. A blackboard with some battle positions marked stands to her right. The hut is full of* WOMEN OFFICERS *and* N.C.O.s. *A few* MEN *are also present.* CHRISTOPHER LOW, *in a smart uniform, stands beside* CONNIE. McTURK *and* RAMSAY *sit with the* AUDIENCE.

CONNIE (*turning from the map with a bright smile*). We move up tomorrow, dears.

A flutter of interest from the WOMEN.

CONNIE. I'm sure we're all terribly excited by the prospect of a real face to face meeting with a man! (*She chews on an unlighted cigarette.*) The front is in a fluid state at the moment so we've no definite news on how things will turn out. The rendezvous will be at Reference 7.

She swings round and prods the map.

CONNIE. Jean and Freddie have prepared haversack rations for us. If any of you are on a diet please let Freddie know. He won't be responsible for that 'extra poundage'. (*She laughs merrily.*) Any questions?

McTURK. Are we winning?

CONNIE. Well, my dear, I'd rather not commit myself at the moment. I had a long chatty letter from 'Pixie' yesterday. And she's heard rumours — whilst having elevenses at Tregunters — that the war will be over in time for the Spring showings. So we mustn't lose heart.

She turns to CHRISTOPHER LOW.

CONNIE. I want two signallers detailed tonight. And pick a good-looking wireless operator for my set, will you?

She leaves the hut with a cheerful wave.

110. Exterior. The battle area. Dawn. *In the distance guns are firing. Not heavy sustained fire, but sporadic bursts of one or two rounds at a time. A jeep is driving rapidly along a road blackened by shellbursts.* CONNIE *is in front.* CHRISTOPHER LOW *is driving. In the back sit* McTURK *and* JACK RAMSAY. *The jeep rounds a corner. The place is deserted. The jeep stops.* CONNIE *steps down.*

CONNIE. Dismount! We're going to establish camp over to the left. Bring the telephone. Quick now!

As they plunge into the scrub, the noise of firing increases. Bren guns chatter from a dozen different points. Sandwiched between comes the thud of INFANTRY MORTARS.

CONNIE. Heads down!

A shower of bullets falls across the path. Everyone ducks. They stumble across the open ground. WOMEN in uniform appear and salute CONNIE. A CONVOY drives up. Five hundred uniformed WOMEN jump down and begin to pitch camp.

111. Exterior. The new camp. Evening. *A little rain is falling. The camp resembles the old camp. McTURK, his head bandaged, his uniform muddy, meets RAMSAY who has his arm in a sling. Both are battle-stained and weary.*

RAMSAY. This camp is no different to the other one.

McTURK. It's nearer the enemy lines. The chances of being killed are greater. It's quite different.

RAMSAY. What happened to that little corporal you were keen on?

McTURK. She was drafted home on compassionate grounds.

RAMSAY. Why?

McTURK. Her husband has dyed his hair and gone on the streets.

RAMSAY. It always happens in wartime when the women are away.

They meet up with CHRISTOPHER LOW. His uniform is spotless.

LOW. The G.O.C. requests the pleasure of your company in the concert tent this evening. Our quota of entertainments has arrived. Now is the time to desert if you've been turning the matter over in your mind.

They turn a corner and meet a number of dancing MEN and WOMEN dressed in Brazilian costumes waving maraccas. Behind the carnival is a white-painted van. On the side of the

van is a painting of a South American scene with the words
'P. DRUMGOOLE. MUSIC IN THE SOUTHERN MANNER'.

The van stops. MISS DRUMGOOLE *steps out. She waves with a gay smile.*

MISS DRUMGOOLE. It's cabaret time!

The uniformed WOMEN *begin dancing with the Brazilian dance troupe.* McTURK, RAMSAY *and* LOW *rush to meet* MISS DRUMGOOLE. *They embrace her. She lingers longest in the arms of* McTURK.

MISS DRUMGOOLE. Oh, Ian McTurk, your kisses haven't altered. You give a girl a most beautiful experience even in public.

RAMSAY. What are you doing here?

MISS DRUMGOOLE. I'm a licensed entertainer. I travel round the battlefields bringing hope and cheer to the weary soldier.

They link arms and take her towards a line of sagging tents.

LOW. We thought you were drowned.

MISS DRUMGOOLE. I was rescued by a passing ferry. When war broke out I formed my Latin American dance band from a group of discontented Welsh Nationalists. I've no talent for South American rhythms, but I don't let this spoil my enjoyment. But how did you escape the fury of the elements?

RAMSAY. It would take too long to explain. Be thankful that we're alive not to tell the story.

MISS DRUMGOOLE. Is there any special number you'd like my band to play tonight. Bear in mind that we specialise in songs with Latin American rhythms.

LOW. We'll have to miss your concert. We intend to desert.

MISS DRUMGOOLE. After my performance I have to cross the enemy lines to sing to a man who is mortally wounded. I have a visa. You'd better come with me.

They kiss her. She remains in IAN McTURK's *arms.*

MISS DRUMGOOLE. Oh, Ian McTurk, you're the nicest man I've ever met. Won't you please marry me when the war is over?

McTURK. No. My heart is broken. Don't ever ask me again.

He turns and walks away. MISS DRUMGOOLE *watches sadly.*

112. Exterior. Night. A road across the battlefields. *Barbed wire. Dug-outs. The sound of shells bursting. Flashes on the horizon.* MISS DRUMGOOLE's *van stops at a checkpoint. A* SENTRY *comes forward holding a rifle. He is revealed, in the dim light, as the* LORD MAYOR (TERENCE O'SCULLION). MISS DRUMGOOLE *hands him some documents.* McTURK *puts his head out of the car.*

McTURK. Aren't you Terence O'Scullion, the one-time Lord Mayor?

The MAYOR *stares hard. Smiles.*

MAYOR. Yes. And you're Ian McTurk. What are you doing here?

McTURK. We're going to join up with the rebels.

MAYOR. How I wish that I could do the same. I don't like working for my sergeant. She's a most unpleasant woman.

MISS DRUMGOOLE. There's room in the back. Why don't you join us?

MAYOR. How kind you are. I don't deserve your friendship after the unkind way I behaved on Bernie's yacht before the war.

They open the door. He gets in.

113. Interior. The van. MISS DRUMGOOLE *is driving. The* MAYOR *sits with the others in the back.*

McTURK. Why are you dressed as a private soldier?

MAYOR. I am a private soldier. When we landed from Bernie's yachting expedition I was arrested on suspicion of having aided the rebels during the riots after the death of the late Prime Minister. Although I was acquitted at my trial, my property was confiscated. I've been penniless ever since.

RAMSAY. What happened to Bernard Coates?

MAYOR. He left Rowena and took to playing the piano professionally.

McTURK. How is Rowena?

MAYOR. She's still the most modern woman in the world. I saw her only yesterday selling war-bonds. She's very much against the establishment.

RAMSAY'S FATHER *is seen on the road waving the car to a halt.* MISS DRUMGOOLE *applies the brakes.*

RAMSAY'S FATHER. Oh, thank God! I'm wounded! Please get me to the nearest hospital.

McTURK. Get in the back. We're going over to the rebels.

114. Interior. The back of the van. RAMSAY'S FATHER *is white-faced and shaken. Blood pours down his ragged tunic.*

McTURK. Aren't you Jack Ramsay's father?

RAMSAY'S FATHER. I was before the war. I don't know who I am now.

RAMSAY. What are you doing wounded by the side of an arterial road? I thought you were leading our boys to victory.

RAMSAY'S FATHER. I made a dreadful mess of leading our boys to victory. They were going to put me before a firing squad only they couldn't afford the bullets. So I was marched into a wood to be hung like a common criminal. As we entered the forest, we were caught in enemy cross-fire and I escaped. I'm going over to the rebels. They know how to make a man feel he's wanted.

McTURK. We'll have you safe and sound in a well-run all-male hospital in next to no time.

RAMSAY'S FATHER *looks horrified.*

RAMSAY'S FATHER. What are you talking about? I'm going to join the rebels.

McTURK. The men.

RAMSAY'S FATHER. No. The women. I can't go back to the men; they've sworn to court martial me. Oh, what a fool I was to get mixed up with you! (*He seizes the wheel of the van.*) Back! Back to the women! Our only hope!

MISS DRUMGOOLE. No! The men! We must go on!

They struggle with the wheel. The van swerves wildly. The MAYOR *leans forward and speaks to* MISS DRUMGOOLE.

MAYOR. This road is heavily mined. Pull into the side road and let's discuss the matter sensibly.

MISS DRUMGOOLE *swings the van into a side road. A loud explosion shakes the van. In a blinding flash of light a sign is seen 'LANDMINES — DANGER!' Another explosion wrecks the van.* McTURK *is flung out onto the road. The van is blown to pieces in succeeding explosions. Blackness.*

115. Interior. A hospital ward. McTURK *is in bed. He is wrapped from head to foot in bandages. A blood transfusion unit is beside him. He stares vacantly at the ceiling. A bell rings. Visitors enter. They go to the other beds.* RAMSAY *and* CHRISTOPHER LOW *enter. They sit next to* McTURK. LOW *unwraps a bunch of grapes he has brought and begins to eat them.*

RAMSAY. We've joined the rebels. We couldn't wait for you to recover. You've been unconscious for weeks.

LOW. Bernard Coates is our commanding officer. Rowena broke his heart.

RAMSAY. My father was left to die by the side of the road. The fortunes of war. We were rescued by a rebel ambulance and he was a declared Government supporter. Miss Drumgoole's hair fell out. She's taken to wearing a wig.

LOW. Yesterday a species of louse caused a whole battalion to report sick. The M.O. had them sprayed with a new kind of drug which killed ten men and brought the others out in a kind of virulent rash.

RAMSAY. The rest of us are enduring the lice.

LOW *scratches himself. A* DOCTOR *hurries up. He picks up a hypodermic syringe and gives* McTURK *an injection. A bell rings.* McTURK *closes his eyes.*

LOW. You're much better. You're to be allowed to join us tomorrow.

116. Exterior. The rebel encampment. MEN *in uniform pass to and fro across the muddy waste. An ambulance drives into the* *centre of the camp. The door is opened and* McTURK *gets down.* RAMSAY *meets him.*

RAMSAY. I'm glad you're well again. We're rather short of rations at the moment. Did you bring any grapes from the hospital?

McTURK. No.

LOW, *in a smart uniform, ambles up.*

LOW. What are we fighting for? We've been having an argument back there.

RAMSAY. Consult the handbook. You'll find a list of things we're fighting for at the back with the map of the London Underground.

BERNARD COATES *hurries up, pulling on his gloves.*

BERNARD COATES. The enemy forces are only a mile away. I've ordered a retreat. Commandeer every vehicle and drive for your lives!

They leap into the ambulance. MEN *are running in all directions. A lorry rumbles into the camp.* McTURK *starts up the ambulance which shoots forward and crashes into the oncoming lorry. The lorry and the ambulance burst into flames and are wrecked. A number of* MEN *run up with stretchers. They take* McTURK, RAMSAY, LOW *and* BERNARD COATES, *pale with shock, from the ambulance and put them on stretchers. They do the same for the driver of the lorry.*

Two ambulances drive into the camp, their bells ringing. Male NURSES *and* DOCTORS *leap from each ambulance. They pick up the stretchers and put them into the ambulances. The two ambulances drive off. They are hardly out of the camp when they run over a landmine which explodes under them. The two ambulances burst into flames. Injured and horrified* MEN *stumble out.*

MEN *run up with stretchers. They take the injured crews and passengers of both ambulances from the shadow of the burning wreckage. They wrap them all in blankets. Four ambulances drive into the camp.* DOCTORS *and* MALE NURSES *leap from them. The* VICTIMS *of the explosion and the motor accident are piled into the four ambulances. They drive off. A retreat is sounded on a trumpet.*

*Lorries rumble into retreat positions and drive with the four
ambulances away from the camp. Outside the camp is a
hump-backed bridge fording a stream. As the lorries and
ambulances drive over it the bridge collapses. Lorries and
ambulances crash into the stream amid the wreckage from the
bridge. Explosions. Flames. Panic.*

MEN *with stretchers rescue the, by now, shocked, injured and
well-nigh senseless,* McTURK, RAMSAY *and* LOW. *They are
placed, wrapped in blankets, with other* VICTIMS *of the
various disasters. The banks of the stream and the approaches
to the camp are lined with the dead and injured. In the stream
are four wrecked and blazing ambulances. Outside the camp
are two wrecked and blazing ambulances. Inside the camp is a
wrecked and blazing ambulance and a wrecked and blazing lorry.*

*With bells ringing furiously eight ambulances drive into the
disaster area.* NURSES *and* DOCTORS *leap from the
ambulances and pile* McTURK, RAMSAY *and* LOW *and the
other* VICTIMS *into them. The eight ambulances drive off.*

*At this point the camp is surrounded and attacked by Govern-
ment troops led by* CONNIE *and* RAMSAY'S FATHER.
*Hand grenades are thrown and the ambulances set on fire.
Hundreds of* MEN *with stretchers attempt to put the injured,
the dying, the sick, unhappy army of* VICTIMS *into some
sort of shape. To the injured of the many disasters are added
the* MEN *wounded by the attacking troops. A whole fleet of
ambulances arrive with their bells ringing.*

*At this point, with snipers' fire, the defence of the camp,
blazing ambulances, the cries of pain, the panic created by the
appearance of the enemy, the stretcher bearers are hard put
to it to know where to turn. Stretcher bearers pick up*
McTURK. *Shots are fired and the stretcher bearers collapse as
badly injured as their patient. More stretcher bearers pick up
the stretcher bearers. They are hit in their turn and collapse.
The victims and the helpers struggle together in the mud of
the battlefield.*

An army of ambulances moves away from the camp.
McTURK, RAMSAY *and* LOW *run after them. At this point,
with a loud roar, the earth caves in and the ambulances, full
of suffering humanity, crash into the hole which has opened
up in the treacherous subsoil.*

*An army of stretcher bearers attempts to bring order to the
scene. Several descend upon McTURK, RAMSAY and LOW.
Seeing what has happened before, they decline to be helped
and fight off the stretcher bearers. The stretcher bearers,
injured now from the blows inflicted by the YOUNG MEN,
are swept away to the First Aid Sections by other stretcher
bearers.*

*All this with the sound of rifle and Bren gun fire. Bells ringing.
Trumpets sounding retreat. Shouts and screams from the
injured. Blood pouring from bleeding wounds. On the edge of
a gaping hole amid the carnage of battle. Onto the scene
steps FATHER BRODIE, holding high the CROSS upon which
OUR LORD died, accompanied by NUNS and CHOIR BOYS
singing a Hymn to the Glory of Immortal God.*

CHRISTOPHER LOW, *struck dumb, kneels.* McTURK
*bursts into tears and sits sobbing among the stretchers and the
blankets.* RAMSAY *shrieks with maniacal laughter and begins
to leap about in a kind of glee.*

The three YOUNG MEN *are surrounded by* WOMEN *armed
with rifles and led away.*

117. Interior. The Government H.Q. CONNIE *and a number of*
WOMEN *officers.* RAMSAY'S FATHER *is with them.* McTURK,
RAMSAY *and* LOW *are led in.* CONNIE *turns to them.*

McTURK. I suppose you're going to have us shot as traitors?

CONNIE. Traitors? (*She looks surprised.*) Of course not.

RAMSAY'S FATHER. You've just won the Military Cross.

RAMSAY. Why?

CONNIE. For exceptional bravery over and above the call of
duty.

RAMSAY'S FATHER. Your strategy in ramming that approaching
lorry resulted in a chain reaction which completely
immobilised the enemy.

CONNIE. The war is over! You're all heroes!

CONNIE, RAMSAY'S FATHER *and the* OFFICERS *all
embrace the* YOUNG MEN *with great emotion.*

CONNIE (*to* LOW). It only remains to announce the date of our wedding.

RAMSAY'S FATHER (*to* RAMSAY). Your mother was shot by a sniper last week. She's to receive the O.B.E. posthumously. My joy is complete.

McTURK. But the peace brings no joy to me. I can never marry the woman I love.

He turns and leaves the room.

118. Exterior. The battlefield, *recently the scene of such horror, is now transformed. Dancing figures reel among the debris, the lorries and ambulances still blazing provide light for courting couples. Among them are one or two bandaged figures. Bloody bandages flutter like ribbons in a light breeze.*

119. Exterior. The Town Hall square. *The victory celebrations. Many people are decorating war heroes.* MRS O'SCULLION *allows the injured to kiss her hand.* FATHER BRODIE *gives them his blessing. Dancing and cheering.*

120. Interior. Money-Box Lodge. *Chandeliers and dancing to a waltz. Crowds of people.* CONNIE, ROWENA, BERNARD COATES *and* RAMSAY'S FATHER (*in a magnificent Field-Marshal's uniform heavy with medals) stand with* RAMSAY *under an enormous oil painting of a pair of feet.*

CONNIE (*to* RAMSAY). And what are you going to get up to now that the war is over?

RAMSAY. I'm going to tell the patrons of the Ritz that the manager is mad.

CONNIE (*turns to* ROWENA *and* BERNARD COATES *with a laugh*). Isn't that absolutely splendid? He's going to tell people that the manager of the Ritz is mad. He's such a convincing liar too.

RAMSAY'S FATHER. It isn't a lie. The manager of the Ritz is mad.

BERNARD COATES (*with a cough*). Any well-regulated society must find room for anti-social activity. (*He smiles in a kindly way to* RAMSAY.) I hope you have a great success in your enterprise.

ROWENA *opens her eyes wide and looks intelligent.*

ROWENA. I'm inclined to believe that perhaps the manager of the Ritz is mad.

CONNIE. You're so bitter against the establishment, aren't you dear?

BERNARD COATES (*to* RAMSAY). My wife, as I expect you know, has been elected the most modern woman in the world for another year.

McTURK, *rather drunk, appears at* ROWENA's *side. He puts an arm round her waist.*

McTURK. Will you marry me?

ROWENA *gives a squeaky laugh and pushes his arm away.*

ROWENA (*smiling to* CONNIE *and* BERNARD COATES). Isn't he terrible? But I think startling people ought to be encouraged.

McTURK. Come for a walk in the garden.

He leads her away.

121. Exterior. A garden. Moonlight. *Dark leaves. Roses. A nightingale. Faintly blown by the wind comes the sound of a waltz.* McTURK *walks with* ROWENA *under a rose arbour.*

McTURK. I love you, Rowena. Through all my sufferings you've been constantly in my thoughts.

ROWENA *smiles an uncomfortable smile.*

ROWENA. Shall we go in? It's turning cold.

McTURK. I've kept this rose you gave me. (*He takes it from his pocket.*) It's been watered with my tears. It was for your sake I did everything. Why did you have to break my heart? I loved you so much.

ROWENA *turns to go. He takes her hand.*

ROWENA. I must go! Love seems out of place in a garden in the moonlight.

McTURK. I'd hoped that some day we might settle down. Even get married.

ROWENA. That's not possible. I've a rich husband whom I love dearly.

McTURK. Then we must part forever. I can't go on seeing you. There's an ache in my heart that can never be eased or satisfied.

She draws near him.

McTURK. Kiss me before we say goodbye.

Petals from a rose fall softly upon them from an overhanging bough. The moonlight folds them in a shining embrace as they kiss before parting forever.

122. Interior. Money-Box Lodge. CHRISTOPHER LOW *is talking to the* MAYOR (TERENCE O'SCULLION).

LOW. What happened to you after the landmine exploded.

MAYOR. I was in the most desperate straits for nearly a year. Then I had a stroke of luck and profited by it. I spent the last six months of the war directing operations from a wheelchair.

LOW. But you were only a private.

MAYOR. I was mistaken for a General who'd been admitted to hospital for a minor surgical operation. I should've owned up, I suppose. But there it is. We're all human and err sometimes.

LOW. How did you get to be Lord Mayor again?

MAYOR. That was due entirely to the influence of the General I was impersonating. He'd been rather badly treated as a private soldier and he paid me a large sum of money to regain his identity. With his cheque in my pocket I was soon up to my old tricks on the stock exchange. I'm now twice as wealthy as I was.

He accepts a glass of champagne from a passing waiter.

MAYOR. But what's been happening to you? You're quite a hero, I'm told.

LOW. Yes. I've been decorated for bravery in the field and now I'm going to marry my commanding officer.

MAYOR. What a unique experience! You'll be able to sell your story to the newspapers.

LOW. I shan't, I'm afraid. You see, my wife will be the President. (*He shows the* MAYOR *his engagement ring.*) My private life will be top secret from now on. I shall probably be offered a post in the cabinet.

The MAYOR *looks surprised.*

MAYOR. But only women qualify for Government office. A new law has just been passed.

LOW. You must be mistaken. Connie would never consent to such inhuman legislation.

He turns to RAMSAY'S FATHER *who happens to be passing.*

LOW. Where's the President?

RAMSAY'S FATHER. She's waiting for you under the little picture of Jesus in the conservatory.

123. Interior. The conservatory. CHRISTOPHER LOW *enters pushing aside the leaves.* CONNIE *stands under a palm tree. She gives him a brief, welcoming smile. Takes out a cigar case.*

CONNIE. Cigar?

LOW. You know I never smoke.

CONNIE. It's a chocolate one. Your favourite brand.

LOW *takes a cigar from the case. He unwraps the band and eats the cigar.* CONNIE *lights a real cigar. They sit together on a rustic seat.*

LOW (*petulantly*). What's this ridiculous new law? The days have gone when I could pass as a woman. I have to shave twice a week now.

CONNIE. Men shouldn't concern themselves with making laws. (*Stroking his hair.*) They should be charming and masculine. Give mummy a kiss and forget about it.

He pushes her away.

LOW. What about the equality of the sexes? Isn't that what Mrs Pankhurst wanted?

CONNIE. I'm sure she didn't, dear. Women have never imagined that they were equal to men. They've always known that they were superior.

LOW *is quite put out by her reply.*

CONNIE. This law is only the first. I hope ultimately to exclude men from Parliament, the armed services, the law, medicine and the Church.

LOW *stands. Tight-lipped.*

LOW. I can't possibly marry a woman who holds those views. (*He pulls off his engagement ring.*) Take back your ring! I never want to see you again.

He flings the ring at her feet and leaves the conservatory.

124. Exterior. The garden. RAMSAY, McTURK *and* **LOW** *wander through the dew-laden foliage under a lightening sky.*

LOW. I'm going to sell the trinkets Connie gave me. I always hated her loud and vulgar presents.

McTURK. What kind of presents were they?

LOW. Diamond cuff-links and the occasional gold cigarette-case.

McTURK. I shall send Rowena a dozen red roses each year on the anniversary of our parting. The card will say simply — 'McTurk — Rowena — Always'. I can't bear to think of the long years of loneliness that lie ahead.

RAMSAY. My father is going to marry the matron of St. Helena's Recovery Home. He hasn't benefited from his past mistakes.

125. Exterior. A deserted street. The sun rising. *The young men wander past closed shops, under an arcade to a memorial commemorating some long forgotten war. Under a badly damaged allegorical statue of 'Peace' stands MISS DRUMGOOLE bathed in early sunlight. She wears spectacles. She has on a plain hat and coat. She is carrying a small case. Her face is stained with tears.*

The YOUNG MEN *run to her. They embrace her.*

McTURK. I thought you'd been killed in the war.

MISS DRUMGOOLE. No. I survived. I was very ill for a time, but I'm glad to say that I'm quite recovered. I can't see as well as I did. And my hair never regained its original lustre. I survived, though, if not in one piece at least in recognisable shapes.

LOW. Where are you going?

MISS DRUMGOOLE. To the railway station. I've accepted a post as children's nurse with a large family in New Guinea. It's rather a hazardous undertaking.

RAMSAY. Why? Do they eat their old nurses?

MISS DRUMGOOLE. In certain circumstances I believe they do.

McTURK *suddenly flings his arms about her.*

McTURK. Who wants to be a Governess in a cannibal kraal? Leave these head-hunters to their own devices and marry me.

MISS DRUMGOOLE *is bowled over by his generous offer.*

MISS DRUMGOOLE. But you love Miss Rowena.

McTURK. My heart is broken, but everything else is in working order. I'd make an excellent husband.

MISS DRUMGOOLE. What would we live on?

LOW. If you married me I'd sell my jewels.

McTURK. The Mayor would be delighted to show us how to make money from dishonest dealings on the Stock Exchange.

MISS DRUMGOOLE. I can't marry both of you.

RAMSAY. Why not? The President has just introduced new legislation to permit a woman to have three husbands. Let's spend the rest of our lives as a quartette.

MISS DRUMGOOLE. No. You'd desert me to raise a rebellion.

RAMSAY. I wouldn't. Getting married and having children is the most rebellious thing a man can do. It shows a disregard for the conventional bourgeois status-quo and a fine, careless anarchic sense of the absurd.

MISS DRUMGOOLE. Very well. As long as its perfectly legal I will marry you.

They hug and kiss her on all parts of her body simultaneously. She gasps for breath and closes her eyes in ecstasy.

126. Interior A church. A fashionable congregation. FATHER BRODIE *stands at the altar with a prayer book open. A rustle of anticipation as the organ begins 'Here comes the bride'. The congregation rises.* RAMSAY, McTURK *and* LOW *are at the altar. With them is the* MAYOR (TERENCE O'SCULLION) *as best man.* MISS DRUMGOOLE *is led down the aisle by* BERNARD COATES. *Bridesmaids and* MRS O'SCULLION *as* MATRON OF HONOUR. *The* BRIDE *reaches the altar. Gives* RAMSAY, McTURK *and* LOW *a smile.* FATHER BRODIE *begins the service.*

FATHER BRODIE. Dearly beloved, we are gathered here in the sight of God, and in the face of this congregation to join together these men and this woman in Holy Matrimony . . .

FATHER BRODIE's *voice becomes fainter. The candles gutter at the altar. The ceremony wears on.* FATHER BRODIE *turns a page in the prayer book. He faces the boys.*

FATHER BRODIE. Ian, John, Christopher wilt thou have this woman to thy wedded wife?

THE BOYS. We will.

FATHER BRODIE. Patricia wilt thou have these men to thy wedded husbands?

MISS DRUMGOOLE. I will.

127. Interior. The church. RAMSAY, McTURK *and* LOW *lead* MISS DRUMGOOLE *down the aisle to the accompaniment of the wedding march.*

128. Exterior. The church steps. *Confetti is thrown. Bridesmaids. Friends. Well-wishers. A photographer runs forward.*

PHOTOGRAPHER (*pushing people aside*). Just the happy quartette, if you don't mind!

He kneels. MISS DRUMGOOLE *and the young men pose for their wedding photograph. A flash.*

129. Interior. A hotel corridor. RAMSAY'S FATHER, *in the uniform of a hotel page, leads* MISS DRUMGOOLE *and the young men up to a door.*

McTURK (*to* RAMSAY'S FATHER). The last time I saw you was at the Victory celebrations. You were wearing a Field Marshal's uniform.

RAMSAY'S FATHER (*wheezing, opening the door*). I was a Field Marshal then, now I'm a hotel page. Only the uniform is the same. I'm married to the ex-Matron of the Recovery Home who treats me with the contempt I deserve. My home life makes sorry telling. You'll find no comfort in marriage. Everything's in a state of flux. (*He shakes his head, coughs a little.*) We live in an era of constant change and extreme conservatism. I'm on duty at six tomorrow. Ring when you require breakfast.

He stumbles away down the corridor. The young men lift their wife up and carry her across the threshold.

130. Interior. The hotel bedroom. Morning. *The sun streams into the room.* MISS DRUMGOOLE *is in bed with* RAMSAY, McTURK *and* LOW.

MISS DRUMGOOLE. It's like a wonderful dream! I hope we have a long and happy married life!

The young men kiss her. There is a struggle. MISS DRUMGOOLE *squeals with delight and disappears under the coverlet with her husbands.*

The end.

Other titles of interest

**THE PARIS DIARY & THE
NEW YORK DIARY, 1951–1961**
Ned Rorem
New introduction by
Richard Howeard
Preface to *The Paris Diary* by
Robert Phelps
431 pp., 29 illus.
80838-2 $16.95

THE ORTON DIARIES
Edited by John Lahr
332 pp., 51 photos
80733-5 $14.95

**THE COMPLETE TALES OF
WASHINGTON IRVING**
Edited by Charles Neider
840 pp.
80840-4 $22.95

**THE FRANCIS
PARKMAN READER**
Edited with an introduction and
notes by Samuel Eliot Morison
544 pp., 1 illus., 5 maps
80823-4 $17.95

HERE AT *THE NEW YORKER*
Brendan Gill
New introd. by the author
428 pp., 131 illus.
80810-2 $15.95

WARHOL
The Biography
Victor Bockris
570 pp., 53 photos
80795-5 $17.95

**THE KINDNESS OF
STRANGERS**
The Life of Tennessee Williams
Donald Spoto
445 pp., 34 photos
80805-6 $15.95

**THE EDMUND WILSON
READER**
Revised and Expanded
Edited by Lewis M. Dabney
808 pp.
80809-9 $18.95

THE DIFFICULTY OF BEING
Jean Cocteau
Introd. by Ned Rorem
174 pp.
80633-9 $13.95

SAM SHEPARD
Updated Edition
Don Shewey
282 pp., 11 photos
80770-X $14.95

**THE THEATER ESSAYS
OF ARTHUR MILLER**
Revised and Expanded
Edited by Robert A. Martin and
Steven R. Centola
Foreword by Arthur Miller
686 pp.80732-7 $17.95

SCREENING THE SEXES
Homosexuality in the Movies
Parker Tyler
New foreword by Andrew Sarris
New afterword by
Charles Boultenhouse
419 pp., 71 photos
80543-X $15.95

THE AMERICAN EARTHQUAKE
**A Chronicle of the Roaring
Twenties, the Great Depression,
and the Dawn of the New Deal**
Edmund Wilson
576 pp.
80696-7$17.95

**BATTLE-PIECES AND
ASPECTS OF THE WAR**
Herman Melville
New introd. by Lee Rust Brown
282 pp.
80655-X $13.95

THE COMPLETE HUMOROUS
SKETCHES AND TALES OF
MARK TWAIN
Edited with an introduction
by Charles Neider
722 pp.
80702-5 $19.95

FACES IN THE CROWD
Musicians, Writers, Actors &
Filmmakers
Gary Giddins
288 pp.
80705-X $13.95

FRANZ KAFKA
A Biography
Max Brod
295 pp., 8 photos,
3 pp of Kafka's sketches
80670-3 $13.95

GEORGE WASHINGTON
A Biography
Washington Irving
Edited and abridged with an
introduction by Charles Neider
790 pp., 3 illus., 5 maps
80593-6 $18.95

HARDBOILED AMERICA
Lurid Paperbacks and the
Masters of Noir
Expanded Edition
Geoffrey O'Brien
216 pp., 137 illus. (8 pp. in color)
80773-4 $16.95

REVOLULATION OF THE MIND
The Life of André Breton
Mark Polizzotti
784 pp., 48 photos, 1 line drawing
80772-6 $20.95

MAPPLETHORPE
A Biography
Patricia Morrisroe
512 pp., 60 photos
80766-1 $16.95

RICHARD WRIGHT READER
Edited by Ellen Wright and
Michel Fabre
910 pp., 66 photos
80774-2 $22.50

SAINT-EXUPÉRY
A Biography
Stacy Schiff
559 pp., 40 illus.
80740-8 $18.95

SURREALISM
Julien Levy
New introd. by Mark Polizzotti
202 pp., 68 illus.
80663-0 $17.95

PRESENT PAST
PAST PRESENT
A Personal Memoir
Eugène Ionesco
New introduction by
Robert Brustein
196 pp.
80803-X $13.95

Available at your bookstore

OR ORDER DIRECTLY FROM

DA CAPO PRESS, INC.

1-800-321-0050